EXPLORA IN CONSCIOUSNESS

A NEW APPROACH TO OUT-OF-BODY EXPERIENCES

FREDERICK AARDEMA

MOUNT ROYAL
PUBLISHING

Explorations in Consciousness
A New Approach to Out-of-Body Experiences

Frederick Aardema

Cover design by Brion Sausser

Image Courtesy NASA, NOAO, ESA, C.R. O'Dell (Vanderbilt University), M. Meixner, P. McCullough, and G. Bacon (STSI)

Mount Royal Publishing
2348 Lucerne #138
Town of Mount Royal, Quebec, H3R 2J8

email: info@mount-royal-publishing.com
www.mount-royal-publishing.com

Library and Archives Canada Cataloguing in Publication

Aardema, Frederick
Explorations in consciousness : a new approach to out-of-body experiences / Frederick Aardema.

Includes bibliographical references and index.
ISBN 978-0-9879119-0-2

1. Astral projection. 2. Consciousness.
3. Aardema, Frederick. I. Title.

BF1389.A7A27 2012   133.9'5   C2012-902251-9

ISBN 978-0-9879119-0-2
6 5 4 3 2 1   15 14 13 12
Printed on acid-free paper

EXPLORATIONS IN CONSCIOUSNESS

For Moni

Contents

Table of Contents

PART 1 – BASIC ISSUES AND CONTROVERSIES

PART 2 - EXPLORATIONS IN THE PHYSICAL

PART 3 - THE HUMAN SPECTRUM OF CONSCIOUSNESS

PART 4 - THEORY AND PRACTICE

Foreword

Dr. Frederick Aardema has been a valued colleague for over ten years, and occasionally OBEs have crept into our discussions, primarily as an academic issue linked to our mutual interest in dissociation, but lately also from his personal experience. So, I'm not surprised to find in this book that Frederick brings the two together, combining personal testimony with a scientific eye. It is a pioneering book in several respects.

Firstly, it brings OBEs into everyday discourse. In psychological jargon, it "normalizes" the experience. Clinical psychology is rather good at normalizing phenomena that psychiatry likes to pathologize: hallucinations, delusions, talking to yourself. These experiences, once hallmarks of madness, are now considered universal to such an extent that people happily join, for example, societies of "voice hearers" as they would a society of beekeepers.

OBEs have likewise been marginalized as either a mysterious, esoteric activity that fits well into New Age guru-style mysticism or as an abnormal psychiatric sign of severe desomatization. With his careful, detailed scientific consideration of the phenomena, Frederick pulls OBEs out from the smoke screen of flimflammery to present them transparently as a comprehensible human experience—in particular, an experience potentially attainable by all.

OBEs tell us about the way consciousness works and bring into question our notions of reality. Does reality really exist as such, or is it constructed rather as a maximum likelihood guided more by our intent and projects, as our possibilistic model suggests?

Even though Frederick provides a comprehensive review of the literature, his own experiences form the mainstay of the book. Instead of placing his subjectivity rather shamefacedly within an objective framework to legitimize it, Fred puts objectivity within his subjective experience. He describes the trials and tribulations encountered, observing this experience like an explorer, and discusses the influence that can unbalance such an observer stance as part of the journey. It's a decentering of the scientific method, in which the observer position is itself recognized as a qualitative experience—a kind of OBE (observer behind experience) of OBEs.

In the same way that Frederick breaks down the barrier between subject and object in his method of observation, the book also provides a quantum leap for the mind-body debate. What implications do OBEs have for our idea of an isolated brain-based consciousness? What about the physical divide between our bodies and the world? Are our bodies really part of our mind?

In many ways, *Explorations in Consciousness* harks back to Wilhelm Wundt's introspectionist explorations of sensory phenomena and Husserl's dictum of "back to things themselves." We have to know a phenomenon in order to measure it. We need to know the dimensions of experience—in this case, the qualitative nature of OBE absorption—in order to quantify it. Frederick's MESS questionnaire, which measures environmental absorption, is a good example of quantifying OBEs via a qualitative approach.

Finally, as a clinical psychologist, Frederick is attuned to the therapeutic practical application of OBEs. What if OBEs could be harnessed as a travel option for people trapped in their bodies? Could we explore our conflicting intents therapeutically in OBEs where feelings appear visually and symbolically around us? Can we manipulate ourselves through our environment? We know already how people can immerse themselves for the better in virtual reality. Could OBEs be the next stage?

As Frederick acknowledges, the book is a start—a very comprehensive start and an up-to-date, state-of-the-art account. We are discovering as we go along. Frederick even needed to invent his own vocabulary along the way. The field of OBEs is literally opening up to those with an open mind. We stand at the frontier of an exciting new venture into inner space. Outer space may be contracting, but consciousness is expanding, the future is boundless, and anything and everything is possible.

Kieron O'Connor, Ph.D., M.Phil.
Research Professor
Faculty of Medicine, Department of Psychiatry
University of Montreal, Canada

Preface

The out-of-body experience (OBE) is an experience in which you find yourself at a location different from that of your physical body. It is an experience in which it appears that you have actually left your body behind. Not surprisingly, for some, the OBE falls within the realm of the strange and uncomfortable.

However, many people have OBEs. It is not a sign of psychopathology. In fact, an increasing number of people actively pursue the experience, hoping to touch something of value, something other than the physical world with which we are all so familiar. After all, the subject is tied up with some fundamental questions about human existence. What is my purpose? Where do I come from? Do I continue after death? Is my existence bound to physical reality? What is reality?

I should probably warn the reader early on that I consider it doubtful that the OBE offers any definite answers to these questions, at least not as things stand now. Yet, unlike some scientific approaches, after more than twenty years of exploring the out-of-body state, I have difficulty dismissing it as merely a hallucinatory experience.

The out-of-body state is more complicated than that.

Nor can I accept many of the more naïve assumptions surrounding the OBE, such as that everything encountered therein should be taken at face value.

Reality is more complicated than that.

The current book is an attempt to bridge the gap between prescientific and scientific approaches to the OBE. It is meant for those who are willing to explore the out-of-body state from both an experiential and critical-based perspective.

I took care not to let theory take precedence over experience. Nothing is ever presented as fact if it is not grounded in experience. Theory aligns itself closely with practice, and as such, the current work can also be considered a comprehensive travel manual for those wishing to explore the entire spectrum of consciousness themselves.

I also wanted the current book to be an accurate reflection of what it is like to experience an OBE. Often, experiences reported in the literature follow the ideal format according to preconceptions of what an OBE *should* be like. I do not doubt the integrity of the many authors in this regard, but I suspect a certain level of selectivity leads some experiences to find their way into print, whereas others do not. I have attempted to provide a more balanced picture by also reporting on those experiences that do not fit the norm.

The reporting was the easy part. Making sense of it was quite the opposite.

Most of the out-of-body experiences reported in the current work occurred between 2000 and 2011. I have been experiencing OBEs since the late '80s, but regrettably, not all my journals have survived up to the present.

During most of the early years, my experiences were few and far between. Inducing an OBE is not that easy, but a lot of trial and error does pay off. Over time, reaching the out-of-body state became a lot easier. I hope what I learned will make it attainable for others as well.

More frequent OBEs allowed me to investigate the experience in a far more systematic fashion than ever before. I could finally test some of the claims others had made about the out-of-body state. On some occasions, I had to come to different conclusions, as I was not able to align myself entirely with traditional scientific approaches nor with those adhering to esoteric assumptions surrounding the out-of-body state. I suppose this runs the risk of satisfying no one, but at the same time, I suspect that many people are already uncomfortably positioned in between these unbending opposites.

At the end of the day, I am a scientist at heart, willing to follow the evidence wherever it leads me. I was originally trained as a clinical researcher following a scientist-practitioner model. This means carefully proceeding from observation to case formulation, followed by theory and empirical analysis, whenever practical and feasible. I have attempted to follow that approach to the out-of-body state as much as possible.

Likewise, in line with solid scientific tradition, you will find frequent references to other authors in the field of the OBE. The practice of referencing gives credit where credit is due, and if opinions and observations collide, it enhances intercommunication and healthy debate, which in turn may assist in the advancement of knowledge of out-of-body states.

There is a lot that still remains to be done. The current work only aims to contribute to an existing field, at times anecdotal, sometimes empirical, and at other times speculative. Regardless, I hope it inspires others to follow up on some of the ideas put forward in the present work, or at least give them the opportunity to enhance their own experience in the out-of-body state.

It is only a beginning.

Frederick Aardema, Ph.D.
Research Assistant Professor
Faculty of Medicine, Department of Psychiatry
University of Montreal, Canada

Acknowledgments

My thanks to everyone who has helped this book come to fruition. It has been a long time in the making, from all the way back to when I was first introduced to the topic up to the last five years, when I have been writing it. I have learned a great deal from many others who have been on a similar path. You have my gratitude.

I also would like to thank all of those who have commented on the present work, especially Dr. Kieron O'Connor, who also graciously accepted my request to write a foreword. A special thanks to my editor, Kira Freed, for her outstanding contributions as well as her enthusiastic comments about topics related to the book.

Finally, a huge thank-you to the love of my life for all the stimulating conversations we have had on the topic. She is a natural scientist, unwilling to take anything at face value, unwavering toward dogma from any source, yet in awe of the mystery that surrounds us all. Her input has been invaluable.

Chapter 1
Setting the Stage

More than two decades ago, I was first introduced to the topic of out-of-body experiences (OBEs) by Robert Monroe through his first book, *Journeys Out of the Body.*[1] In that book, Monroe described how he one day, out of the blue, began to experience strange vibrations coursing through his body while lying down and preparing for sleep.

Initially, these sensations provoked a great deal of fear, especially when Monroe discovered that the vibrations allowed him to leave his body. Over time, however, his fear subsided, and he set out to actively explore the out-of-body state. He moved through walls, flew through the air, talked to the dead, and visited all kinds of exotic locations.

At seventeen years old, I believed that anything was possible, and with much naïveté and enthusiasm I made it my first priority to experience the same thing. I carefully read the method Monroe prescribed for leaving the body, which required approaching the borderline of sleep while simultaneously trying to keep one's mind awake. For several weeks, every night before bedtime, I attempted to leave my body.

I was not successful at first—I would always fall asleep prematurely. It was not easy to remain awake while lying in bed, especially when trying to relax my mind at the same time. I decided that more drastic measures were needed. What I lacked in skill I would make up for with sheer effort and determination. I vowed that in my next attempt, I would not give up, no matter how long it took.

That same night, I spent what seemed like ages twisting and turning in my bed, trying every possible method I could come up with. I even quite literally tried to will myself out of my body. Of course, this method failed as well. It was exhausting, and five or six hours later, unable to keep sleep at bay, I slipped into unconsciousness.

Only a couple of minutes later, I awoke. I heard the sounds of bells—the most delicate tones I had ever heard. Each vibrated at a unique frequency, combining into a beautiful arrangement. They were exquisite. A broad smile appeared on my face. I had finally made some progress!

Barely able to contain my excitement as deep and vibrant colors flashed before my eyes with each tone, I focused on the sounds. They began to speed up, slowly at first, but quickly reaching a peak. I braced myself.

Suddenly, my body began to vibrate violently. A strong current of energy coursed through me. It felt like what I imagine being electrocuted feels like, but without the pain. I felt excited, afraid, and elated all at once. But what was I supposed to do next?

I remembered the instructions provided by Monroe. They involved getting the vibrations to form a circle around my body. Then I needed to move the circle of energy upward along the axis of my body. This would somehow allow me to leave my body.

It seemed like a scary prospect, but I couldn't take the vibrations much longer. They were beginning to feel more and more like a real electric current. Every molecule in my body was shaking.

I requested the vibrations to form a circle around my legs. To my surprise, they responded almost instantly, settling into a circle around my body, just above the knees. I had not expected it to be that easy. They were still the same heavy pulsations but were much easier to bear in a more localized area.

I looked down at my body, seeing through closed eyelids. It was an incredible sight. Wrapped around my legs was a brilliant golden circle of light with multicolored sparks flying off in all directions. I had never seen anything like it. It was out of this world!

So far, the vibrations had been like a steady, low-frequency thumping. But I knew that in order to be able to leave my body, they needed to pulse much faster. I asked for the vibrations to increase in frequency.

Once again, the vibrations responded immediately. Their frequency increased until it became difficult to tell one beat from another. The shift made the sensations a lot smoother and more comfortable. They were as strong as before, but all the roughness had now disappeared.

I asked for the ring of vibrating light to move upward.

It responded.

The ring began to move along the axis of my body, its pace steady and unwavering. I got a sense that I would not be able to stop it, even if I were to try.

I felt some trepidation as the ring of energy approached my loins, but it passed uneventfully. The energy flowed past my belly and chest and then moved farther upward. I assumed it would continue all the way to my head. But then, suddenly, it stopped at my neck, right near the suprasternal notch. I felt pressure there, as if it was trying to find an entry point.

I became anxious. I had not expected the energy to actually get inside of me! There was no way all that energy would fit through that tiny hole in my neck. But I had no say in the matter. The pressure continued until I felt the energy worming its way inside like a snake. I felt some tension as it did so, but nothing cracked. There was no pain.

Then something happened I was completely unprepared for. My head roared—a deafening noise, as if the entire Niagara Falls had descended into my brain. The energy was all inside of me now. The sheer power of it was enormous. I was on the edge of panic. It was all too much. Then, abrupt silence!

I felt good, very good. A comfortable tingling sensation had spread across my body, like the feeling of a thousand soft, warm raindrops falling on my skin. It was blissful. My mind felt light. A little *too* light.

The sky had opened in front of me as if I were looking into deep space. Not outer space, but something entirely different. Far in the distance were wispy clouds of a purple hue. I began to hear whispering sounds—thousands of voices. It was eerie, nonhuman, not of this world. I felt my mind extending there. Almost like *being* there.

I became afraid again and quickly focused back on my body. Everything seemed normal. The tingling had disappeared. The only thing out of the ordinary was my leg. It was touching the wall beside my bed. Then it hit me. My leg was floating outside of my body! But I was not ready yet! I did not want to leave my body!

Moments later, I felt my regular leg again, on the bed as it should be. I immediately jumped out of bed. I couldn't believe the magnitude of what just happened. I had read about the vibrations and about some sort of electric current preceding an OBE, but I had never imagined anything like what I just experienced. This was the real thing!

Rarely has an OBE felt as vibrant as it did that first time. I never fully left my body, but that was inconsequential. For many years to come, this experience had me in its grasp; I sought to recapture the sense of freedom, bliss, and delicacy of that journey into the unknown. The sheer sense of euphoria was beyond my wildest imaginings.

In the years that followed, my OBE quest was similar to those described by others. In the beginning, I was only able to partially leave my body. Often, I would get "stuck" with a phantom arm or leg sticking out of my physical body, while the rest of me was unable to complete the exit.

However, as time went by, separating from my body became easier. "Rolling out" of the physical body was a favorite method for a long time. Eventually, I no longer even needed an exit procedure. I would fly up and away as soon as the vibrations allowed. Other times, I simply lifted myself out of bed as if I were getting up in the morning.

My experience of the vibrations also changed. Right from the start, they pulsated at a much higher frequency. I certainly did not mind that. It was a lot more comfortable than the extremely heavy and slow vibrations I had experienced the first time. Also, the direct manipulation of these sensations was no longer necessary to achieve separation. I only needed to mentally relax into them, and they would automatically intensify until separation was possible.

Like many others who explore OBEs, I initially found myself experimenting in the immediate environment of my bedroom. However, moving through walls and examining the specific attributes of the nonphysical body can only hold one's interest for so long. I soon found myself venturing farther out. Some of these experiences had a physical flavor to them, while others seemed to take place "elsewhere."

I never had any problems with returning to my body. Staying out of my body was the more difficult task. Often, I would suddenly find myself back in bed during an OBE. The slightest thought about my physical body would cause this to happen. I was able to remedy the problem somewhat by keeping myself ultra-focused on the environment, but it was far from ideal. Over time, however, thoughts about my physical body seemed to have less of an effect.

Traveling for long distances in the out-of-body state was also quite difficult, I discovered. This problem became especially acute while I was still living in the Netherlands, physically separated from my girlfriend, who was in Canada.

Standing in front of the Atlantic and having to cross it by flight is a pretty overwhelming prospect. My attempts to travel such long distances often failed. I was either pulled back into my body prematurely, or I would completely forget about my initial purpose on my way there by getting distracted by something else. I had to find a simpler and more straightforward mode of travel. The "void" seemed like a good candidate for doing just that.

In the out-of-body state, I would frequently find myself floating in an empty black space with nothing around me. It was not unpleasant except that very little ever seemed to happen there. It was like floating in a space of nothingness. But then something occurred to me. If distance is an illusion in the out-of-body state—and it certainly appeared that way in the void—then why not use it to travel from one location to another? I would simply fly through it for a while, keep my destination in mind, and then arbitrarily touch ground somewhere.

With this method, I had better success in reaching my girlfriend. It certainly was a lot cheaper than taking an airplane. Mind you, the method was far from foolproof. More often than not, I would end up in what appeared to be a foreign city, but not always close to the house where my girlfriend lived. It is not that easy finding your way in the out-of-body state, even if you are relatively close to your destination. Yet, despite all these difficulties, I was able to reach my girlfriend on several occasions.

Apart from traveling issues, what I also came to realize during these early experiences was that the OBE is not at all as straightforward as it is often proposed. Usually, the environment I encountered was quite different from the real environment that I knew to be there. Proof of the reality of the OBE was difficult to come by, and even if there was some sort of validation, it was usually different from what I expected. For example, during one projection, I found my girlfriend's house filled with vampires. This was odd, since vampires had never before figured in my out-of-body experiences, nor were they particularly in vogue at the time. Needless to say, I did not stick around for long during that particular visit, but the next day I asked my girlfriend what she had been doing at the time. She told me she had been watching a horror movie, and indeed vampires were a part of it. Assuming that this was more than just coincidence, I had apparently perceived her state of mind rather than the actual environment. It was one of the first indications I had that the content of consciousness takes precedence over everything, including physical reality itself.

One of the most popular interpretations of the OBE is that you are roaming the physical world quite literally as if you were a ghost. However, what is assumed to be physical reality in the out-of-body state does not always act like physical reality. Often, objects that should be there are absent or displaced (windows, furniture, doors, and so on). Or you may encounter events and people that are not really there. Other inconsistencies include being able to open doors and windows while out of the body. The latter is obviously not an ability that a ghost is supposed to have.

In the OBE literature, these inconsistencies are often referred to as "reality fluctuations" or "perceptual distortions." It is said that the out-of-body environment is more fluid than regular physical reality, more easily responding to thoughts and expectations of the projector. This did not seem such a bad explanation except that these distortions were the norm rather than the exception. Where *was* reality located in all of this? I had to find other accounts of the OBE, so I began to read up on the scientific literature.

I quickly discovered that the problems I experienced were hardly unique to me. Of particular interest were several parapsychological investigations carried out in the 1970s. These experiments usually involved asking a talented subject to establish the out-of-body state and then try to perceive an object in another room, with the object itself unbeknownst to the projector. Surprisingly, even the most famous and adept projectors were unable to correctly view the object in the other room. There were a few exceptions, but overall, results showed that accurate perception in the out-of-body state was not as straightforward as is often suggested in the popular literature. Without prior knowledge of the environment, physical reality was almost impossible to perceive correctly.

My skepticism regarding the reality of the OBE grew. I'd had a few experiences that were difficult to relegate to the realm of coincidence. Yet, none of these explained the vast number of occurrences in which my experience in the out-of-body state was different from physical reality. It didn't seem to fit this quite literal idea of roaming the physical world as a ghost, give or take a few perceptual distortions. I became increasingly interested in more scientific and conventional explanations for the OBE.

One of these explanations suggested that that the OBE is a lucid dream, which is a dream during which you are entirely alert and aware, just as you are in ordinary waking consciousness. Yet, you are actually only occupying a dream world that is recreated from your own mental model of the world, perhaps even including hovering over your own body located on the bed. In other words, according to this explanation, when you have an OBE, you are not really out of your body—you are dreaming it.

This "dreaming hypothesis," as we might call it, sounded pretty convincing to me when I first learned about it. After all, my body seemed to be asleep during these experiences, and it would certainly account for the many inconsistencies I encountered. So was I just dreaming during my experiences? And if so, what would that imply?

Whatever the terminology used, dream or otherwise, most scientific approaches try to make the point that the OBE is an unreal experience. Some, for example, hold that the OBE is a hallucination of some sort that has nothing to do with reality. Others argue that the OBE is produced by the brain; they assume that consciousness is a product of the brain and is therefore ultimately located inside of the body, so therefore nothing is leaving the body. Still others consider the OBE the result of a distortion in various psychological and perceptual processes. In all of these perspectives, the OBE is viewed as entirely *internally* generated, not related to objective reality as we know it. Nothing is leaving the body, and the out-of-body environment is entirely created by the projector. But what does the idea that the OBE is internally generated really tell us about the reality of the OBE?

As noted by Charles Tart, we already live in a virtual world in which our perception is a simulation of reality rather than reality itself.[2] We do not experience reality directly, but instead, energies of sound and light travel down our sensory apparatus and through our central nervous system, eventually resulting in the conscious perception of physical reality. So physical reality, as we *perceive* it, is internally generated as well. Senses obviously function as senses, but ultimately, what you perceive as the world comes from within, not from the outside. We do not really know what is "out there" on an objective level. In Tart's words: "We sit, as it were, in a movie theatre of our own, lost in the show created by the usually hidden mechanisms of the World Simulation Process."[3]

No matter how you turn it, the OBE fundamentally challenges your outlook on what is real. I am presented with experiences that have a definite *feeling* of reality to them. There are many inconsistencies, and even a high level of lucidity may not always be guaranteed, but the out-of-body experience is able to closely simulate physical experience. Thus, inevitably the question arises as to what makes anything real or unreal, including physical reality itself. After all, scientific rigor, if applied to one end of the spectrum, should work in the opposite direction as well.

In the end, the experience of floating in the air while looking down upon your physical body, at the very least, opens up your mind to the possibility that consciousness may have less to do with corporeal existence than previously assumed. Even so, as convincing as the experience may be, I still cannot be certain I am really out of the body. I may merely be looking down at a replication of my physical body, produced by my own expectations and lacking any real significance. Does it end with my imagination—the inner experienced as if coming from outside—or is there something else about the out-of-body state that makes it real? We will have to make up our minds as we go along, with all our expectations and beliefs and their confounding influence on everything that we encounter in the out-of-body state.

PART ONE

Basic Issues and Controversies

Chapter 2
Theoretical Approaches

DEFINING THE EXPERIENCE

Defining the out-of-body experience is a fairly straightforward matter. First and foremost, the OBE is an *experience* in which you find yourself located outside of the physical body. There is surprisingly little controversy there, as reflected in the following definitions of the OBE that have been proposed over the years:

> "An experience in which a person seems to perceive the world from a location outside his physical body."
> — Susan Blackmore[1]

> "...in which the objects of perception are apparently organized in such a way that the observer seems to himself to be observing them from a point of view which is not coincident with his physical body."
> — Celia Green[2]

> "An out-of-body experience is an experience where you find yourself outside of your physical body, fully conscious and able to perceive and act as if you were functioning physically..."
> — Robert Monroe[3]

"An out-of-body experience is one in which the center of consciousness appears to the experient to occupy temporarily a position which is spatially remote from his/her body."
— Harvey Irwin[4]

"...the experience where the subject perceives himself as experientially located at some other location than where he knows his physical body to be."
— Charles Tart[5]

What all these definitions have in common is that the environment you find yourself in during an OBE is not the same as what you would perceive from the *perspective* of the physical body. In other words, they are all remarkably similar with regard to the central requirement that you experience yourself in a different location than that of the physical body. However, it is also important to note what is *not* included in these definitions.

First, the manner in which you establish the out-of-body state is not essential to the experience. It does not matter whether you experience yourself separating from the physical body (moving out of it in a very literal way) or whether you find yourself beyond the body through other means. Second, there is no requirement that the OBE must occur in any particular environment; the experience is not restricted to environments that resemble the physical world, but may occur "elsewhere" as well. And finally, there is no suggestion that you are really out of body during the OBE. It is an experience—not a fact.

Overall, then, the definition of the OBE is simple and clear-cut, at least as far as the experience of it. But, of course, the controversy does not lie in the experience. Rather, it lies in the *interpretation* of the experience. We will begin with mystical and occult traditions and, most notably, theosophical approaches to the OBE.

MYSTICAL AND OCCULT TRADITIONS

One of the most influential approaches to the OBE finds its origin in various theosophical writings from the early twentieth century inspired by a rather ambitious mixture of Eastern mysticism, religion, occultism, psychology, science, and alchemy.[6] Theosophy suggests that during an

OBE, you quite literally leave the body in a "double"—a vehicle of consciousness—made up of finer particles than physical matter. It also proposes an elaborate scheme of different planes of existence, each of which may be visited during an OBE (see Table 2.1).

Table 2.1. Planes of Existence and Vehicles of Consciousness[7–10]

Plane	Characteristics	Vehicle
Physical	The world of matter as well as invisible forms of etheric matter	Etheric Body
Astral	The world of emotion and desire manifested as real objects, events, and creatures	Astral Body
Mental	The world of thoughts and ideas manifested as "thought-forms"	Mental Body
Buddhi	The world of intuition, inspiration, creativity, and wisdom	Buddhic Body
Atma	The world of spirituality, heaven, bliss, and Nirvana—the highest human aspect of God within us	Atmic Body
Anupadaka	The world of the Soul, True Self, or Higher Self (i.e., The Monad)	Anupadaka Body
Adi	The Source, The Divine, God, Ultimate Reality	Adi Body

According to theosophical doctrine, whether you are aware of it or not, each person exists inside of the different planes of existence simultaneously. Physical actions exist on the physical plane, emotions exist on the astral plane, thoughts and ideas exist on the mental plane, and so forth. In other words, the theosophists divided the mind into different aspects, according to prevailing views on the nature of the human psyche at the time, and consequently transposed these aspects by use of a geographic metaphor onto different planes of existence. Of course, the more exalted aspects of the human mind, such as spirituality and bliss, were allocated to higher planes of existence.

The physical plane of existence was said to have the lowest "vibration" corresponding to the highest density of matter. This also included "ethereal matter"—one of the lighter and higher forms of matter permeating the physical world. The planes beyond the physical world were made up of an even finer matter than ethereal matter. They were considered to be "atomic" in nature—the smallest particle known in science at the time. All these different planes of existence could be accessed during the OBE as long as you occupied the appropriate "vehicle" of consciousness. For example, the astral body was required to enter the astral plane of existence, the mental body was required to enter the mental plane of existence, and so on. What differentiated these different bodies across the different planes was that the higher the plane of existence, the higher the "vibration" of the body needed to be in order to access it.

Interestingly, albeit rather confusingly, the etheric body was not really considered part of the OBE. It was a body that was not viewed as a viable energy to carry consciousness. Rather, the etheric body was closely affiliated with the physical body as a *vehicle of vitality*, unable to separate from the physical body except during anesthesia, trauma, and illness.[11] So even though the etheric body was closely affiliated with the physical world, this was not the body you would occupy during a projection that occurred on the physical plane. If you did access the physical plane, you were visiting the astral portion of the physical world utilizing the *astral body*. In the words of Arthur E. Powell, a well-known theosophist at the time:

> "Not only man's physical body, but everything physical, has its corresponding order of astral matter in association with it, not to be separated from it except by a very considerable exertion of occult force, and even then only to be held apart from it as long as force is being definitely exerted to that end. In other words, every physical object has its astral counterpart. But as astral particles are constantly moving among one another as easily as those of a physical liquid, there is no permanent association between any one physical particle and that amount of astral matter which happens at any given moment to be acting as its counterpart."[12]

Even while the physical world had a fluid astral counterpart, the astral realms were considered to extend far beyond it, including into the afterlife. Upon death, depending on one's spiritual development, so the theosophists argued, the average person takes up residence in one of the subplanes of the astral, ranging from lower astral ("Hell") to intermediate ("Purgatory") and finally to higher astral ("Summerland"). These locations were considered very similar to the physical world, complete with inhabitants, scenery, and wildlife.[13] Unlike the physical world, however, the astral plane was entirely made up of astral matter, which could be actively controlled by inhabitants of the higher astral planes.

> "Those living on the higher subplanes usually provide themselves with whatever scenes they desire. Thus in one portion of the astral men surround themselves with whatever scenes they desire: others accept ready-made the landscapes which have already been constructed by others."[14]

Regrettably, those on the lower planes were not so fortunate to be able to control their environment:

> "The vivisector also has his "hell", where he lives among the crowding forms of his mutilated victims—moaning, quivering, howling. These are vivified, not by the animal souls, but by elemental life pulsing with hatred to the tormentor, rehearsing his worst experiments with automatic regularity, conscious of all their horror, and yet impelled to the self-torture by the habits set up during life."[15]

Beyond the astral, the theosophists locate the *mental plane*—the world of thoughts and ideas.[16] The mental plane was believed to be composed of very fine mental atoms, which consequently infused this plane with a great deal of fluidity. It had no permanent scenery, as the astral planes did—at least not in the normal sense of the word.

> "...he will experience bliss, indescribable vitality, enormously increased power, and the perfect confidence which flows from these. He finds himself in the midst of what seems to him a whole universe of ever changing light, colour and sound. He will seem to be floating in a sea of living light, surrounded by every conceivable variety of loveliness in colour and form, the whole changing with every wave of

thought that he sends out from his mind, and being indeed, as he will discover, only the expression of his thought in the matter of the plane and its elemental essence. Concrete thoughts...take the shapes of their objects, while abstract ideas usually represent themselves by all kinds of perfect and most beautiful geometrical forms. In this connection it should be remembered that many thoughts, which to us on the physical plane are little more than mere abstractions, are on the mental plane concrete facts."[17]

While the mental planes could not entirely be understood in three-dimensional terms, you were still considered to occupy a body of sorts—an ovoid-shaped mental body. No ordinary body was required because thoughts no longer needed to be articulated in a physical manner in order to be received. Rather, communication between inhabitants of the mental planes was considered to be "telepathic."

"Instead of their hearing words, articulate sounds that reach the ears, and convey so imperfectly and inadequately but a small portion of the thought, they would see thought as it really is; thought springing out before their eyes radiant in color, beautiful in sound, exquisite in shape, and they would be spoken to as it were in music, they would be spoken to in color and in form, until the whole hall would be full of perfect music and perfect colour and perfect shapes."[18]

Several more planes of existence have been identified by the theosophists beyond the mental planes. However, they were considered extremely difficult to reach and access. Descriptions tend to be abstract, and little is known about them. For example, the atmic plane of existence, also referred to as Nirvana, was described as follows by George Arundale:

"Trying to describe what I must call down here the nirvanic body, the only word that comes to me in substantiation for "body" is radiance. I am radiance, for it indicates the going beyond every single limitation word by the planes beneath. Time, space, form—these are transcended. They have ceased to manifest, though remaining in potentiality, or I would not assume them as I descend, as I pass outwards. ...In some ways, from the standpoint of the lower planes, the word transcendence is more appropriate even than radiance."[19]

There is little doubt that theosophy has been extremely influential in shaping thought on the out-of-body experience. One of its main problems, however, is the heavy use of outdated scientific theories and antiquated language to explain the out-of-body experience. For example, the notion of *atomic* planes of existence makes no sense in contemporary physics. Similar objections can be made with respect to the use of geographic metaphors to describe different states of consciousness as if they were analogous to objective locations in the physical world. Likewise, the notion of various different "bodies" being required to reach their corresponding plane of existence borrows upon outdated scientific concepts on the nature of matter.

While the imposition of outdated physical concepts on an experience that primarily occurs in consciousness can perhaps be forgiven, a more crucial issue is that many of the ideas proposed by theosophists simply do not correspond to experience without a subscription to this particular belief system. For example, a significant portion of people find themselves to be in a formless state during an OBE, not occupying any sort of body.[20] Yet, the theosophical system of thought continues to insist on ascribing objective, energetic characteristics to the various vehicles of consciousness, even though they may be completely absent during an OBE.

Overall, one is left with the impression of a pseudoscientific and ideological movement in which concepts and ideas have become solidified into a strict hierarchically organized doctrine that disallows fresh inquiry and experience. This is not to say that theosophy does not contain elements of authenticity since, after all, part of the model is based on actual experiences, whether by translating works of Eastern mysticism or by the active exploration of consciousness by theosophists and occultists themselves. At the same time, many of its theoretical concepts and divisions seem to have evolved in a rather arbitrary and even opportunistic manner in order to make it all "fit." Nonetheless, the theosophical system of thought is a tenacious rhetorical marvel, and there is no avoiding the fact that it still resonates strongly in the work of many authors who followed.

POPULAR CONTEMPORARY APPROACHES

While the theosophical model of the OBE is still very influential, many of the original divisions and concepts proposed by the theosophists have been abandoned in later writings. In particular, the notions of multiple layers of fine matter and subtle bodies do not figure strongly in later accounts. For example, quite early on, Sylvan Muldoon popularized the theosophical term *astral projection* to signify projections into the physical world.[21] More recently, the term *OBE* has found more frequent use, denoting an experience that applies to *all* forms of projection, regardless of the particular location that is visited. The term is certainly preferable to any other since it does not automatically imply an interpretation of an otherwise straightforward experience, such as is the case when it is referred to as an astral projection or a dream.

Most contemporary OBE authors incorporate a rather eclectic mix of influences in trying to reach an understanding of the OBE experience. William Buhlman, for example, relates nonphysical dimensions to quantum theory rather than to various densities of matter, as proposed by the theosophists.[22] Others, like Robert Bruce, while still strongly associated with occult and mystical traditions, have attempted to make these concepts more understandable to the general public using a more modern-day language.[23] Ultimately, however, the current popularity of the OBE, as well as the widening gap between contemporary and occult traditions, has to be credited to Robert Monroe.

Monroe, a businessman and media executive, began having spontaneous out-of-body experiences in 1957, starting with strange vibrations coursing through his body whenever he lay down to sleep. Initially, these experiences provoked a great deal of fear, and Monroe thought he might have a neurological or psychological problem. However, physical examinations and talks with psychologist friends failed to come up with an adequate explanation. There was no conventional explanation for his experiences, and once fear retreated to the background, curiosity took over, and Monroe began to explore the out-of-body state in a systematic fashion. These early experiences have been documented in his first book, *Journeys Out of the Body*.[24]

In his descriptions, Monroe made a valiant attempt to distance himself from occult and mystical notions surrounding the OBE. He wanted to demystify the experience and take it outside of the realm of the occult and supernatural. In doing so, he invented a whole new terminology that struck a chord with mainstream Western culture. For example, Monroe never used the term *astral projection*. Instead, together with Charles Tart, he popularized the term *OBE* to describe his experiences. Likewise, Monroe does not use the term *astral body*. Rather, he talks of a *second body* with different attributes than those of the physical body during his experiences.

Most of the early experiences described in *Journeys Out of the Body* occurred in the physical world; Monroe experimented with the different attributes of the second body as well as visited neighbors and friends to find proof of the reality of his experiences. In his second book, *Far Journeys,* however, Monroe more frequently describes experiences that seem to occur "elsewhere."[25] He identifies different "nonphysical energy systems" that are structured as layered rings surrounding Earth's atmosphere, inhabited by people both living and dead.

Unlike many others before him, Monroe did not explicitly organize nonphysical dimensions in terms of levels of spirituality. He actively avoided any sort of religious or value-laden connotations. Instead, he located himself in the wider spectrum of consciousness according to the level of "human time-space illusion." The inner rings were considered to be the ones most affected by human illusions, either in the form of inhabitants who held limiting beliefs or in the nature of perception in these nonphysical realities.

Moving outward through the rings, the forces of nonphysical reality became increasingly prevalent up to the point at which environments could no longer be entirely understood in human terms. In the outermost rings, inhabitants had lost most of their humanoid form and were "nearly white in radiation with occasional sparkling patterns around them."[26] These were the "last timers," as Monroe referred to them, preparing for their final in-human experience on the physical plane of existence before "winking out" to other planes of existence. The idea of reincarnation figured strongly in the work of Monroe.

Up until Monroe's second book, *Far Journeys,* many of the differences between Monroe and the occult traditions mostly seem of a semantic nature. However, Monroe's last work, titled *Ultimate Journey,* represents more of a conceptual break with many of the ideas in occult and mystical traditions.[27] In particular, while Monroe's earlier experiences were often characterized by a sensation of quite literally *leaving* the body, his development took a different turn in later years. Monroe discovered what he called the "quick-switch," which allowed him to move from one location to another in an instant by stretching or reaching out with his consciousness. This ultimately led Monroe to consider the second body to be no more than "local traffic"—mere habit due to the physical experience.[28] Indeed, in his last book, *Ultimate Journey*, Monroe no longer speaks in terms of "something" leaving the body. Instead, he emphasizes the relatively uneventful transition into the out-of-body state, likening it to the process of falling asleep and the fading of sensorial input.[29]

The term *phasing* is a metaphor derived from physics that conceptualizes consciousness as a waveform that can either be aligned or nonaligned with physical reality. According to Monroe, when we are 100% "phased" into the physical, we are perfectly aligned with normal physical input and waking reality. However, as consciousness moves further away from the physical (and the senses), consciousness is said to phase into other *focuses of attention*. One of the first of these focus levels is called *focus 10*—the state of mind awake/body asleep. A further phase shift leads to what Monroe calls *focus 12*—a state of expanded awareness in which the person begins to perceive beyond the physical world. These focus levels continue up until 28 (+), each one increasingly further removed from ordinary physical awareness (see Table 2.2).

Despite a reconceptualization of the OBE state as involving primarily a *phase shift* in consciousness that does not require the semi-physical mechanics of a second body, the notion of the afterlife continued to feature strongly in Monroe's conception of consciousness. In particular, focus levels 23 to 27 represent different areas of consciousness in which your own consciousness may touch upon the fields of consciousness of the deceased. These focus levels include several "belief system territories" occupied by those who inhabit physical-like environments created out of their own belief systems. These belief system territories are organized according to the principle "...like attracts like." In other words, upon death, you will occupy the kind of environment that resonates most strongly with you.

Table 2.2. The Focus Levels of Consciousness Across the (M) Field[27]

Focus	Description
Focus 10	A state of awareness in which the mind is awake, while the physical body is asleep. The mind is a little "out of phase" with physical reality, while sensory input is significantly reduced.
Focus 12	A phase shift located further away from the physical, often including all manner of visual perceptions, vibrations, or auditory phenomena.
Focus 15	An intermediary stage toward nonphysical perception where the concept of linear time no longer applies.
Focus 21	The edge of physical time-space.
Focus 22	A level occupied by living human beings with only partial awareness. According to Monroe, experiences here might also be remembered as dreams.
Focus 23	An area inhabited by those who have died but who are unaware of or unwilling to accept their true condition.
Focus 24–26	The next focus levels contain those who have accepted their death and have consequently taken up residence in the "Belief System Territories."
Focus 27	Focus 27 is described as an artificial, physical-like environment. The area is believed to have been created for the deceased in order to ease any shock and trauma. The center of focus 27 is referred to as "The Park."
Focus 28 (+)	An area of consciousness that lies beyond human consciousness. According to Monroe, projecting into this area or beyond limits a return to the physical body.

Beyond the belief system territories, Monroe identifies an area of consciousness termed *focus 27* ("The Park"). Focus 27 is considered different from the belief system territories. The Park, so Monroe was told by an inhabitant, is a creation that is there regardless of your beliefs. It will not disappear even if you don't believe it exists.[30] In one of his visits to focus 27, he describes how everything felt extremely real, more authentic than he had ever felt it before, including the breeze on his skin, the sounds of birds, and the taste of a maple leaf.

Focus 27 was also believed to differ in function from the belief system territories. Monroe defines it as "...an artificial synthesis created by human minds, a way station designed to ease the trauma and shock of the transition of physical reality."[31] Ronald Russell, in his authoritative biography on the life of Robert Monroe, likens the area to the Sufi notion of the afterlife, "a world created solely out of the subtle matter of *alam almithal*, or thought...a plane of existence created by the imagination of many people and yet one that still had its own corporality and dimension, its own forest, mountains and even cities."[32]

Beyond focus 27, Monroe identifies an even wider area of consciousness that is only remotely related to human consciousness. It was also beyond focus 27 that Monroe located the presence of his "I-There," consisting of a conglomeration of reincarnational selves. Like many others before him, Monroe struggled to put these experiences into words, as they often went beyond ordinary human thought and emotion.

According to Monroe, consciousness forms part of a wider spectrum of energy, or what he terms the (M) field—"a nonphysical energy field that permeates time-space, including our Earth Life System."[33] Monroe fails to elaborate in great detail on the (M) field, but it is clearly reminiscent of modern-day notions of quantum fields, or the zero-point field.[34] In quantum field theory, the zero-point field refers to the ground state, or lowest energy point of a field, that can be considered background electromagnetic energy filling the vacuum of space.

It could be argued that the work of Robert Monroe did not offer a new approach to the OBE at all, but rather merely rephrased mystical terminology into a more palatable scientific or engineering type of slant. Even the notion of the (M) field, or quantum fields for that matter, is not entirely unlike references by occultists and mystics to an underlying cosmic life force that permeates our wider reality. Likewise, the idea of belief system territories is quite similar to "astral planes" in occult and mystical writings.

In the end, however, Monroe far more explicitly recognizes the role of consciousness in understanding the OBE, and does so in a manner that is more compatible with modern-day science than the concepts and language used in mystical and occult traditions. Most crucially, due to his work, no longer is the OBE understood in terms of a complicated, almost mechanical interaction between various "subtle" bodies and various densities of matter; rather, you are journeying through consciousness itself. As such, Robert Monroe has rightly been recognized as a true pioneer in the exploration of consciousness, transforming the OBE into a semirespectable topic for scientists to study.[35]

MATERIALISTIC THEORIES

The OBE as a Lucid Dream

Materialistic accounts provide a more sobering account of the OBE than those proposed by mystical and popular contemporary approaches. For example, one of the more well-known scientific theories proposed by the neurophysiologist Stephen LaBerge claims that the OBE is a lucid dream.[36,37,38] In other words, you are not really out of body during the experience. Rather, everything you perceive during an OBE is no more than a dream environment—a replica recreated from your memory and your own expectations. It holds no objective reality whatsoever.

The term *lucid dream* originates from Frederik Van Eeden, who defined it as a dream during which mental clarity is very similar to that of waking consciousness.[39] Stephen LaBerge expanded on these observations by differentiating between two forms of lucid dreaming according to the particular way each is induced. The first type of lucid dreaming he refers to as a *Dream-Induced Lucid Dream* (DILD). During a DILD, you usually notice some kind of oddity or impossible event in the dream, which reminds you of the fact that you are dreaming. As a result, you will be completely awake and alert inside of the dream, seemingly located elsewhere than in your physical body, much like during an OBE.

Moreover, it is also claimed that lucid dreaming can occur straight from the waking state, or what is also referred to as a *Wake-Induced Lucid Dream* (WILD). During a WILD, you actually begin to dream straight from the waking state while remaining lucid in the process. You may even experience floating sensations, feeling yourself separating from the physical body in the process and eventually moving around in your own bedroom—the dream environment. Not surprisingly, a WILD is almost impossible to differentiate from the OBE.

One of the arguments seemingly in favor of the "dream hypothesis" is that those who experience OBEs tend to experience the more typical DILD as well.[40,41] For example, LaBerge reports that only 8% of his experiences were wake-induced, while 92% resulted from becoming lucid within a dream. Likewise, Donald DeGracia reports that 43% of his experiences were wake-induced, while 57% were induced from within a dream. A count of my own journal in one particularly active year (72 in total) showed 83% of my experiences to be wake-induced, while 17% were dream-induced experiences. So while there appears to be a great deal of variance in these numbers between individuals, they do indicate that the OBE and lucid dreams tend to co-occur.

Another argument is that many people are unable to distinguish between lucid dreams and OBEs. The environments encountered in the two states can be virtually identical, and a high level of mental clarity may characterize both. It is also not uncommon to lose lucidity *during* an OBE, in which case the experience will closely resemble the typical non-lucid dream. Or alternatively, an OBE can be initiated from *within* the dreaming state, which may even include leaving the dream body in yet another nonphysical body.[41]

So are the OBE and lucid dreaming entirely identical experiences? Is the person always dreaming during an OBE? Quite frankly, as convincing as the proposition might be, especially given the phenomenological similarities, the empirical evidence simply does not support it.

Firstly, it is well known that the OBE occurs in a wide variety of circumstances completely unrelated to sleep, such as physical trauma, extreme sports, stress, and drug use.[42] It seems difficult to claim that all these experiences involve dreaming. Secondly, even if the OBE occurs under circumstances related to sleep, the available psychophysiological data goes *against* the idea that the person is dreaming during an OBE.

In an overview, Susan Blackmore discusses several cases of adepts who subjected themselves to psychophysiological measurements while in the out-of-body state.[43] In all of these cases, the OBE did not occur during REM sleep, as measured with an electroencephalograph (EEG)—

an objective indicator of dreaming. The EEG revealed a variety of complex patterns, but nothing that could easily be classified as dreaming. In fact, in some instances, the EEG even showed an alert and awake mind.[44] Scott Rogo concludes: "...while LaBerge is correct in pointing out the many similarities between OBEs and lucid dreaming, objective EEG criteria suggest that these resemblances are purely superficial or artifactual."[45]

The finding that the OBE is not associated with a distinct psychophysiological profile does not bode well for the hypothesis that the OBE is a lucid dream. Of course, one could make the point that not all dreams occur in REM sleep. However, this widens the scope of dreaming to such an extent that the "dreaming hypothesis" no longer has any explanatory power. In fact, for the argument to remain coherent, any definition of dreaming would have to include waking life as well.

Let me also reiterate that the OBE is first and foremost an *experience*. It is defined as an experience in which one finds oneself in a location that is incongruent with the location of the physical body. Dreams fall *within* the scope of that definition. So rather than designating OBEs as dreams, it is far more accurate to refer to dreams as a form of OBE.

This might upset those who wish to make a clearer distinction between dreams and OBEs, as well as those who are unwilling to consider dreams as OBEs, but it is the only coherent conceptualization of the issue. Keep in mind that determining whether you are really out of body during any of these experiences, dreams or otherwise, is a separate consideration.

The notion that dreams are a form of OBE also provides a coherent explanation for the fact that the two experiences *can* be very similar. Dreaming would simply represent one of many modes of consciousness that a person may adopt in the out-of-body state. To some extent, this has already been recognized in some of the popular out-of-body literature. For example, Robert Monroe designates a specific area of consciousness where dreams occur in the out-of-body state.[46] Likewise, the projector Robert Bruce considers lucid dreams to be a valid form of OBE.[23]

The OBE as an Illusion

Like Stephen LaBerge, others have attempted to link the OBE with brain activity, but without direct reference to dreaming. For example, Michael Persinger found that magnetic stimulation applied to the right temporal lobe of the brain might produce religious and out-of-body-like sensations.[47] In a similar study, Olaf Blanke and colleagues found that stimulating certain parts of the brain led to various OBE-like sensations in an epilepsy patient.[48] These included falling sensations, sensations of sinking into the bed, and viewing oneself from above, separate from the physical body.

These experiences are noteworthy, and they strongly suggest an association between brain activity and the OBE. However, the main problem with many neurophysiological accounts is that they also often take the default position that consciousness is a *product* of the brain. Therefore, these studies often conclude that the OBE cannot be anything other than an illusion or hallucination. But should we assume that consciousness is produced by the brain and is therefore fixated in the body?

Clearly, the brain is related to out-of-body activity in some way. This is recognized by almost everyone. Why else would many OBE enthusiasts use all manner of supplements and brainwave entrainment technology to induce the experience? What *is* a point of contention, however, is the appropriateness of a neurobiological reductionist's approach to the OBE, including premature assumptions about consciousness being located in the body.

For example, one could interpret the manipulations carried out in various neurophysiological experiments as a disturbance of regular brain activity, as opposed to producing any particular type of experience. In fact, the changes in brain activity observed during these experiments may very well represent an *interference* with those brain functions that normally keep us positioned and fixated in three-dimensional space. Put in those terms, the brain primarily acts as a restraining influence on consciousness, and without it, you do not cease to be, but instead become more of what you truly are—a mobile, free-floating consciousness.

PSYCHOLOGICAL ACCOUNTS

Several psychological theories have also been put forth to explain the OBE without immediately relegating the experience to a neurobiological substrate. John Palmer, for example, holds that the OBE is caused by a change in your body image.[49] This change subsequently threatens the self and causes the person to recreate a new body image (or "second body") to alleviate the threat. Susan Blackmore expands on this account by focusing on the role of sensory reduction and attention in establishing the out-of-body state.[50]

According to Blackmore, during an OBE, you separate from sensory input while recreating a body image and perceptual environment from memory. Under normal circumstances, sensory stimulation keeps your body image coincident with your actual body location. However, in the absence of sensory input, your body image no longer needs to correspond to the actual location of the physical body. Instead, you recreate a new body (the double or second body) able to "leave" the physical body. Then, you will see the room as it is stored in memory, but from the perspective of being outside of your body.

Blackmore rejects the notion of being able to perceive an environment in the out-of-body state correctly without any prior knowledge (i.e., veridical perception). Instead, she claims that the environment one perceives in the out-of-body state is solely constructed on the basis of memory and imagination, often from a bird's-eye perspective. Yet, Blackmore does recognize that most of our ordinary perception operates in an almost identical manner. In both situations, the person constructs a world "out there" on the basis of the best model of the world available at the time. According to Blackmore, this makes the OBE "...as real as anything ever is."[50]

Essentially, Blackmore views the OBE as a *change in perspective* adopted by consciousness, and despite her rejection of extrasensory perception during the OBE, it is not at all incompatible with accounts that deem such perception to be possible in the out-of-body state. For example, the later work of Monroe also views the OBE as the result of adopting different perspectives, or more precisely, focuses of attention, as the person detaches from sensory input. Neither does the claim that the OBE is generated from within automatically make it unreal. There is actually very little that does not come from within, including our perception of physical reality itself.

More recently, these deliberations on the mobility of consciousness have led to an ingenious experiment by Henrik Ehrsson in the application of virtual reality to induce various OBE-like sensations.[51] During this experiment, participants viewed themselves through a camera, located behind them, that transmits the image to the virtual-reality goggles the person is wearing. Hence, participants are looking at themselves from behind as if being in a different location than their actual body. These sensations of being elsewhere than the physical body were enhanced by touching the real person, as well as the illusory person they were viewing from behind, with a plastic rod on the chest. Consequently, participants felt that they were actually located behind their physical body, as if watching a dummy or a body that belonged to someone else.

Interestingly, these types of perceptual shifts, albeit quite rudimentary in comparison to a full-fledged OBE, may also occur in everyday life. For example, the philosopher Thomas Metzinger describes the situation in which you sit inside a stationary train right next to another person on a different track.[52] Then, as the other train begins to move, it will feel as if your own train is in motion—a movement that can be felt in your body.

Overall, phenomenological and psychological approaches have the potential to provide an important contribution to an understanding of the out-of-body experience. They do not necessarily imply that the OBE is merely a "perceptual quirk."[53] Quite the opposite, they illuminate the ability and flexibility of consciousness to take on varying perceptual perspectives toward reality. This brings us to the nonlocal perspectives of consciousness, in which consciousness is neither ever really inside nor outside of the body. Rather, consciousness is "located" wherever it *constructs* itself to be.

NONLOCAL PERSPECTIVES

Nonlocal perspectives of consciousness have received an increasing amount of interest in recent years. In particular, some have argued that the relationship between mind and brain should be solved with a completely different approach that takes into account modern developments in quantum physics to explain consciousness. Christopher Clarke, for example, proposes that consciousness or mind is a nonlocal phenomenon that precedes time-space, similar to matter being a nonlocal phenomenon in quantum physics.[54] Others have suggested that consciousness causes probabilistic and nonlocal phenomena to collapse into a single possibility within our deterministic and local universe (i.e., regular time-space).[55] Yet others suggest that consciousness is the result of quantum coherence in the microtubules of the brain.[56]

Interestingly, Robert Monroe also proposed a nonlocal perspective of consciousness to understand the interaction between consciousness and the brain. He views the brain as a "tuning mechanism" that allows consciousness to operate in the physical world.[57] Ordinarily, the brain processes relevant physical sensory patterns into form, while filtering out any distracting signals. However, consciousness can tune in to different signals as well as shift away from the original "station." In this model, the brain does not create consciousness, nor is it located anywhere in particular. Rather, the brain solely acts as a filter of information, while consciousness itself exists apart.

The view that consciousness is able to exist apart from the brain has found some support in a recent study carried out by the researcher Van Lommel on Near Death Experiences (NDEs) in 344 patients with cardiac arrest.[58] The significance of this study lies in the fact that patients were clinically dead. In other words, because brain activity had ceased, there was no medical factor to account for conscious experience during the NDE. Likewise, anoxia, or the NDE being the result of a dying brain, was argued not to provide a credible explanation for the results. Given the similarities between the NDE and the OBE, this study may have implications for the out-of-body state as well.

Van Lommel also proposes a quantum mechanical interaction between consciousness and the brain.[59] Like some of the other quantum mechanical approaches, he argues that the brain itself does not contain any information, nor does it produce consciousness. Instead, again quite similar to Monroe's views, the brain acts solely as a transmitter and receiver of invisible phase-space fields. Van Lommel compares this interaction between brain and phase-space fields to modern worldwide communication. Similar to receiving information through a radio or computer, the brain receives signals from a larger electromagnetic field that then become observable and perceived as the world around us. This information is not stored inside the brain any more than the sounds produced by a radio are stored inside of it. Even as the reception ends, such as in the case of a dying brain, the transmission still continues.

Despite the attractiveness of quantum mechanical explanations to understand mind-brain interaction, their scientific status remains unclear. One scientist from a materialistic perspective criticized a particular quantum account as explaining little more than the idea that conscious experience is created by pixie dust in the synapses.[60] Of course, the appropriate rebuttal was that a materialistic account of consciousness, explained by chemicals in the brain carrying consciousness, is exactly that—pixie dust in the synapses.

Whatever the scientific merits of quantum physical accounts of mind-brain interaction, the notion of a nonlocal consciousness fits quite well with psychological and phenomenological accounts of perception in particular.[61] That is, unlike materialistic perspectives, these accounts do not automatically fixate consciousness in any particular location. They would recognize that the particular location in which consciousness perceives itself to be is an active and simulated phenomenon, whether inside or outside of the physical body. Different rules may apply in each circumstance, but the perceptual environments encountered in either situation are still both constructed by consciousness.

However, a nonlocal approach to consciousness does raise an important question with respect to the phenomenology of the OBE. If the OBE is primarily a change in perspective, or attention, that is an act performed by a nonlocal consciousness, why do many experience themselves so clearly *leaving* the physical body? Would this not suggest that *something* is leaving the physical body? Is it really all about consciousness? Or is there some sort of objective second body involved? This question brings us to a more detailed investigation of the transition process leading into the out-of-body state.

Chapter 3
The Transition Process

MAKING SENSE OF NO SENSES

An investigation of the transition process leading into the out-of-body state is fraught with difficulties. Typically, the OBE occurs during borderline states of sleep in which lucidity is compromised, and as a result, you will be unable to report on the transition process from beginning to end. Even if the transition is entirely lucid, attentional limits still complicate a full understanding. You may, for example, try to observe various tactile sensations during the transition process, such as vibrations coursing through your body that typically precede the onset of an OBE. Yet, in the meantime, you are unable to pay much attention to any visual phenomena, so some important aspects of the transition process will go unnoticed. To complicate matters further, the act of attention in itself changes the experience of the transition process. For example, directing attention toward visual transition phenomena creates an entirely different experience than focusing on tactile sensations. Consequently, the manner in which you may arrive at the out-of-body state is wide and varied, and relatively little is known about exactly how these differences come about.

Notwithstanding the difficulties in identifying the exact factors involved in the onset of the OBE, it is quite clear that *sensory reduction* is related to the OBE. The importance of sensory reduction was initially noted by Robert Monroe, who reported how the various sensory modalities (touch, seeing, hearing) diminish in strength during the transition phase leading into the out-of-body state.[1] Likewise, scientific approaches, which generally view the OBE as an altered state of consciousness or a form of dreaming, tend to agree that the OBE occurs under circumstances in which sensorial input is reduced or not attended to.[2,3] Even most traditional approaches recognize that one is temporarily cut off from the sensory apparatus of the physical body during the OBE.

Because of its association with sensory reduction, the borderline of sleep is also often considered an important factor in the voluntary induction of the OBE, and various OBE authors advocate entering the hypnagogic stage of sleep in an effort to induce the OBE. The hypnagogic stage of sleep can be considered a transition period between waking and sleeping. It is a stage of sleep in which you are half asleep, thought patterns start to become incoherent, and dreamlike imagery may begin to occur. Meanwhile, in order to induce the OBE, the goal is to keep your mind alert and awake while the physical body falls asleep more deeply. This state of mind has also been described as Mind Awake/Body Asleep (MABA)—a state of consciousness in which sensory input is significantly reduced, yet the person is wide awake and alert.[4]

It may be worthwhile to note here that it is as yet unclear whether the OBE always occurs *during* the hypnagogic stage of sleep. EEG measurements with some gifted subjects during the onset of an OBE showed that brain activity more closely resembled a waking than a hypnagogic state of mind.[5,6] Harary and Weintraub describe it as a paradoxical state of consciousness in which deep physical relaxation is accompanied by an underlying heightened sense of arousal.[7] Hence, even though entering the hypnagogic stage of sleep may be a facilitating factor in the voluntary induction of the OBE, the person may not always remain in a hypnagogic state of mind at the onset of the OBE. Regardless, there is little doubt that the OBE is facilitated by mentally approaching the borderline of sleep while the physical body falls asleep.

Despite overall consensus on the importance of sensory reduction and its association with the borderline of sleep, many aspects of OBE induction remain a mystery. What is the origin of energy sensations? Do you leave the physical body with an objective second body? What if you experience no sense of separation from the physical body? The following sections are an attempt to address some of the main factors involved in the process of transition as well as to provide an initial account of the wide variety of experiences that may be encountered.

Table 3.1. Common Transition Phenomena Associated with the Onset of the OBE

Modality	Common Sensations and Perceptions
Tactile	Tingling, buzzing, fizzling, vibrations, electricity, chills, heat, cold, goose bumps, trembling, raindrops, numbing, shaking, throbbing, swirling, spinning, cobwebs, weightlessness, surges, rising, fluttering, numbness, falling, sinking, enlargement, pressure, squeezing, shrinking, swelling, heaviness, lightness, rocking, spinning, rapid heartbeat
Visual	Whirling colors, light flashes, stroboscopic light effects, imagery with "special effects," tunnels, portals, symbols, textures, geometric shapes, fog, mosaics, points of light, stars, tunnel vision
Auditory	Engine-like sounds, squeaking, screeching, tapping, humming, metallic sounds, buzzing, roaring, bells, voices, static, wind blowing, ringing, chorals, tones, music

THE ORIGIN OF ENERGY SENSATIONS

Common transition phenomena associated with the onset of the OBE include a wide variety of different *energy-like* sensations (see Table 3.1). There are many variations in these energy sensations, which occur across different sensory modalities, including vibrations, heat, heaviness, light effects, colors, voices, buzzing, bells, and roaring. And while these sensations may feel incredibly real, there is no apparent physical cause. For example, if you feel your body shaking or vibrating, it would not be visible to an outside observer. Rather, you would appear to be soundly asleep, even as your mind is entirely wrapped up in a wide array of strange perceptual events.

Energy sensations also occur quite frequently during "sleep paralysis," a condition in which you find yourself at the borderline of sleep, unable to move your physical body. Not surprisingly, scientific accounts generally refer to these energy sensations as *hypnagogic hallucinations*, although there is no consensus on their exact origin. Indeed, the lack of any obvious physical cause for energy sensations has led many authors to conclude that they have an "otherworldly" origin.

Sylvan Muldoon, for example, was convinced that energy sensations originated from the astral body.[8] Others, such as Robert Bruce, have based a great deal of their work on the Eastern concept of nonphysical energy pathways in the body, claiming that "energy work" facilitates the separation of a projected double from the physical body."[9,10]

More modern accounts of the OBE, however, have increasingly recognized the second body as a *construction of mind* that is recreated from memory and therefore not necessarily associated with finer energetic matter.[11,12] Yet, if the "second body" is a body image recreated from memory, what *is* the source of energy sensations? Consider the following experiences:

Journal Entry — Thursday, May 13, 2004, 6:00 am

I awoke at around 6 am after a vivid and powerful dream. I quickly made some mental notes of the dream and then began to feel for energy sensations. There were none, except for a slow pulse in my chest—my heartbeat. It was unusual to actually feel my own heartbeat, but the feeling was not unpleasant, and I relaxed into the sensation.

Suddenly, with my heartbeat at the center, circular waves of energy began to move across my body, rippling outward in concentric circles like the waves caused by a pebble thrown in water. With each pulse, I fell a little bit deeper into the trance state, until my entire body seemed enveloped in a fog that effectively blocked out the physical world... *[Continued on p. 87]*

Journal Entry — Friday, April 1, 2005, 2:35 am

Last night, the energy sensations came on easily, which allowed me to observe their onset more closely. I left my body several times, staying in close vicinity to my physical body. Each time I returned, I provoked the energy sensations again, while paying close attention to their source.

Several exits later, it became clear to me that the energy sensations always started somewhere in between my shoulder blades. From there, they would quickly move up my spine and neck, and then spread out further as a tingling and buzzing sensation across my body. Still, I wasn't too sure about the exact point of origin and decided to slow down the process even further.

In the following attempt, as soon as I felt the first inkling of energy sensations, I prevented the sensations from spreading out. Again, they seemed to start somewhere in between my shoulder blades. However, I was able to keep the sensation more localized this time—a tingling sensation in my upper spine and neck region. This all occurred in less than one second.

Next, I focused on what appeared to be the epicenter of these sensations, located near the heart area. Doing so made the sensations retract to their point of origin. I no longer felt anything in the neck area. Rather, nothing remained except for a peculiar fluttering sensation fairly deep underneath my skin—no more than an inch wide. It seemed as though I had found the epicenter. It was at the exact location of my heart, as if a butterfly were inside of it!

Journal Entry — Tuesday, July 4, 2006, 4:10 am

Having an experiment in mind before bedtime, I awoke in the middle of the night. Conditions were excellent. I only needed to touch slightly on the hypnagogic stage of sleep to trigger the vibrations, which, as usual, spread out across my body, quickly reaching a frequency of around 200 beats per minute. I knew better than to think that my physical body was shaking—at least not in a visible manner—but what if I could feel the vibrations with my hands?

Carefully, I moved my physical hand toward my abdomen. Luckily, the physical movement of my hand did not interfere with the vibrations, and without any interruption in the energy sensations, I placed my fingertips on the skin of my abdomen.

What I felt was most interesting. Right underneath my skin, I could feel my blood rushing through zillions of tiny blood vessels. It flowed in a strong rhythmic, pulsating pattern. It was pulsating at a much faster rate than would be physically possible. If these pulses did originate from my heartbeat, they were clearly distorted.

I observed these physiological sensations for a while longer, as well as the vibrations, which continued without interruption. Then it suddenly became clear to me. The blood pulsed at <u>exactly</u> the same frequency as the vibrations. They were one and the same thing, both of them a distorted version of reality... [Continued on p. 59]

Journal Entry — Sunday, March 11, 2007, 5:20 am

I had a bit of a scare last night. Following my usual pattern, I entered the hypnagogic stage of sleep to induce the vibrations. Then suddenly, my heart began to thump inside my chest at an almost impossible rate (approximately 220 beats per minute). Worse, my chest tightened, and for a short while, I had a strong impression of a heavy wooden beam pressing down on me.

I almost panicked with the thought of a heart attack but remembered similar accounts in which such a rapid heartbeat always turned out to be an illusory phenomenon. I was able to compose myself. Yet, I had never experienced anything like this before, at least not with the tightness in my chest. I was not at all sure if I would come out of this unscathed. I had really done it this time, I thought.

Carefully, so as not to upset anything further, I began to move out of the hypnagogic state at a very measured pace. Slowly but surely, the rapid heartbeat was replaced by the pulse of a regular heartbeat. For a while, I experienced a dual type of perception in which one sensation fades into awareness (i.e., the normal heartbeat) and the other sensation fades out of awareness (i.e., the rapid heartbeat). Eventually, I returned to full wakefulness, in which everything seemed completely normal—as if nothing out of the ordinary had ever taken place.

Others have noted an increased sensitivity to internal stimuli when the physical body is about to fall asleep, which may manifest as "...an awareness that the pores of your skin breathe, hearing the swish of blood flow behind your ears, feeling your heartbeat."[13] If this seems difficult to imagine, consider a medical disorder of the inner ear such as *superior canal dehiscence syndrome,* which leads the sufferer to hear the eyeballs moving in their sockets like "...sandpaper on wood."[14] In the case of energy sensations, we are dealing with the perception of internal bodily phenomena as well, except that they are often experienced in a distorted format. In particular, my own observations are remarkably consistent with those noted by the late physicist and philosopher Isaac Bentov, who holds that energy sensations can be traced back to pressure pulses traveling through the vascular system, ultimately originating from the heart muscle—the "noisiest" organ in the body.[15] Interestingly, in this regard, people with quadriplegia have reported energy sensations as well while trying to induce the out-of-body state, confirming that not every torso and limb sensation reaches the brain through the spinal cord. Some predictions can also be derived from the current conceptualization, such as that those individuals with a stronger cardiovascular system will experience stronger energy sensations. Gender differences likely apply as well.

Most people are probably familiar with the sensation of just being about to fall asleep and, when poked by someone else, jolting wide awake as if hit with a sledgehammer. Alternatively, you might be just about to doze off when an outside noise is experienced as if the world has come crashing down. These distortions generally occur because a state of sensory reduction disallows for the proper integration and perception of external stimuli. Similar distortions and translation factors seem to occur in the case of "energy sensations," in which normal bodily phenomena are experienced as vibrations, shaking, buzzing, light flashes, noises, voices, and so on.

The psychophysiological translation of internal stimuli into energy sensations may also cross sensory boundaries, causing objective tactile sensations to translate into visual imagery and vice versa. This is a form of synesthesia in which, for example, hearing the blood rushing behind your ears translates perceptually as an image of an exploding light bulb or a feeling of glass shattering against your face. Alternatively, you may perceive your own breathing as the sound of wind or even experience a sensation of wind blowing against your skin.

The exact manner in which bodily stimuli are perceptually translated is often dependent on your psychological mindset at the time.

In some cases, they give rise to more complex hallucinatory types of experiences only very remotely related to the original bodily sensation. For example, a fearful attitude might lead you to hear a screaming or threatening voice. Likewise, marginal pressure on your skin from the sheets could lead to a sensation of pressure on the chest as if an "entity" were sitting on your chest, especially if this occurs in combination with sleep paralysis. Suffice to say, a multitude of variations can occur in which normal internal bodily phenomena are perceptually translated into energy sensations.

It should be recognized that there are still several unknowns with respect to the distorted perception of normal internal bodily phenomena. The exact mechanisms responsible for hypersensitivity to internal stimuli are not known, either, except that they seem associated with sensory reduction and attention. It seems quite clear, however, that in the vast majority of instances, energy sensations do find their origin in marginal sensory input, usually of an internal origin.

I do not wish to exclude the possibility that these sensations relate to "energy" on some level since, after all, as quantum physics teaches us, all mass is energy.[16] However, trivial references to potential quantum mechanical factors do not really clarify the issue, especially if energy sensations are also coherently explained on a materialistic, macro level, an explanation generally rejected in more esoteric accounts.

Mainstream scientific accounts do not fare much better than esoteric accounts by almost always referring to energy sensations as hypnagogic hallucinations. Energy sensations do not always involve the perception of completely imaginary phenomena. A more appropriate term for scientific approaches to adopt would be *hypnagogic illusions*. To avoid confusion, however, I will continue to use the term *energy sensations,* which, at least from an experiential perspective, describes these sensations quite well. Besides, energy sensations do not solely occur in a hypnagogic state of mind; consequently, using the term *hypnagogic* to describe these sensations is inappropriate to begin with.

THE INDUCTION OF ENERGY SENSATIONS

The induction of energy sensations is rather vague and complex in most of the OBE literature. Some propose meditative techniques or trance techniques, which are simply variants of techniques aimed at reducing sensory input. Robert Monroe suggests entering the hypnagogic stage of sleep and reaching for and drawing in "vibrations" from above the head.[17] Likewise, the projector Robert Bruce notes that all techniques for OBEs involve the person focusing outside of the body, away from any inner movement.[9] My own observations, however, suggest that it is not merely a focus of attention directed *outside* of the body that triggers energy sensations. Rather, energy sensations, and somatosensory sensations in particular, typically occur when you direct attention *toward* physical body awareness from an otherwise inward-oriented focus. This is not surprising since, as discussed earlier, energy sensations are associated with events occurring in the physical body (heartbeat, pressure pulses, blood flow, and so on). Consequently, attention needs to be focused on the body (at least to a certain extent) in order to trigger energy sensations. Often, directing attention outside of the body will be quite sufficient as well, but this is only because outward-directed attention often implies some level of physical body awareness.

Journal Entry — Saturday, June 17, 2006, 3:05 am

Last night, as part of my regular routine, I let my mind drift and began to approach the sleep border. For a while, I moved in and out of sleep while trying to maintain that delicate balance between waking and sleeping. I was tired and had difficulty preventing myself from falling asleep. However, right before losing lucidity altogether, a hypnagogic image caught my attention, and I regained a significant amount of lucidity in the process.

The image itself, now forgotten, was insignificant. It did, however, startle me enough to focus my attention back toward my body. Almost immediately, a wave of energy moved across my body. Interestingly, I could clearly discern that it was not the hypnagogic image, but rather my <u>attention</u> directed toward bodily sensations, that triggered the energy sensations...

Journal Entry — Saturday, June 24, 2006, 3:35 am

I was able to put several ideas regarding the transition process to a final test last night. In particular, I wanted to pay close attention to any changes in physical bodily sensations in the course of the transition process. I began by moving toward the sleep border.

Initially, I had trouble maintaining lucidity, and each time I drifted off into sleep, I forgot to divert attention back to my body. I frequently woke up, reminded myself of my purpose, and then repeated the process over and over again. However, over time, perhaps for more than an hour, I began to notice an interesting effect of my activity. It became progressively easier to move into sleep without losing consciousness.

Eventually, I became so lucid that it was difficult to discern any difference between waking and sleeping. It felt as if the veil between waking and sleeping had collapsed. No longer was it I who had to mentally approach the borderline of sleep. Rather, the borderline of sleep was encroaching upon me.

I felt a very subtle rocking or trembling sensation accompanied by an almost liquid sense of mental and physical relaxation. Right then and there, I knew I could easily move into sleep without losing any lucidity in the process. I relaxed my awareness and kept my attention loosely focused on my physical body. Almost immediately, the transition process was set into motion, with several chill-like sensations spreading across my body... [Continued on p. 45]

Ideally, energy sensations are induced from a state very similar to the waking state, without any break in consciousness. It is a feeling quite similar (if not identical) to the state of mind that may occur after tossing and turning in bed for hours due to insomnia, when eventually there is a sudden increase in sleep pressure, and all physical tension and mental chatter come to an abrupt halt. Often, this coincides with a slight trembling or rocking sensation, presumably the result of extreme physical relaxation preceding the onset of sleep. Yet, despite the proximity of sleep under these circumstances, you are wide awake, with full physical body awareness.

Because this situation occurs under highly lucid conditions, you are in an excellent position to establish a completely lucid transition into the OBE state. Often, energy sensations will be pronounced. Conversely, energy sensations are far less likely to occur if the transition process is initiated from deep *within* the hypnagogic stage of sleep. Usually, in these cases, the physical body has fallen asleep completely, and the level of sensory input has already decreased significantly. There may not be a sufficient level of sensory input left to allow for the perception of energy sensations. This is unproblematic as long as you are sufficiently lucid and able to make a controlled entry into a specific out-of-body environment.

THE INTENSIFICATION OF ENERGY SENSATIONS

Whether energy sensations are triggered from deep within the hypnagogic stage of sleep with a more pronounced reduction in sensory input, or from full waking consciousness with the physical senses on the *verge* of retraction, in order to complete the process of sensory reduction, you need to allow the physical body to fall asleep until no sensory input remains. This may often be accomplished by relaxing into the energy sensations, both mentally and physically, and allowing them to unfold on their own terms.

Journal Entry — Monday, July 10, 2006, 3:45 am

I once again woke up with energy sensations—fairly slow, coarse vibrations throughout my body. I relaxed into the sensations, and they quickly began to intensify, turning into higher-frequency buzzing sensations.

During the intensification process, I got the idea to suddenly break off my mental movement toward sleep. Doing so almost made me wake up completely. For a while, the energy sensations wavered like a stalling engine.

However, after I regained my mental balance by positioning my mind somewhere around the midway point toward sleep, the energy sensations settled into a steady pattern without intensifying.

Satisfied that I could keep hold while still in the middle of the transition process, I proceeded to move deeper into sleep until the energy sensations reached that familiar pitch at which I could fly off into the sky...

As the physical body falls asleep while your mind remains alert, awake, and focused on energy sensations, you will notice the intensification of these sensations. The term *intensification* does not simply refer to energy sensations becoming stronger, which may occur as well, but rather to an increase in the *frequency* of the sensations.

For example, energy sensations that start out as strong, heavy vibrations typically increase in frequency up until the point that they are experienced as buzzlike or tingling sensations. If you were to increase the frequency even further, the sensations might transform to a more generalized feeling of heat or cold (the highest frequency). Sometimes, a numbing or clouding effect may occur as well, as if the physical senses are enveloped in a haze—a relatively direct representation of the actual process that is occurring.

There are many variations, which are also subject to psychological influences such as the state of mind of the projector at the time. From a practical viewpoint, however, the exact manner in which energy sensations evolve, both over time as you become practiced and during the process of sensory retraction itself, is not that important.

The intensification of energy sensations is a by-product of the process of sensory retraction that automatically occurs as the physical body falls asleep. The more deeply the body falls asleep, the more energy sensations will intensify as you remain focused on them. Your mind allows this by mentally relaxing into these sensations. Hence, it is unnecessary to manipulate energy sensations *directly* in order to effectuate an OBE. You are far better off learning how to relax into these sensations.

SENSORY REDUCTION AND BODY AWARENESS

Do you literally separate from the physical body with an objective second body during an OBE? My own observations do not indicate that there is an objective second body involved the transition process, nor is there any need to "exit" the physical body in order to establish the out-of-body state. Rather, you "separate" from sensory input while maintaining the same body image you occupy in normal consciousness. It is a transition that can therefore also be appropriately referred to as a *parasomatic* transition, during which some sense of body awareness is maintained.[18]

Journal Entry — Saturday, June 24, 2006, 3:35 am

[Continued from p. 42] ...I relaxed even more, and the energy sensations intensified. All the while, I remained highly attentive to any changes in body awareness. I expected that perhaps any physical sensations would fade away, including my sense of having a physical body. Yet, as the transition process unfolded, nothing truly changed. I remained aware of everything: my body, the sheets, the mattress, the bed I was lying in.

The situation was no different at the end of the transition process. I still felt my body, the bed, even the pillow against my face. Yet, I knew for certain that I was ready to move out; the energy sensations had intensified quite sufficiently.

I slowly moved my head up. Again, I remained focused on any change in sensation. There was nothing to indicate any sort of separation. Nothing was moving "out." Yet, I was certain I had reached the out-of-body state. It was not my physical head that I was moving, even though it was the same head I had felt just a moment ago.

I then moved my head back onto the pillow. There was no sense of a return to the body, either. I moved my head up and down a few more times just to see if I had missed anything, but there was nothing to suggest any sort of separation. Eventually, I lifted myself up completely and sat on the edge of the bed, puzzled.

I took a quick glance back at the bed and noticed there was no body lying in bed. Oddly enough, this was the only thing that made sense so far. I had never left the body. I had simply gotten up! With that last observation, I decided to leave my experimentation behind, walked up to bedroom window, and flew outside into the garden...

There is nothing that leaves the physical body in this experience. There was no second body, nor was there any transferal of consciousness from one body to another. Instead, there was a complete *continuity* of body awareness during the transition despite a pronounced reduction in sensory input during the course of the transition process. Under these circumstances, because of the continuity of body awareness, you will usually not see your physical body lying in bed after having established the out-of-body state. This makes sense since, except for the absence of sensory input, you are walking around in the same body image you "occupy" in ordinary consciousness, with no image of the physical body left behind.

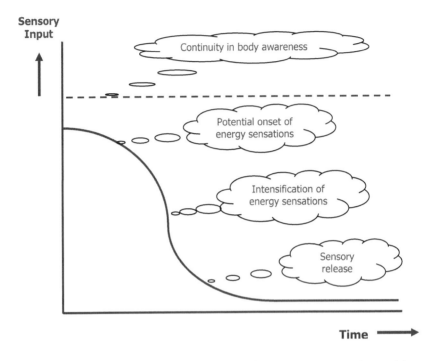

Figure 3.2. Graphical Representation of Sensory Retraction with Continuity in Body Awareness During the Transition Process

As shown in Figure 3.2, you start out with sensorial-informed body awareness with the physical senses on the edge of retraction, which, given sufficient sleep pressure, leads to the onset of energy sensations. Typically, energy sensations under these circumstances are of a somatosensory nature (vibrations, electricity, waves, and so on) and will intensify once the physical body falls more deeply asleep. Sensory input may diminish rapidly, but body awareness does not falter because consciousness fills up any potential gaps left behind by the absence of sensory input (i.e., your own body image). Eventually, once sensory input has decreased sufficiently, you are free of physical limitations without having gone through any "exit procedure" (i.e., sensory release).

SEPARATION

The idea that you do not have to *leave* the physical body to establish the out-of-body state may seem at odds with a strong feeling of separation from the physical body that projectors sometimes experience. In fact, many of my own earlier out-of-body experiences often did involve a strong sense of separation, including seeing a second body separating from what appeared to be my physical body. There appeared to be two bodies, not just one. Yet, even under these circumstances, there is no second body leaving from the *physical* body. This claim, of course, requires further elaboration.

Journal Entry — Tuesday, October 17, 2006, 2:40 am

I had difficulty getting to sleep, but after several hours of tossing and turning, I began to feel light rocking and trembling sensations. I recognized the sensations as a sign that sleep was just around the corner. My mind was still restless, however, and the rocking sensations soon disappeared.

Yet, ten minutes later, the rocking sensations returned. This time, I found myself able to relax my mind until the full-fledged energy sensations were triggered. I soon reached the point of sensory release and flew up into the void, which is my usual pattern. However, just as I was about to set a destination, I was suddenly pulled back and found myself back in bed.

Everything was quiet. If there had been an outside disturbance leading to my premature return, it was no longer there. Luckily, I still felt the energy sensations. I was still fairly deep in and probably could separate again. This time, however, rather than flying away, I decided to conduct an experiment.

I looked down my body. The light was dim, but I could clearly make out the outline of what I assumed was my physical body underneath the comforter, with my arms dropped on top. Without meeting any resistance, I lifted two phantom arms out of my physical body. I could clearly discern the outline of my two phantom arms, as well as my physical arms, lying immobile on top of the sheets. Except for the two phantom arms, there was nothing to indicate that the rest of me was not in the physical body.

I woke up shortly after and began to analyze the entire experience. Then it suddenly hit me. I was no longer lying on my back as I had been earlier. I was lying on my side with my right arm firmly locked underneath my body. I had never been physical in any way to begin with. Every part of me had been "out" during the experience.

This experience does not make any sense from the perspective that you are leaving the physical body during an OBE. It started out as a fairly typical OBE during which I flew up into the void immediately following sensory release. Once back in bed, I assumed I was back in the physical, so I began to experiment with moving my phantom arms out from what appeared to be my physical body. Yet, this was not my physical body at all. My actual physical body turned out to be in an entirely different position. I had been separating my phantom arms from a phantom body that *posed* as my physical body!

I would suggest that this scenario always occurs when you "leave the body." You start out with sensorial-informed body awareness (the physical body) while lying in bed (see Figure 3.3A). Once sensory input starts to retract, consciousness continues to provide a completely realistic body image (see Figure 3.3B). This body image is the *same* body image we "occupy" in ordinary consciousness except that it is no longer sensorial informed. Effectively, you have reached the out-of-body state by separating from sensory input. However, once released from sensory input, you may still engage in some form of separation, thereby needlessly creating yet another body image (see Figure 3.3C). The latter typically occurs when you operate under the assumption that leaving the body is still necessary to achieve the out-of-body state, even while you have already separated from physical input. Upon separation, the phantom body that is left behind may be found lying in bed posing as a physical body, or alternatively, it may disappear altogether, with the bed left empty. Whatever the case may be, in none of these instances do you leave the physical body (see Figure 3.3D). In fact, once the process of sensory reduction is completed, you may simply get out of bed in your phantom body as per figure 3.3B. There is no need to create another body image.

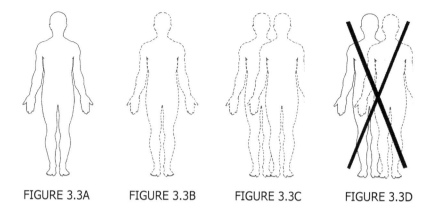

FIGURE 3.3A   FIGURE 3.3B   FIGURE 3.3C   FIGURE 3.3D

Figure 3.3. Graphical Representation of Separation from Sensory Input

Occasionally, the belief that one still needs to separate, while already completely free from physical limitations, leads to confusing but amusing situations. The same phenomenon has also been referred to as a *false awakening*, in which one fails to realize that one is no longer part of ordinary physical reality, such as in the following experience:

Journal Entry — Saturday, October 28, 2006, 3:15 am

I had a confusing OBE last night. I woke up at around 3 am and for a while hovered near the borderline of sleep, until the energy sensations started. A few seconds later, I reached the point of sensory release, and as a matter of habit, I rolled over in bed to complete the process.

I must have been lying at the edge of the bed, since as I rolled over, I promptly landed in between the nightstand and the bed. It felt quite uncomfortable, with the edges of the nightstand digging into my skin.

I immediately reasoned that I must have rolled over physically and fallen out of bed. I stood up, feeling a little foolish. How I had managed to roll over physically was beyond me. I could have sworn I had reached the point of sensory release. Luckily, my wife was still soundly asleep.

I got back into bed, and once again, after going though all the motions before separation, I continued to roll over several times more in an attempt to separate. I did not fall out of the bed this time, but each time I rolled over, it felt as if I was moving my physical body.

Something clearly was not right.

Eventually, I simply gave up, moving back to full wakefulness. Only then did I realize I had been "out" all along.

VARIATIONS IN SENSORY REDUCTION

What about experiences in which you exit the physical through *selective* parts of the physical body? Ernst Waelti, for example, reports leaving the physical body through the head.[19] Would this not indicate that you are separating from the physical body rather than merely separating from sensory input? Indeed, on the surface, an experience in which you exit the physical body through selective parts of the body seems to suggest that you are literally leaving the body. Again, however, you are not exiting the *physical* body in these instances.

Journal Entry — Monday, April 18, 2005, 4:20 am

Last night, I once again found myself back in the vibrational stage. I decided to watch the process of separation more carefully and try something different. I began by bringing down the vibrations to a localized area in my body as I had done on a previous occasion. Doing so was more a matter of mental acrobatics than anything else— remaining poised at the borderline of sleep very close to complete physical body awareness. I managed to do so, and soon the only sensation that remained was a fluttering sensation near my heart. Again, it felt like a butterfly flapping its wings inside of me.

I then tried to separate and squeeze my way through the tiny area of fluttering sensations. Not entirely surprised, I soon figured out that this was impossible. The space to "move through" was far too small. Besides, I was still far too physical. I moved deeper into sleep, using the same mental acrobatics, until the vibrations had expanded to my upper body. Like a liquid whirling across my chest, they now covered most of my upper body.

Again, I tried to move out—successfully this time. There was some resistance, and it felt as if I were worming my way through a hollow tube, but I managed to get out through the upper body region. Once out, I quickly realigned with the physical and repeated the process while keeping the vibrations limited to the upper part of my body. This time, however, I attempted to move out by going downward. However, the absence of any vibrations in that region made moving out through my lower body impossible...

The main reason you find yourself leaving the body through a selective body part is because of an *unequal* distribution in sensory reduction in the physical body. Consequently, you are only able to exit the body through those parts where energy sensations have intensified sufficiently. So while it may feel as if you are moving out of the physical body, you are not really exiting through a physical body part. Rather, you are exiting through a *selective* phantom body part that is no longer informed by sensory input. This is the same situation as depicted in Figure 3.3C, except that it involves a much smaller phantom area through which you exit.

A variation on the theme of an unequal distribution of sensory reduction across the physical body is the situation in which you find yourself "stuck." You may, for example, after almost having "left" the physical body, suddenly get stuck at the feet. None of these difficulties are the result of "energy blockages," as is sometimes suggested in esoteric accounts of the OBE. They merely represent the incomplete retraction of the physical senses in certain parts of the physical body. You will get stuck in exactly those places where too high a level of sensory input is still present.

Incomplete sensory retraction in selected body parts may also translate into complex illusions. One person, for example, reported finding her feet entangled in the bedsheets, which prevented her from completing the process of separation. Here, incomplete sensory retraction of the feet, and the inability to separate from the senses at the feet, leads to a perception of the most probable cause in the mind of the projector (e.g., "the sheets must be wrapped around my feet").

Another variation of incomplete sensory retraction is a sensation of "peeling out" during the process of "moving out" of the body. You may experience friction, perhaps even complete with sounds effects, such as a crackling sound. Again, however, these perceptions are due to incomplete sensory reduction that creates the illusion of friction. The source of the "friction" is, of course, quite real. It's just that its symbolic manifestation is not.

A final variant of incomplete sensory retraction is *sleep paralysis*, during which you find yourself either partially or completely paralyzed, unable to move. It represents a situation in which you have progressed quite far into the transition process to the extent that sensory reduction no longer allows you to move physically. At the same time, sensory input has not decreased sufficiently for you to be entirely free of physical limitations and move "out of the body." In other words, you are not just immobilized in a physical sense but in a nonphysical sense as well, which occurs within a very narrow band of consciousness, somewhere in between the intensification of energy sensations and sensory release (see Figure 3.2, p. 46).

Sleep paralysis is by no means a frequent precursor of the OBE, but expect it to occur now and then. The inability to move may give rise to fear, which can lead to various hallucinatory types of experiences. For example, it is not uncommon to hallucinate being held (down) by a presence.

Journal Entry — Sunday, February 8, 2004, 3:00 am

I got stuck in sleep paralysis last night. It started out with inviting several hypnagogic images into my awareness. I'm not sure what happened next except that I ended up lucid and alert while lying in bed, surrounded by voidlike darkness. Next, as soon as I was about to fly off, I felt a pair of foreign arms locked tightly around my waist. I was utterly unable to move.

Strangely enough, the pair of arms did not have a body to go along with them. It was like being held by "Thing" (a character in the form of a disembodied hand) from the The Addams Family. It was far too surreal to panic about, and I quickly surmised that I must be in sleep paralysis, hallucinating a pair of arms in the process.

The arms were locked around my waist, leaving my own arms free to move. However, there was little I could do. They did not give an inch. I even went so far as to grab the fingers, trying to bend them backward to force them to let go, but even a pinky was stronger than I. If I was going to get out of this, I needed to be smart rather than try to use force... [Continued on p. 283]

Journal Entry — Wednesday, May 17, 2006, 4:40 am

Last night's experience began right after a dream. I woke up, remembered my intent to project, and immediately slipped back into the borderland between waking and sleeping. Energy sensations quickly followed. However, while still lying in bed, I received an unexpected percept of a dark figure that was trying to make its way into the house. I perceived this in my mind's eye, remotely viewing what was outside.

The scene made me quite uncomfortable, especially since the dream I had just woken up from revolved around a similar theme. It felt like an intrusion of some kind. Immediately following the impression, I focused back on my surroundings to find the stranger sitting on the side of the bed right next to me. His hand was holding mine in an iron grip.

I did not detect any animosity, but it was dark, and I could not identify the visitor. Yet, I had no intent to open up my vision for fear of what could reveal itself.

I tried to get up but found myself unable to move. Apparently, however, I could still move my arms and hands, and in a battle of wills, I squeezed his hand as hard as I could. There was no reaction despite the strong pressure I applied.

Then it spoke.

"Who do you think I am?" the dark figure asked. It sounded far too ominous.

"Yes, who are you?!" I shouted.

For some reason, the paralysis broke with my outburst of anger.

No longer held down, I was in a fight-or-flight response and got very mad, promising the stranger that his life was soon to end. I quickly rose toward the ceiling to gain the advantage.

With some distance between myself and the figure, I finally opened up my vision and looked down into the bedroom. There was nothing. The figure had vanished into thin air. I soon decided I had enough for the night and proceeded to wake up.

Back in bed, I noticed a faint sensation in my hand—the kind of sensation you would be left with after making a fist and squeezing as hard as you can. I probably had been squeezing my own hand. I'm now *left wondering if I missed some sort of opportunity.*

It can be quite difficult to break out of sleep paralysis, especially if fear and hallucinations are part of it. To break out of sleep paralysis in a physical manner, it is generally best to attempt to move a small body part, such as your fingers, and press them down hard on the mattress of the bed. Often, there will be faint impressions of underlying physical sensations. This will help you to return to physical-based awareness. Alternatively, if you still want to engage in an OBE, you will have to find a visual exit point without any interfering body awareness. This brings us to asomatic pathways into the out-of-body state.

ASOMATIC PATHWAYS INTO THE OUT-OF-BODY STATE

During the transitions described so far, you maintain some level of body awareness, or what can also be referred to as *parasomatic* transitions. However, an entirely different class of transition is the *asomatic* transition, during which no body awareness is maintained. There will be no continuity in body image as sensory input is reduced; rather, any awareness of having a body will disappear in the process.

To induce an asomatic transition, you maintain a solely visual focus toward inner phenomena associated with the onset of sleep. You pay no attention to your body image, nor should any of the visual imagery occurring at the onset of sleep relate to having a body. Then, as the physical senses retract, energy sensations may begin to occur, but none that relate to your body. Instead, energy sensations will remain limited to stroboscopic effects, light flashes, swirling colors, symbols, explosions, voices, and so on (see Table 3.1, p. 35).

Often, as soon as energy sensations of a visual nature occur, you will find that your attention automatically focuses on your physical safety. This may have the outcome of body awareness returning, accompanied by energy sensations such as vibrations, electricity, buzzing, and chills. You can still complete the transition into the out-of-body state, but it is no longer an asomatic transition.

The visual focus required for the asomatic transition can make it a difficult act to perform, at least in any controlled manner. However, do expect asomatic transitions to become more frequent in the course of your out-of-body activity. They are part of a natural progression in which you find yourself increasingly at ease with strange phenomena and less interested in bodily awareness.

Journal Entry — Sunday, June 18, 2006, 10:00 am

I slept in this morning and had an unusually late OBE. I had already been drifting in and out of sleep for a while without intending to project. Eventually, I decided to give it a try.

I allowed myself to drift gently while maintaining a relaxed visual focus, trying not to get too involved with the imagery and dreamscapes passing by. Then, once I felt I had entered deep enough, I brought in full awareness without diverting any attention to body awareness. Doing so almost immediately filled up my entire visual field with a gray-blue color.

The abruptness of the visual effect almost shocked me back into full wakefulness. But I managed to stay with it and continued to push ahead by allowing it to unfold further. Then, just as quickly as the colors had appeared, they vanished from view. My entire field of vision "blacked out," and I found myself staring off into a familiar space. I was formless, suspended in the void...

Journal Entry — Saturday, August 19, 2006, 3:25 am

I made an effort to have an OBE last night. I had already woken up twice before, after which I tried to remain lucid while drifting off. The third time, I felt rather bored and drifted off deeply into the hypnagogic stage without any attention directed toward my physical body. Instead, once I entered deep enough, I found myself quite automatically "transported" into the bedroom environment as if I was phasing into it. This all happened quite accidentally, and lucidity was less than usual, perhaps the result of the suddenness of the transition. But I still knew what I was doing and proceeded to make my way through the bedroom door and went downstairs...

Journal Entry — Sunday, March 11, 2007, 6:10 am

In my second attempt of the night, I entered deeper into the hypnagogic stage of sleep, quickly losing any sense of body in the process. Energy sensations were fairly minimal. There were no somatosensory sensations. Even visual sensations were kept at a minimum until a "screen effect" appeared. My entire perceptual field filled up with horizontal lines of black and red, which then morphed into a surreal-looking room. I saw myself standing in the middle of the room. It did not take me long to become part of the environment as an active participant. No longer was I viewing the event from a distance, but instead, I was inside of it...

Journal Entry — Saturday, May 7, 2005, 4:05 am

I spent some time doing several imagination exercises last night. I was trying to imagine the color white as vividly as possible as I drifted off to sleep. At first, the color was difficult to imagine, but as I relaxed more and more, I began to see it with less effort. However, it was not until I drifted off even further that a bright light began to fill my entire field of vision as if it existed entirely independent of me. From there, my mind plunged forward toward the light. I did not feel a body, and yet I moved forward deeper into it.

One or two seconds later, I began to see a texture. The light was like a piece of fabric with crossing threads of white linen. In between the threads—empty black space. I had moved in microscopically close by now. The empty black space began to expand. Soon, I would be able to move my mind through the threads. I began to hear a thousand whispering voices, but I ignored them, continuing to move toward the black space in between the linen—ever increasing in size until I no longer could discern any of the white threads. I had arrived at the void...

Journal Entry — Tuesday, August 23, 2005, 2:10 am

I woke up often last night—an activity I have been cultivating lately. Then, at around 2 am, I felt the familiar energy sensations. It was like an inaudible high-pitched wave of energy, neither entirely tactile nor auditory in nature. I was ready for the sensation to increase, and it did, until all physical sensation disappeared. I felt nothing. No second body. No bed. There was no sensation whatsoever. Instead, I found myself staring off into a wide expanse of blackness—the void.

Not having a second body was a peculiar feeling. It was like staring off into a mental abyss without anything concrete to hold onto. Yet, I was able to "move" around in the 3D blackness—not in any physical sense, however. I was rotating and moving my own consciousness through space.

After playing around with these rotations for a while, I decided to try to trigger some scenery from within the void. Doing so gave me a vague impression of a "lighted" humanoid shape hidden behind the veil of darkness. Nothing really manifested, however, and I returned to the physical context not long after.

No sense of separation is experienced during an asomatic transition. This is not surprising since during this type of transition, there is no body awareness to experience a sense of separation *from*. Consequently, you typically end up in a formless state—floating in an empty void as pure awareness.

The void is a truly remarkable state of consciousness in which practically all contact with the physical senses is severed. It represents the end result of sensory retraction, with almost all of the physical senses disengaged. At most, the auditory senses may still be partially operational, with sounds from the outside perceived in a muffled and distorted format. Otherwise, all contact with the physical senses has been lost, providing you with a great deal of freedom to move wherever you want.

Aptly, the void has also been referred to as a *minimum perceptual environment*.[20] In general, very little is ever perceived inside of the void. It is often completely dark. However, this darkness should not be confused with the flat, two-dimensional type of darkness that occurs when you close your eyes. Rather, the void has a spatial depth as if you were staring into outer space.

In fact, it is not uncommon to perceive various pinpoints of colored lights in the void, leaving one with the impression of stars. It is unclear to me what these lights signify, except that they add to the spatial depth of the void, making it appear more massive and increasing one's overall sense of mobility (see Figure 3.4).

Figure 3.4. Graphical Illustration of a Minimum Perceptual Environment with Spatial Depth (i.e., the Void)

It should be noted that the emergence of the void is by no means limited to the asomatic transition. It also commonly occurs after a parasomatic transition. It is more difficult to recognize, however, because following a parasomatic transition, you would generally seamlessly replace the physical environment with its nonphysical version, more or less bypassing the void in the process. However, any darkness you perceive following a parasomatic transition is actually closely related to the void. Usually, this phenomenon is interpreted as "blindness" as you stumble around your bedroom. Yet, do not be surprised to sometimes find yourself in a completely different environment than that of your bedroom as your vision opens up. You may, for example, step out of your own bed on top of the Himalayas. So despite appearances, until you have engaged visually with your surroundings, do not make the assumption of being in your bedroom, not even when you can feel yourself lying in bed. You are in fact inside of the void, which occurs *before* the actual manifestation of an out-of-body environment.

EXOTIC MODES OF TRANSITION

Environmental Transitions

There are many more rare and exotic modes of transitioning, quite reminiscent of popular means of transportation in science fiction movies. For example, you may also engage in what might be called an *environmental transition,* which involves the entire dissolution of the environment in the course of the transition process. So rather than you moving anywhere, it is the environment around you that is transitioning, eventually leaving you "elsewhere."

Environmental transitions into the void tend to be very disorienting and are perhaps not recommended to establish the out-of-body state. They interfere with spatial orientation in a rather fundamental manner. They may even temporarily compromise your ability to *think* in spatial terms. However, if there was any doubt that you do not have to go through an "exit procedure" to establish the out-of-body state, consider the following:

Journal Entry — Tuesday, July 4, 2006, 4:10 am

[Continued from p. 38] ...I then proceeded to separate several times. However, each time I had almost detached, I got pulled back and found myself lying on the bed. Then something unexpected happened.

Without warning, I lost all sensations of lying in bed, and the entire environment around me dissolved into thin air. Quite literally, I felt as if the ground had been swept away from underneath me and found myself suspended in pure blackness.

I realized I was in the void but was utterly disoriented. I was unable to position myself relative to the bed that was there just a moment ago. It was a most peculiar situation to be unable to even think in spatial terms. I still knew the difference between up and down, left and right, but I was entirely out of touch with the concept of "there-where-I-came-from."

I continued to mentally struggle for a while, trying to get a hold of the concept of "there-where-I-came-from," and luckily, my understanding eventually returned. Once it did, it did not take long for physical awareness to return, and I found myself back in bed.

Auditory Transitions

An auditory transition is yet another exotic type of transition. Of course, energy sensations of an auditory nature may occur during both asomatic and parasomatic transitions. However, if attention is focused on listening for sound, while keeping visual and tactile sensations at bay, you might be able to effectuate a purely auditory transition.

Journal Entry — Monday, November 17, 2008, 5:25 am

I was lying in bed hovering near the borderline of sleep. It was one of those states of mind in which it seemed easy to move in and out of sleep. But something was slightly different this time. Each time I moved closer to sleep and initiated the process of sensory retraction, there were no vibrations or any other kinds of somatosensory sensations. Instead, there was only a metallic screeching sound that got louder and more intense as I moved more deeply into sleep.

I continued to move in and out of sleep, manipulating the intensity of the sounds in the process, while wondering why there were no other kinds of energy sensations. Then I realized my attention was fully focused on my head region, as it would be when you try to hear. I did not pay any attention to any other body part, nor did I look into the blackness in front of my eyes. It made sense that only auditory sensations would occur.

I continued to complete the transition and intensified the energy sensations until they stopped. It felt as if all auditory senses had now retracted, and outside sounds were blocked off, for the most part. The only sensation of sound that remained was similar to what you hear when you yawn. Soon, that disappeared as well.

I then moved out of sleep, activating my physical senses once again and, this time, diverting my attention toward the rest of my body. Sure enough, there were no auditory sensations, and all I could feel was a mild sensation of chills across my body.

Auditory transitions can be very smooth if executed in a controlled manner. Uncontrolled, however, they have the potential to be very disconcerting. In particular, if the transition is quick and violent, you may be catapulted out of the body. Usually, this is accompanied by a loud explosion or a frightening noise of something snapping inside of your brain. On rare occasions, the focus toward the head region may lead your phantom head to be violently disconnected from the rest of you. The sensation is not unlike that of "flying head," eerily reminiscent of the guillotine.

SENSORY "BLEEDTHROUGH"

A final aspect that deserves mentioning here is *sensory bleedthrough* following perceptual engagement into an out-of-body environment. To understand the process, you have to realize that sensory input never completely disappears; it can still exert an influence, even from the farthest margins of consciousness (Figure 3.2, p. 46). If sensory information remains below a certain threshold, it does not disturb the OBE in any noticeable way. Occasionally, however, situations may arise in which sensory input penetrates the out-of-body environment. Consider the following:

Journal Entry — Friday, October 6, 2006, 2:30 am

I had difficulty falling asleep last night, tossing and turning in bed for around two hours. Eventually, however, sleep pressure caught up with me, and the vibrations hit me. I rolled out of body easily and stood beside the bed soon after.

Then, without warning, I suddenly got pulled back in my body. I quickly realized the reason for my premature return—one of the dogs was snoring loudly.

I mentally blocked out the sound and was able to induce the vibrations once again. This time, however, instead of rolling out of my body, I floated upward, turned around in midair, and hovered a couple of feet above the bed, looking down.

The dogs were lying in between my own body and that of my wife. One of them was still snoring, lying on her back—oblivious to my presence. Her snoring did not seem to wake me up this time, but I was concerned that it might do so later on.

I moved in more closely and snuggled her belly with my face. She grunted happily and quieted down soon after. I wondered if she had actually stopped her snoring. However, I did not want to abort the OBE to find out. So instead, I tried to make my way toward the window... [Continued on p. 79]

Journal Entry — Monday, February 12, 2007, 4:50 am

I woke up with a firm intent to project and quickly began to feel for the vibrations. They came on strong, but I managed to relax sufficiently for my body to fall asleep. Soon, at a high pitch, I gently floated upward without having had any intent to do so. At the same time, the bedroom environment faded from view, and I found myself floating in the void.

I continued to float aimlessly for a while, postponing any intent to go anywhere. My lack of ambition seemed to result in a sensation of falling deeper into the void below me. I did not resist it despite some trepidation about the idea of "going down."

I kept falling into the void, streaks of blue occasionally surrounding me. I did not seem to get anywhere, however, and eventually I decided it was time to engage. I moved from my inert horizontal position into an upward position and began to feel for the ground under my feet.

There was a hard surface, and before I knew it, I stood in the middle of a dark environment. I had not yet engaged visually, and I was still partially inside of the void. I peered into the pitch-dark surroundings, hoping this would trigger my vision, but it remained completely dark.

I then began to walk anyway—blind to my surroundings. This seemed to help my vision, and a large green field appeared around me. It was still rather dark, and twilight had almost ended to make way for an evening sky, but I could see. In the distance was something that looked like a farm or compound. The building was surrounded by a high fence made of barbed wire.

Intrigued, I decided to get a closer look. However, as soon as I began to walk, I found myself unable to move—my left foot pinned to the ground. I looked down. There was nothing there that I could see. I jerked forward, but it was useless. I could not move my foot, as if an invisible force kept it firmly in place. I woke up a few seconds later and became aware of a pressure against my left foot. The dog had draped its paws on top of my foot, pressing down on it intermittently while stretching its paws.

A related phenomenon to sensory bleedthrough is the sensation of having a "hitchhiker" on your back. You feel someone, or something, clamped around your body, ready to go along for the ride. This may occur inside of the void or even while in an out-of-body environment. It may also occur during the transition process, when you have a sense that someone is lying below or beside you in the bed. This is not something to fear. It is merely the sensation of your physical body in the background of your awareness, bleeding into your experience in a distorted format. The best course of action is to simply ignore it because interaction will only increase the hold that a "hitchhiker" has on you.

A FINAL MODEL OF THE TRANSITION PROCESS

So what does it really mean to be out of the body? It means we *construct* ourselves to be out of the body. We adopt a different perceptual perspective toward the world and ourselves. Such a perspective is not necessarily any less real than the perspective we adopt when we construct ourselves to be in the body. Neither situation, in terms of the constructive abilities of a nonlocal consciousness, is fundamentally different from the other.

Because our position and perception of being "inside the body" is a construction created by our own consciousness, there is also nothing actually *leaving* the physical body. After all, you cannot leave something that you are not really inside of. Therefore, all that is required to establish the out-of-body state is to get up out of bed once the process of sensory retraction has been completed. You can try to leave what appears to be your physical body, but you would be trying to leave a body image that is already free of physical limitations.

The manner in which consciousness is able to construct and experience itself at locations different from that of the physical body is wide and varied, including exotic modes of transitioning such as the dissolution of the external environment. Overall, however, we can identify two major pathways leading into the out-of-body state—the parasomatic and asomatic transition (see Figure 3.5).

Both the parasomatic and asomatic transition involve a reduction in sensory input as the physical body falls asleep. During a parasomatic transition, you maintain body awareness, while no body awareness is maintained during an asomatic transition. In either scenario, you will eventually experience yourself as separate from the location of the physical body.

Once the physical senses have fully disengaged, you may encounter the void—a minimum perceptual environment. In the case of a parasomatic transition, you will typically find yourself in bed, with darkness surrounding you. In the case of an asomatic transition, you will find your mind floating in darkness. In either of these situations, a new perceptual environment may be entered—the out-of-body environment.

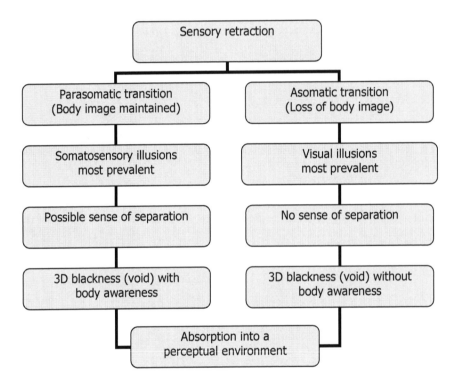

Figure 3.5. Diagram Representing Sensory Retraction and the Subsequent Sequence of Events in Parasomatic and Asomatic Transitions

PART TWO

Explorations in the Physical

Chapter 4
The Physical Field of Consciousness

PROJECTIONS INTO THE PHYSICAL FIELD

During many out-of-body experiences, the environments you encounter will resemble the physical world. This is especially the case following a parasomatic transition, in which your own bedroom environment will usually seamlessly appear at the end of the transition process. From there, you can explore your own neighborhood and the town or city where you live, or you may try to venture out further and visit the Rocky Mountains, the Pyramids at Giza, the Amazon, or even outer space, if these destinations interest you.

Some traditional approaches argue that these kinds of OBEs are exactly as they seem, namely, that you are roaming the physical world as if you were a ghost. They claim that the projector is unable to manipulate any objects because the person occupies a ghostly form that moves straight through objects and matter. You are invisible to other people in the out-of-body state, unable to interact with the living.

On the surface, this account seems straightforward enough, but it does not fit very well with actual experience. You *will* be able to manipulate objects in the out-of-body state. This includes opening doors and windows, all, of course, without any real effect on the physical world.

Likewise, you are often visible to people you encounter in the out-of-body state. None of this fits the idea of occupying the physical world as a ghost.

These inconsistencies have led some to argue that the OBE does not take place in the actual physical world. Rather, it is proposed that these types of OBEs occur somewhere between the physical and nonphysical dimension—in a buffer zone of sorts.[1]

The notion of a buffer zone ties in, of course, with the theosophical claim of "astral matter" directly underlying the physical world, a more fluid layer of matter than dense physical matter (see pp. 15–16). So, for example, when picking up an object in the out-of-body state, you are not actually picking up the physical object but rather its astral counterpart.

The fluidity of astral matter is also often blamed for so-called "perceptual distortions" or "reality fluctuations" in the out-of-body state. For example, you will often find the out-of-body environment to deviate from ordinary physical reality, such as, for example, the layout of furniture in a bedroom, the absence of objects that should be there, or the occurrence of events that did not actually take place in physical reality.

Metaphorically speaking, the idea of an "astral buffer zone" is not entirely incorrect. However, from a nonlocal perspective, any attempt to blame a particular location for inconsistencies is ultimately mistaken. Perceptual distortions have very little to do with any inherent characteristics of the environment itself (i.e., "the fluidity of astral matter"). Rather, the question is whether you are able to *construct* physical reality in a manner that closely resembles ordinary perception, which is an act performed by your own consciousness. In fact, from such a perspective, phenomena such as opening doors and handling objects in the out-of-body state are not really inconsistencies or distortions at all. They indicate a *more* accurate reflection of physical reality than the ability to walk through walls.

So instead of a buffer zone, it would be more correct to refer to it as a *field of consciousness* made up of your own constructions of physical reality. I use the term *field* not to automatically imply an adherence to quantum-physical notions of consciousness, although obviously the connection may be made. You may also quite simply think of it as a physically oriented state of consciousness—a *mode* of consciousness that is focused on the physical world. The exact same mode of consciousness would apply when you occupy so-called objective reality. The only difference lies in the absence of sensory input in the out-of-body state.

Ideally, with sensory input taken out of the equation, the environment you construct is the same as physical reality. This is indeed quite often the case in the initial stages of the OBE, such as when you are in your bedroom immediately following separation. However, sensory input does contribute significantly in maintaining environmental stability. Without it, the ability of your consciousness to construct physical reality in an accurate manner, especially over prolonged periods of time, is not at all guaranteed.

Keep in mind that we're not even talking about projecting into an environment *without* any prior knowledge and then trying to perceive it in an accurate manner. We're only talking about those situations in which you are already familiar with your surroundings before embarking upon an OBE. You often even know that your perception is incorrect, and yet you still perceive it differently. So what is really happening here? What makes perception so unstable that it may only show a remote resemblance to actual physical reality?

FAILURES IN THE RECONSTRUCTION OF PHYSICAL REALITY

The majority of threats to environmental stability almost always originate from within. Broadly speaking, and with considerable overlap between them, the threats to stable perception in the physical field can be categorized as follows:

- Externalization of the Inner Psyche
- Remote Representation
- Faltering Cognitive Functions
- Displacement
- Perceptual Collapse
- Atmospheric Influences

Externalization of the Inner Psyche

Externalization of the inner psyche refers to those instances in which the mental content of your own mind finds itself manifested in the out-of-body environment as external objects, events, and people. They include memories, transient thought and emotion, and hopes and fears, each of which can manifest in the environment surrounding you. For example, a joyful mood might translate as a bright, sunny day, even while in reality it is dark outside. Likewise, a spiritual attitude may lead to the appearance of a church down the street, while fear may manifest as a boogeyman out to get you.

Many projectors fail to notice the relationship between their psyche and the environment, especially under conditions of fear. This is unfortunate, since a failure to recognize the relationship between the content of the personal psyche and the external environment may lead the projector to treat manifestations of the inner psyche as actual danger. Luckily, lucidity is usually compromised under these circumstances, insulating the projector from a potentially traumatic experience.

One of the reasons that the externalization of the inner psyche can be difficult to recognize is that these manifestations are not solely the result of *immediate* thoughts and concerns. For example, with some awareness of the mechanisms involved, most people would probably make the connection between a conscious wish to interact with someone and subsequently noticing a person walking in your direction. Obviously, the connection between the wish and its subsequent occurrence is not a coincidence.

However, the externalization of the inner psyche also includes the manifestation of thoughts you had during the day. For example, a fleeting worry about having forgotten to lock the front door before going to sleep may bleed into an OBE in which you find someone breaking into your house as if it were an actuality. You may not even remember having had the thought, let alone make the connection with the manifestation of that worry in the out-of-body state.

Even more difficult to recognize are more stable and structural aspects of your inner psyche finding their way into the OBE environment. For example, a persistent belief in danger can lead to manifestations in the out-of-body environment that conform to this belief. This problem is further compounded by the fact that structural aspects of the psyche often manifest in a remote and symbolic format. It is one thing to be able to recognize a boogeyman as a manifestation of your own belief system, but it is quite another to interpret, for example, the meaning of prehistoric birds or dancing elephants in your neighborhood.

Externalization of the inner psyche into the environment sometimes coincides with a loss of lucidity. However, this is by no means always the case. It is possible to construct an entirely imaginary scenario originating from your own psyche without losing lucidity. Nonetheless, do expect loss of lucidity and awareness to occur now and then, especially when you become heavily immersed in events surrounding you and fail to recognize the bizarreness of events.

Journal Entry — Friday, August 11, 2006, 2:10 am

It was my second OBE of the night. After the last one, a failed experiment, I had briefly gone downstairs to get some juice. On my way back upstairs, I noticed that the back door to the garden had been left unlocked. This was not good since there have been a couple of break-ins in the neighborhood recently.

After locking the door, I went back to bed. It did not take long for the vibrations to start again. I had not intended to project again, but the opportunity was there, so I quickly separated. My lucidity was rather poor right from the start. I felt a little paranoid and stressed.

I quickly made my way downstairs, this time out of body, and looked out the window. Sure enough, there was a car driving into the driveway with two unsavory-looking characters inside.

I did not question the reality of it. I accepted it as a real danger. It looked like a home invasion. I went into the kitchen and grabbed one of the knives. Then the doorbell rang. I thought this was odd, since burglars usually don't ring doorbells.

I carefully walked to the front door, knife in hand, and looked through the small window next to the door. To my surprise, there were two people with colorful balloons in their hands. I heard music coming from outside. I awoke soon after.

Journal Entry — Saturday, April 4, 2009, 9:45 am

I was moving in and out of sleep this morning. Monique had already gotten up. I knew she was busy working downstairs on the computer in the kitchen. It was tax time for her business. I felt a little bit guilty still lying in bed.

After hovering around the borderline of sleep for a while, I felt a vibrational pattern emerging. I had not intended to project, but given the opportunity, I decided to try. I was fairly deep in already, and after I let myself slide into sleep, the vibrations intensified.

Wanting to do a small experiment, I then partially rolled out of body. Half of me was inside my body, while the other half was out. Next, I moved my physical hand across the sheet, which felt as would be expected. I then did the same thing with my phantom hand. There was barely any noticeable difference, except that the movement with the phantom hand felt slightly more fluid and less defined.

Satisfied that it was possible to move physically even when partially separated, I completed the separation and made my way downstairs. I was vigilant about the occurrence of any distortions in the process. Everything was as it was supposed to be until I reached the kitchen.

The kitchen was in disarray. Clothes were all over the floor, some of them still needing to be washed and others that needed ironing. The ironing board stood ready in the middle of the kitchen. I very much doubted that Monique was doing laundry at the time and felt slightly disappointed to not be perceiving things more correctly. I woke up soon after.

After I went downstairs, I found out that the kitchen was indeed in disarray, but not with any laundry. Instead, there was paperwork everywhere from Monique working on her taxes. Apparently, I got the laundry mixed up with paperwork. This made sense since I'm more likely to feel guilty about her doing laundry than her doing taxes for her own business.

Remote Representation and Perceptual Degradation

Remote representation is one of the strongest destabilizing influences in the out-of-body state. This situation occurs when, for example, furniture is out of place, familiar objects are absent, walls have rearranged themselves, and entire rooms are in different locations in the house. Your perceptions are still reminiscent of the original, yet not quite the same—a more remote version of it. This often co-occurs with externalization of the inner psyche, in which your perception is not only remote but is also symbolic of your state of mind (see previous journal entry).

Remote perception can come about quite suddenly and unexpectedly in the out-of-body state. For example, you may be running down the street and, as you pick up speed, abruptly find yourself driving a motorcycle on the interstate. Often, such incidences are accompanied by *perceptual degradation,* with the environment no longer being perceived as vividly as before. Everything suddenly starts to look a little bleak and washed out.

When this occurs, expect a significant loss in your overall level of lucidity and alertness. You will have entered a subjective reality of your own making—a dreaming state of consciousness. By definition, you are still in the out-of-body state, experiencing yourself as located elsewhere than your physical body, but under these circumstances, very little of what you will perceive has anything to do with physical reality. This may already occur during the transition process itself, before you actually become part of a regular out-of-body environment, as in the following experience:

Journal Entry — Early 2000s, date and time unknown

I awoke with energy sensations. I was lucid but quite drowsy and tired. Still, I proceeded to relax my awareness in order to intensify the energy sensations. It did not take long for my mind to slip into a semi-lucid state. Thought became incoherent. I had moved too quickly. For a short while, I was able to hold onto a sliver of lucidity, but I soon lost it altogether and started dreaming.

I found myself inside the basement of my house. Large wooden beams and slabs of concrete were suspended above me, blocking my way upward. It looked like a total mess. Yet, nothing about this felt strange to me. I felt I needed to get past these beams. I was still in the process of leaving my body.

I struggled and wiggled my body through the narrow openings in between the wooden beams. Meanwhile, water coming from above was crushing down on me, making it difficult to breathe. I felt as if I was drowning as I struggled to reach higher ground. It was too much. The fear of drowning was strong enough to wake me up.

Journal Entry — Mid-2000s, date and time unknown

I woke up several times last night. Each time, I immediately felt for the vibrations. It took a while, but by early morning I was finally able to shift into the hypnanogic stage of sleep with relative ease.

There were no vibrations, perhaps because I was not lucid enough, but I managed to let my body fall asleep as my mind slid through the cracks. I was soon flying down the street, the familiar tall oak trees lined up on both sides.

It was summer. The branches of the trees formed a canopy of foliage as I whisked by underneath. I would have appreciated it more if I had been fully lucid, but all I could think of was to make sure not to hit any of the branches.

Suddenly, the environment shifted, and I lost any remaining lucidity. I found myself in the cockpit of a jet plane, struggling to control the rudder to the best of my ability. I worried that the wing tips would hit the tree branches.

I continued to fly below the trees for a while, not questioning the situation, until it finally occurred to me that something strange had just happened. Why was I frantically trying to fly a jet plane through the trees? I woke up before I had the chance to answer my own question.

Journal Entry — Friday, December 28, 2007, 3:05 am

I had a disappointing OBE last night. I easily triggered the energy sensations, but whatever mental clarity I started with was gone soon after. Initially, it felt as if I was lying in my own bed, but the environment soon shifted, and instead I was lying in a bunk somewhere with other people sleeping around me.

I got out of the bunk and made my way to a doorway at the end of the room. This was all quite robotic and dreamy. I was going through the motions of an OBE without really knowing what I was doing.

Behind the door I found a staircase, as is the case in our real house, but it did not lead toward the garden door. Instead, there was no end to the stairs. Each time I had descended one level, there was another one.

Luckily, I was sufficiently lucid to recognize the repetitive pattern. I held the firm intention to perceive a door leading outside as soon as I reached the next level going down. And indeed, there was a door when I arrived at the next level.

I opened it, but to my surprise there was no back garden, as there should have been. Instead, right in front of me was an airfield. I was surprised. I had never expected an airfield at the other end...

Faltering Cognitive Functions

Occasionally, mental faculties will falter in the out-of-body state. For example, loss of memory may suddenly occur. Under these circumstances, you are likely to misconstrue the environment. Even if the anomaly is recognized, you still won't be able to "correct" the environment since you do not remember what it is supposed to look like.

Memory is clearly important in the accurate reconstruction of physical reality. It has also been implicated in maintaining lucidity.[2] Without proper recall of waking life, lucidity is likely to be compromised.

Interestingly, however, lucidity does not *always* degrade with an inability to remember aspects of your waking life. You can be entirely lucid during such circumstances, as long as you are aware of the fact that you fail to remember.

For example, if you cannot remember what your neighborhood is supposed to look like, and yet you are aware of the fact that you fail to remember correctly, your level of lucidity will not be threatened. It will only be threatened if you fail to recognize the anomaly.

Incomplete access to waking memory does, however, almost always coincide with an inaccurate reconstruction of the physical field of consciousness, such as in the following experiences:

Journal Entry — Tuesday, May 15, 2007, 4:10 am

I had a couple of OBEs last night. The last one was interesting, as I was preparing for an experiment. The experiment required me to feel for a hidden object inside of a box on the nightstand. I decided on some preliminary practice involving pushing my hand through the box.

I had no problem doing so, except that I saw right through the solid box as I pushed my hand through it. In any case, I experienced no difficulty pushing my hand through the box and decided to do something else.

This time, I wanted to ensure that the environment outside would be entirely similar to the physical environment in real life. However, as I set that intent on my way toward the window, I had a great deal of difficulty remembering what our house looked like from the outside. I tried imagining several different houses, hoping one of them would trigger the correct memory. None of them did. All the while, I experienced no problems with lucidity.

Eventually, I gave up and decided to go outside. I jumped through the window, walked up the street, and turned around to see what the house looked like. The walls were made of thick wooden beams that provided a framework for smaller slats of wood. I knew it looked nothing like our real house. The next moment, I promptly remembered what our house looked like...

Displacement

Displacement is a situation in which you find yourself in a different location than you expected or intended. It usually occurs immediately after you have established the out-of-body state. For example, a common occurrence is finding yourself in the bedroom you had as a child. Displacement may also coincide with "time warps" in which you find yourself in a different time than you intended.

Displacement is usually just a psychological phenomenon that threatens the accurate reconstruction of physical reality. The phenomenon deserves separate mention, however, not only because it occurs quite frequently, but also because projectors often mistakenly interpret the phenomenon to signify that they have entered a parallel world or have traveled through time to their childhood. This is not really the case.

For example, if you have been thinking about your childhood, you have just increased the chance that you will find yourself in the bedroom of your childhood following the transition process. Remote perception is often involved as well, in which you subconsciously draw upon memories of the past in order to construct the environment. Under these circumstances, there are almost always problems with lucidity.

Displacement is also often symbolic in nature. You may, for example, find your bed suddenly located in the basement or attic of your house. The overall atmosphere of the environment during the OBE often provides several clues as to its symbolic meaning.

As a simplistic example, if you find yourself in a creepy basement, background fear has likely contributed to the displacement. It all depends on your own symbol bank and personal associations. You will often have to use your intuition to get to the bottom of it.

Journal Entry — Sunday, March 25, 2007, 5:05 am

Last night, I went to bed feeling happy and excited. Monique was due home the next day following a weeklong business trip to China. After spending a week in an empty and lonely house, I was looking forward to her return.

I went to bed late, at around 3 am. I did not intend to project but nonetheless woke up two hours later in the right state of consciousness to project. I established the out-of-body state by merely stepping out of bed. Initially, I had a clear sense of my surroundings. However, as soon as I stood next to the bed, I found myself in the basement, the bed still beside me, but otherwise entirely elsewhere.

It had not been a sudden transition from one location to another. I did not find myself suddenly "transported" to a different environment. Rather, the transition was quite seamless. I did not even notice the oddity of the event. It did not register as significant, and apparently some critical mental faculty was missing. Yet, I knew I was projecting and was ready to explore the environment.

I left the basement and moved up the stairs leading to the back door of the house and into the garden. It was a bright, sunny day, the garden fresh and lush. It looked familiar enough, even though the actual layout of the garden only barely resembled our real garden.

I walked up a little elevation in the garden and watched some neighborhood children and teenagers play on the street in the distance. The energy was strong. I felt alive.

To my left, not too far from my location, the sound of rustling leaves caught my attention. I looked up and saw a large tree filled with bluebirds. There were literally hundreds of them!

It did not take long before they made their exit, flying upward toward the heavens in a stunning helix pattern. The symbolism of the scene did not escape me. It was a spectacular sight.

I felt energized. I wanted to fly myself and stared off toward the horizon, where I saw the outline of St. Joseph's Oratory, a religious landmark in Montreal built on the slope of a mountain. Memory of my whereabouts was returning. I lived in Montreal.

I began to run, hoping to become airborne with the speed, but to no avail. As soon as I gained some lift, I was propelled back into the basement—lying in the bed that did not exist.

Partially aware that I had "awoken" in the wrong environment, I quickly moved into an upright position. I was not alone. Monique was lying beside me.

Monique turned and, half asleep, draped her legs over mine. Almost immediately, a force of irresistible magnitude threw me back into a lying position as the basement environment dissolved into thin air. I had awoken for real this time. I was back in the master bedroom.

Perceptual Collapse

Perceptual collapse is the complete breakdown of perception in the out-of-body state. One moment, you are inside an out-of-body environment, and the next moment, the entire environment disappears into thin air.

Often, you will wake up immediately, or alternatively, you may find yourself in the void.

Perceptual collapse is mostly due to excessive detachment, a state in which you are not sufficiently focused on your environment. It is a problem that is more likely to plague frequent projectors as boredom with familiar environments begins to set in.

The risk of perceptual collapse is further enhanced when crossing a particular perceptual boundary, such as when crossing a wall, door, or window. The reason is that you might not be quite sure what is behind the boundary, and as such, your level of engagement with the environment is reduced. Hence, it is important to maintain a strong sense of purpose when crossing a boundary to compensate for these destabilizing effects.

Journal Entry — Friday, October 6, 2006, 2:30 am

[Continued from p. 61] ...Suddenly, however, I was unable to move. I felt extremely heavy, as if I were trying to walk through the surf. But then I received a sudden percept—a "knowing" about how to get out of it.

I stretched out my arms sideways and made a pirouette by spinning around the axis of my body. Simultaneously, I began to move toward the window, spinning my way toward it. This seemed to work well. By the time I had reached the window, I was able to move normally again.

I then remembered an experiment I had planned before the experience—to clap my hands in order to heighten my level of lucidity. I clapped my hands a couple of times. I could hear the sound loud and clear. It gave me a nice jolt of lucidity.

Next, I flew through the window, but all the hand clapping had left me distracted. I forgot to focus on what lay ahead, beyond the window. Not surprisingly, as soon as I had gone through it, I ended up directly in the void. There was nothing behind it.

Inside the void, I clapped my hands again. Strangely, contrary to my expectation, there was no sound this time. I truly had ended up in the void...

Atmospheric Influences and Shadow Images

A more controversial threat to stable perception in the physical field is the notion of *atmospheric influences*. It is controversial because atmospheric influences do not originate from the mind of the projector, but rather appear to have an external and independent origin.

I feel obliged to mention them here, however, since you will likely come across them. Each one on its own is easy to relegate to the realm of coincidence, but as they continue to pile up in your experiences, you will inevitably feel more reluctant to do so.

Essentially, atmospheric influences are those manifestations in the physical field that originate from the consciousness of other people, events that have occurred in the past, or events that are about to happen in the future. Jane Roberts describes atmospheric influences as follows:

> "Form is the result of concentrated energy, the pattern for it caused by vividly directed emotional or psychic idea images. The intensity is important. If you have, for example, a highly vivid desire to be somewhere else, then without realizing it consciously a pseudophysical form, identical with your own, may appear in that spot...you might think of them as ghost images, or shadow images, though this is only for the sake of analogy, forms, for example, that have not emerged completely into physical reality as you know it, but are nevertheless vivid enough to be constructed."[3]

One example of atmospheric influences is related by the Dutch psychiatrist Frederik Van Eeden who, during a lecture tour, stayed in an unfamiliar bedroom as a guest of a family.[5] Even though his mood was excellent at the time, he reports having "...a night full of the most horrid dreams, one long confused nightmare, with a strong sentiment that it meant something." The next day, the family informed him that he had slept in the room of their daughter, who had recently been committed for mental problems. She used to refer to the bedroom as her "den of torture."

Most people who regularly remember their dreams are probably familiar with the phenomenon of having unfamiliar dreams when sleeping in a previously occupied bedroom. These types of dreams are not always disturbing, but are quite ego-alien nonetheless. Of course, this can also be attributed to unfamiliarity with one's surroundings bleeding into the content of the dream. The level of unfamiliarity encountered during such dreams appears to go quite a bit further, however.

In any case, while you can expect to come across atmospheric influences, it would be a mistake to attribute every strange occurrence to such influences. In the majority of cases, you are simply dealing with the (unrecognized) externalization of your own personal psyche. If you suspect an atmospheric influence may have occurred, it is generally a good idea to start out with the simplest explanation and, only if that fails, work your way outward toward more unconventional hypotheses.

Journal Entry — Wednesday, January 17, 2007, 6:00 am

I had a bit of a sleepless night with a lot of waking up throughout the night. Each time I woke up, I reminded myself about my goal to have an OBE, but the energy sensations never seemed to arrive. Then finally, at around 6 am, I had a chance to separate.

Monique had just gotten up for a business meeting. I did not know what the meeting was about—just that it was taking place early in the morning.

I stayed in bed a little while longer, even though I wasn't getting a whole lot of sleep. I heard footsteps in the hallway, and I assumed she was getting ready.

Eventually, the noise subsided. I felt pretty awake by that time. My body was still tired, however, and I soon found myself in the proper state to separate from the physical.

I wanted to go downstairs and see what corresponded to reality later on. I quickly made my way toward the bedroom door. It seemed like a good opportunity to find some sort of validation.

For a brief moment, I considered running straight through the door, but I remembered bumping my head the last time I tried that. So I simply opened the door in the usual manner by turning the handle.

I then made my way down the stairs and through the hallway. So far, everything corresponded quite well except for the front door of the house. It seemed to be a bit larger than usual. Otherwise, everything appeared to be the same. That all changed once I entered the home office area.

Everywhere I could see, the walls were decorated with grape-sized balloons. It looked very festive, yet tasteful at the same time. The grapes were in deep, rich colors of blue, green, and violet. It was quite pretty.

Then Monique walked in from the other side of the room. She greeted me with a smile, wearing a light blue bathrobe. Apparently, contrary to my expectations, she was not yet ready.

I soon felt my awareness slip back into my body.

Note: After the OBE, I went downstairs to check things out. Monique was indeed wearing the same light blue bathrobe. Some further news came later in the day. Monique called me to say that the meeting was very successful with a big order. I told her about the experience I had this morning and the balloons I had seen. She added that it was not just the balloons that were significant, but also the fact that they were shaped like grapes—a symbol of abundance.

MAINTAINING THE PROPER CONSTRUCTION

Clearly, despite many interesting and thought-provoking phenomena you may encounter in the out-of-body state, sensory input is very much needed to maintain stable perception in the physical field of consciousness. Of course, this is the function of sensory input to begin with—to act as both an informative and restrictive influence on your awareness to keep other perceptual possibilities at bay. Without it, the environment easily deviates from ordinary physical reality. Yet, there are a number of actions you can engage in to keep perception in the physical field relatively stable. None of these actions are entirely foolproof, especially not over a prolonged period of time, but they will assist in temporary maintaining or restoring the proper construction of physical reality. These include 1) remaining detached, 2) improving wakefulness and alertness, and 3) "rebooting" perception.

Remaining Detached

Maintaining a certain level of detachment from the environment will help to keep the environment relatively stable. In contrast, excessive preoccupation with a particular aspect of your environment easily leads it to take on a life of its own, overtaking your entire awareness, like a temptress leading you straight into a dreaming state of consciousness.

For example, if you find yourself in a building with a confusing layout of hallways and doors, excessive absorption can easily lead you to run through a never-ending maze of hallways and doors. Maintain a strong sense of your *overall* purpose rather than focusing on the details you are presented with.

To remain detached, it is often helpful to have a constant commentary going on in your mind as you keep an eye on your own performance. Often remind yourself 1) that you are having an OBE, 2) how you got where you are, 3) where you are, and 4) where you are planning to go. This will ensure that you do not become too absorbed in all manner of distractions that are in conflict with those goals.

Do keep in mind that too much detachment will lead the environment to collapse, so you need to find a balance between absorption and detachment. Unless you want the environment to disappear, never give up all interest in it. The main thing to avoid is a robotic state of awareness.

Journal Entry — Saturday, April 12, 2008, 7:10 am

Last night, after waking up a few times, I let myself fall into the hypnagogic stage of sleep with the intent to obtain lucidity later in the process. It's a little bit of a lazy approach, but I did not have the motivation to wait for the energy sensations to occur in the waking state.

I was able to maintain a sliver of lucidity, and luckily, once the energy sensations occurred, I regained all the lucidity I needed. I got out of bed and sat on the floor with my back against the wall. The plan was to do nothing except to remain lucid.

In the beginning, it was not too hard. I could barely see anything to distract me to begin with. It was quite dark, and if there was any light outside, the double curtains kept most of it out.

After a while of telling myself to remain focused, I began to get a little bored. I traced my fingers across the wooden floor, just for the sake of the sensation itself. It was completely lifelike as usual.

Then I felt a thin piece of carpet that ran along the wall, attached to the floor. I wasn't sure whether it was supposed to be there. Still, it was quite possible it was there. We had removed the carpet a while ago and stained the wooden floor. Perhaps someone had forgotten to cut away that small piece of carpet.

I felt for the piece of carpet again and then traced my fingers along the wall. In fact, it was a lot more than a small piece of carpet. It seemed to extend along the entire wall. I began to be fascinated by this piece of carpet that should have been removed.

Next, I found myself crawling along the wall, following the strip of carpet. I had almost reached the closet door, where the carpet seemed to bend along the wall into the closet. Then I came to my senses. Why was I on a wild goose chase, going after a carpet strip? I reminded myself again of my purpose and removed all of my attention from the carpet.

I probably should have stared into the darkness, as I had done before, but an investigative mood had taken over. So I moved in front of the nightstand, which was made of mirrored glass. There was nothing out of ordinary, which I liked, since my goal had been to keep the environment stable.

I then noticed that the nightstand door stood slightly open. It was a small detail, but I did not remember leaving the door open. It might be worthwhile to check later, I thought to myself.

I stood up and looked at the top of the nightstand. To the left was a white crystal for decorative purposes. In the middle of the table was the lamp, and to the right was the alarm clock. Everything was as it was supposed to look, and I got bored again.

I placed my hand above the crystal, just to see what would happen. Almost immediately, a burst of light jumped from the crystal into my hand. I quickly pulled my hand away. I had not expected that!

I decided to leave the crystal for another time, and I turned around. On the other side of the room was an LED alarm clock. It was difficult to read due to the distance. I could only make out the first number. It was a seven.

I woke up after this.

Note: Immediately following the OBE, I checked the real time on the LED alarm clock on the other side of the room, as I usually do. It was still difficult to read the clock, but I was able to do so. It said 7:12 am. Later that morning, I also checked up on my other observations during the OBE. There was indeed a small piece of carpet near the bathroom door, close to where I had sat down during the OBE. It obviously did not extent all the way along the wall, but it was there. In addition, the door of the nightstand stood open around an inch. None of it makes for a high-quality validation, given "subconscious memory" as an alternative explanation. In any case, keeping the environment stable had worked out relatively well.

Improving Wakefulness and Alertness

Initiating the OBE straight from the waking state is generally a good guarantee of a high level of wakefulness, at least initially. However, never underestimate how easy it is to lose alertness in the out-of-body state, especially when your mind is tired to begin with. To maintain or even heighten your level of wakefulness, you will need to keep a strong check on your level of wakefulness throughout the experience.

Wakefulness is closely associated with your overall level of arousal in the out-of-body state. For example, it should come as no surprise that fearful dreams, and nightmares in particular, generally coincide with a higher level of lucidity than ordinary dreams. Of course, you do not want to use fear in this manner, but keeping up a steady pace helps to maintain a relatively high level of wakefulness.

Also, frequently clap your hands as if you were a coach cheering yourself on. Simultaneously, remind yourself that you are out of body and have a task to perform that you set for yourself. If lucidity is truly threatened, run around until you once again feel comfortable with your level of wakefulness.

Another method to increase the level of wakefulness for more experienced projectors is to tense your nonphysical muscles while thinking of your physical body. If you make a fist and tense the muscles in your arm, you will experience vibrations, swirls of energy, or similar types of sensations. These energy sensations will subsequently "reenergize" your level of wakefulness, at least to a certain extent. You can also tense your entire upper torso, which will make the sensations more global.

The reason for the occurrence of energy sensations is that you are actually tensing your physical body, but without being directly aware of it. So, in essence, you bring yourself back into contact with sensory input while simultaneously remaining in the out-of-body state. As a result, the physical body will produce energy sensations, which are experienced in the nonphysical body due to bleedthrough effects.

Keep in mind that when using this method, you are in effect taunting your physical body to wake up. So only gradually increase the tension in your nonphysical muscles until you begin to feel energy sensations. Never use all of your strength since the physical body does sometimes overreact, and you run the risk of cramping and sore muscles upon waking.

"Rebooting" Perception

"Rebooting" the environment is a fairly efficient way to deal with any discrepancies you may encounter in the out-of-body state. You will reset the environment and replace it with another one. This should be done early, before the various threats to stable perception begin to pile up and loss of alertness and wakefulness begin to ensue.

The manner in which you reboot your perception is entirely up to you. The main idea is to temporarily "blind" yourself to the surrounding environment. My own preference is to wave an entire arm across my visual field as if I were wiping a window. The same effect is obtained with a different type of movement, such as a quick 360-degree turn, so choose something you are comfortable doing.

As you engage in some sort of rebooting movement, it is important to have a clear intent in your mind of what you *want* to perceive. Otherwise, random perceptions will occur, which can be useful, but not if you're trying to perceive inside the physical field of consciousness. So intent is very important, while the movement itself is mostly symbolic.

One of the drawbacks of rebooting the environment is that it can lead to an *increase* in environmental instability. You may be able to update the environment, but if you're not careful, threats to environmental stability come back with a vengeance. After all, the rebooting of your visual field relies on environmental instability to begin with. You might therefore be left with an environment that is in greater flux than it was before.

Destabilization following a reboot of your environment can be circumvented by increasing your level of wakefulness and maintaining detachment immediately afterward. Try not to engage with anything until you have reminded yourself of your purpose and the environment has stabilized. Likewise, unless you are practiced, avoid rebooting the environment several times in a row, which creates so many fluctuations that it will be difficult for consciousness to recover from.

Journal Entry — Thursday, May 13, 2004, 6:00 am

[Continued from p. 36] ... I quickly rolled out of body and proceeded to walk toward the bedroom window—my regular exit point from the house. I had intended to explore the neighborhood again, but that plan was short lived. As soon as I reached the window, I was abruptly jerked back to my physical location in bed.

There was nothing I could discern that might have caused such a forceful pull. I had no choice but to go through my usual routine to establish the out-of-body state again. Luckily, I was still in the proper state of mind, and my body soon lost all physical sensation. However, it was more difficult to separate this time. I really had to squirm out of my body as if moving through a narrow hollow tube.

After wiggling for a while, I felt the point of release, rolled over in bed, and promptly landed on the floor beside the bed. I tried to get up, but a strong resistance accompanied my every movement. I could just as well have been trying to move through thick mud. The only way I was able to move forward was by crawling. However, once I reached the foot end of the bed, I was able to get up.

I then noticed a movement on the bed. It was Monique trying to leave her body! Her body was moving in a contorted manner as if trying to escape a cocoon. It looked like a very nonhuman, alien movement. I knew what it felt like. I had just done it. I had just never seen anything like it. Not from this perspective, at any rate.

Interestingly, I only saw one body. It was not as if she was trying to leave the physical body in a second one. Instead, she was squirming, until eventually she managed to break free of something invisible that had been holding her back. Like me, she eventually landed on the floor beside the bed, unable to stand up.

She began to move toward my position. She had not yet seen me, and I moved to a dark corner so as not to frighten her. I was not sure what to think of it. Was it her dream body?

I decided not to disturb her. But just as I was about to leave, she looked straight at me. She was signaling for me to come over and help her get up.

I picked her up from the floor and carried her in my arms toward the window. Then I jumped out the window.

Going down, I sensed a little trepidation from Monique. The descent was faster than usual, as there was more weight. However, right before touching the ground, I was able to flare. All things considered, it wasn't a bad landing.

I placed Monique on her feet, and she no longer appeared to have any trouble standing on her own. Still a little apprehensive about frightening her, I refrained from asking her any questions. Instead, both of us looked around.

It was already light outside—a crisp spring morning with a great deal of humidity in the air. I liked being outside at this early time of the day, especially with my body still asleep. Everything was always so quiet and calm.

"Yes, this is what it looks like if the energy is clean," Monique said, as if reading my mind.

I was mesmerized. My mind had never felt quite so clear. This was hyper-lucidity. The world was brilliant.

We began to stroll along the street. The neighborhood looked quite beautiful with its old oak trees flanking the road on each side. Neither of us felt the need to say anything.

We continued to walk halfway down the street until a few pedestrians came walking by. I did not think anything of it initially, but then it occurred to me that it was unusual for anyone to be walking here at this hour.

I began to observe the pedestrians, and it did not take long for many more of them to appear. None of them seemed to be concerned *with us, although they seemed to be aware of our presence. It was as one would expect from a fellow pedestrian.*

Several cars began to pass by on the street, and the street continued to get busier. I noticed a bus stop on the side of the street, and sure enough, a bus came just around the corner. Yet, there is no bus stop on our street.

The environment was rapidly deteriorating. My lucidity began to wane as well. More importantly, the peace and quiet of only moments earlier was now all gone.

Then, without any sort of deliberation, I lifted my arm, and in one wiping motion, I moved it across my field of vision. As I did, everything in the neighborhood that did not belong there suddenly disappeared— the people, the cars, and the buses were wiped out. Everything returned to normal again. It was like cleaning a magic crayon board.

"You can do that?" she asked.

"Yeah," I said, feeling rather proud of myself. In reality, I was quite surprised. I never even considered doing anything like it. It just "came" to me.

We turned and walked back to the house, and for a while, everything remained quiet and calm. But as we reached the front garden of our house, I noticed a little squirrel on the lawn near a tree. It was munching on something it held between its tiny paws.

I looked more closely, and I experienced something of a "zooming-in effect," seeing the squirrel up close. Then, the little squirrel growled, like a dog with a bone. It seemed unnatural.

I began to wonder whether I could make it bigger with my thoughts, but lucidity degraded quickly, and things became nonsensical once again. I found myself waking up in bed.

Note: I awoke Monique immediately after. She had dreamed about trying to catch an airplane but was unable to make it in time.

COGNITIVE AND PERCEPTUAL ABILITIES

Although faltering cognitive and perceptual faculties are common in the out-of-body state, you may experience several potential enhancements as well. They are certainly not present during every OBE, but they do tend to function in a fairly coherent and stable manner and should therefore probably not be considered mere anomalies. Rather, they appear to reflect the innate functioning of consciousness when it is free of the limiting influence of the physical senses. They include:

- 360-Degree Vision
- Zooming In
- X-Ray Vision
- Bilocation
- Inner Sense Percepts

360-Degree Vision

Having *360-degree vision* allows you to view your environment from every possible angle at the same time. This vision usually remains horizontal, allowing you to see your environment from your left, right, front, and back all at once. However, 360-degree vision can be entirely three dimensional as well. In addition to viewing the entire environment on a horizontal plane, you also perceive it from above and below. This can be a fairly overwhelming experience because of the associated information overload.

The experience of 360-degree vision is quite difficult to imagine in ordinary waking consciousness and, in fact, it occurs only rarely in the out-of-body state. Most of the time, the habit of ordinary human vision, which perceives the environment with a 200-degree horizontal field of view, will take over. Of those 200 degrees, around 120 degrees make up the binocular field of view, seen by both eyes, which allows for depth perception. This is a pretty wide field of vision to begin with, especially in comparison to many predator animals. For example, owls only have a 110-degree horizontal field of view, with 70 degrees being binocular perception.

From the perspective that sensory input (as well as anatomy) tends to limit perception, the ability to perceive with 360-degree vision in the out-of-body state makes a great deal of sense. After all, why not perceive with 360-degree vision if there are no external restrictions on consciousness to do so? In fact, a very wide field of vision is already quite common in nature if anatomy allows for it.

For example, pigs have a 310-degree field of vision, while rabbits are able to see danger coming from just about any direction, including above the head, with virtually 360 degrees of vision. These species tend to sacrifice poor depth perception (limited binocular vision) for a wider field of vision to better perceive predators. As far as I have been able to determine, 360-degree vision in the out-of-body state does not co-occur with poor depth perception.

Zooming In

Zooming in refers to a perceptual ability in the out-of-body state that allows you to quite literally perceive an object in the distance from up close by merely focusing your attention on it. The effect is much like pressing the zoom function of a camera, which will bring the object up closer, while the remainder of the environment falls out of view.

A great deal of distance is not required to experience a zooming-in effect. For example, trying to read text that is only a foot away from you often leads to a zooming-in effect. You can experience a mild version of the same effect in an ordinary state of consciousness by focusing on a single word or letter right now.

The effect of zooming in is the same in the out-of-body state except that visual acuity does not degrade, no matter how far the object is removed from you. Acuity is normally limited by the physical senses, whereas that limitation does not exist in the out-of-body state.

As in ordinary life, zooming in tends to occur quite naturally in the out-of-body state. This ability can be useful if it is your purpose. Otherwise, it is a distraction that easily leads to environmental instability. The reason is that a large portion of the environment is no longer paid much attention to, which can lead the environment to collapse entirely.

Environmental collapse can be avoided by not completely forgetting about the surrounding environment. You can remind yourself that there is a wider environment out there as you zoom into a smaller aspect of the environment.

X-Ray Vision

X-ray vision involves the ability to see straight through objects in the out-of-body state. You will quite frequently come across situations in which you can see behind walls and other objects during an OBE.

X-ray vision arises when you direct your attention beyond the particular barrier that blocks your view while simultaneously maintaining some awareness of your surroundings. If you remain partially aware of the barrier, it will generally look transparent.

Unlike zooming in, x-ray vision does not make the environment unstable because you are usually only making a smaller aspect of the environment disappear, such as a door or wall that is blocking your view. The wider environment remains intact.

Journal Entry — Wednesday, February 28, 2007, 4:50 am

I had a brief OBE last night. I found myself in a position to easily detach from my physical body. After exiting, I stood in front of the bed for a while, watching myself sleep. It was rather dark, and I was unable to see much except for the dark outline of my physical body, sleeping on its back.

While watching it lie there, I got an idea for an experiment. I have been a little worried about my smoking habit lately, hoping that it has not done too much damage over the years. So why not check it out? I knew I might get more than I bargained for, but the reality of anything I would perceive was very much up for grabs.

As soon as I decided on this experiment, I began to move my arms in an abrupt fashion, as if I were a conductor in front of an orchestra. I had no idea where the idea to do so came from. It was one of those percepts and strange behaviors that so often occur in the out-of-body state when an action, completely unpremeditated, seems important to perform.

Soon, I was staring at the upper half of my chest without any skin covering it. It was no longer dark in the room, either. It was as if someone had pointed a flashlight at the area. It was not bright white— more like a sienna (yellowish-brown) color. It made my skinned physical body appear much less bloody than it would have looked otherwise.

I focused on what lay behind the muscles, and both the heart and lungs appeared, moving and throbbing in my chest. The muscles had entirely disappeared from view, as if my mind had just peeled off another layer beyond the muscles and ribcage. It all looked remarkably detailed. My perception seemed quite clear, and I felt no anxiety about what I might perceive despite my previous concerns. It felt like an intimate, delicate experience.

I carefully looked at the lungs but could discern no dark spots anywhere. The lungs looked pretty healthy—nothing like the pictures of the lungs of deceased smokers that I've seen. It all seemed very clean, unlike anything I had expected.

Satisfied with the results of my brief inspection, I turned away from my body and spent the rest of the time flying over the city before I returned to my physical body. Somehow, the next day, the experience only reaffirmed my wish to quit smoking. I wanted to keep my body the way it had looked in the out-of-body state.

Bilocation

Bilocation is the situation in which you find your awareness to be located in two (or more) different places. In its most rudimentary form, bilocation is a fairly common phenomenon in which you are *intermittently* aware of your physical body and nonphysical body. One moment you are aware of your physical body, and the next moment you feel yourself elsewhere.

A stronger form of bilocation involves being aware of your physical body and nonphysical body at the same time. Often, this phenomenon coincides with bleedthrough effects. For example, if someone poked your physical body, you would likely feel it in your nonphysical body with a simultaneous awareness of your physical body.

The rarest and perhaps truest form of bilocation involves simultaneously being in two entirely different environments, without any apparent connection or interaction between them. You would be engaged in different activities inside of them, with separate streams of consciousness. It is a very rare experience that is mind-boggling.

Inner Sense Percepts

The use of *inner sense percepts* constitutes a mental faculty in the out-of-body state that revolves around some form of direct knowing or perception. For example, while speaking to a person in the out-of-body state, you may suddenly experience a strong impression or knowing that the person you are speaking to is dead. Alternatively, you may be able to sense the personality or character of the person you are speaking with as if they were "radiating" their own energy outwardly.

Usually, however, inner sense percepts are experienced as coming from within. They are not easily traced back to your own reasoning, knowledge, memory, or the immediate environment. For example, you may find yourself stuck somewhere, and suddenly the percept will arrive of the type of action you need to perform to escape it, even while that action might be entirely unfamiliar to you. In fact, much of the information in these chapters originates from *procedural* inner sense percepts experienced in the out-of-body state—a knowing about how to perform a certain action to achieve an effect.

Another variant of inner sense percepts is *perceptual* in nature. You experience an image or sound arising from within yourself that provides you with information regarding a certain situation, person, or location. For example, while inside of the void, you may experience a sudden percept on a particular location you could visit in the form of an image representing that particular environment. This is rather like "remote viewing" a particular location. Similar perceptual percepts may involve hearing voices coming from within that provide you with information on a particular situation.

The different forms of inner sense percepts (conceptual, procedural, and perceptual) often occur simultaneously. You may, for example, see an image and simultaneously know of a particular action you need to perform. As such, in practice, the variants of inner sense percepts tend to complement each other. If you experience an image and have no idea what it means, you have likely failed to access the accompanying conceptual percept.

The combined use of variants of these percepts also plays an important role in advanced forms of communication in the out-of-body state. Often, such communication involves flowing imagery, combined with a complete knowing of the circumstances in which those events occurred. Some projectors have referred to them as "rotes" or "thoughtballs" that are able to encapsulate a large amount of information, thereby allowing for far more effective communication in the out-of-body state than the ordinary spoken word.

Journal Entry — Late 1990s, date and time unknown

I had one of the strangest, most fascinating experiences last night. After trying to have an OBE for a long time, I finally seemed to be getting somewhere. I was lying fully awake in bed, alone, and felt close to being ready to project. I could tell because of vibrations and the high level of arousal that I felt throughout my body.

I still had to let myself fall into it, however. As I did so, I again encountered a strong barrier of fear. It was really bad this time—a strong sense of evil. Worse, it was not just a feeling. This time, I really did feel as if there was something next to me. Something terrible was lying next to me in the bed.

I knew I had to push through it. I had felt this sense of evil before, and it meant nothing. Usually, everything was calm on the other side. I hoped it would be the same this time. The vibrations intensified, and soon I felt myself free of my physical body. All the bad vibes had disappeared. But there really was someone lying next to me!

It was a woman. She looked quite beautiful, and almost immediately she began to talk to me in an excited voice.

"Finally, I found you! I can't believe I found you!" she said.

"Found me...?" I had no idea who she was.

"Yes, don't you know?!"

I had no chance to answer. There was a sudden shift in communication, and a bombardment of images, thoughts, and emotions filled my mind. It was like experiencing the trailer of a movie.

I knew it was she who was doing the "talking." We had lived together as a couple, somewhere, a long time ago. We were not human, although quite humanoid in shape. The environment was subtropical, with many waterways and small lakes interspersed with tiny islands.

We lived in the water most of time, as if it was our natural environment. I saw us playing, living there. The water was so incredibly safe. It was home. Our anatomy was slight different than human—bodies that were made to live in the water, at least partially. We were in the water for hours at a time.

I broke off the connection. I looked straight at her.

"We really lived together?" I could not believe how real this all felt. This was more convincing than talking to someone in real life.

"Yes, we did!" she said, while trying to embrace me. The sexual tension became evident immediately. Reluctantly, I pushed her back.

"I'm really glad we met. But I'm with someone already," I said.

She was quiet for a moment, as if searching for something in either my or her own mind.

"Oh, yes, I see."

"What do you see?" I asked.

"I understand," she said without any disappointment. "It's okay."

With those last words, she dissolved and disappeared.

BODY AWARENESS AND APPEARANCE

The second body is primarily a construction of consciousness, with some relatively stable characteristics nonetheless, due to the habits of your awareness. You will generally look as you do in ordinary waking consciousness. The same holds true of your attire; you will most likely be wearing what you are used to wearing in daily waking life (or nightlife). Nonetheless, the second body, including your attire, does not benefit from the stabilizing influence of the physical senses and is therefore much more malleable than the physical body.

The malleability of the second body is a clear indication of its constructed nature. You can move through walls, levitate, stretch your limbs, fly, and even change into the shape of your favorite animal. Meanwhile, however, the second body is still capable of perfectly mimicking physical-like sensations.

For example, touching your phantom skin will generally result in sensations very similar to touching your real-life physical skin. It is also perfectly possible to simulate pain in the out-of-body state, although it is not something you want to become good at.

Interestingly, over time, in the course of OBE activity, the richness of sensation felt by the phantom body may diminish somewhat. You stop paying attention to it. In a similar vein, your phantom body may become less defined over time. Slowly but surely, you become less interested in maintaining the human form. It is easily brought back, however, when you do start paying attention.

Initially, you are most likely to experience the lack of a human form in the void. You may experience yourself as a wisp of smoke, occupying an undefined area of consciousness, or even as a point of consciousness. You may also experience yourself as transparent, as if the second body has yet to be built up into its usual solid shape and form. The latter phenomenon may also occur when you are in the process of a parasomatic separation from the physical body.

Journal Entry — Tuesday, May 19, 2008, 4:50 am

I awoke with energy sensations across my body last night. Instead of going anywhere, I decided to observe the separation process. I was pretty deep in already, seeing through closed eyelids while looking down my body.

It was an interesting sight. I was able to look down my entire body and see a variety of transparent wispy pastel colors swirling around my body. My entire body seemed transparent, as if made up of energy rather than consisting of an actual physical form. I could actually see the mattress underneath it.

I set the intent for the energy to swirl around the transparent shape of my body. It quickly responded in a swirling movement around my body. It looked like vibrating hot air.

Eventually, I decided to get up and step out of body. This must have finalized the process, since my second body was no longer transparent and was now fully formed...

Journal Entry — Tuesday, July 24, 2001, 3:45 am

Last night, after watching the movie Godzilla, *I continued with the method I used the previous night—trying to remain as alert as possible in the hypnagogic state. Yet, I do not remember transitioning, except for eventually finding myself inside an unknown house close to what appeared to be a highway.*

As soon as I was outside, I felt different than usual. My shape began to change, and before I knew it, I stood what felt like more than 15 feet tall, walking with four legs alongside the highway. As I moved forward, I covered perhaps 8 feet of ground with each step I took.

Whatever I was, I was not human! I was enormous.

I began to wonder what I was. I felt like an elephant, perhaps, but I was much larger than that. This was something prehistoric.

I looked down at my front feet while swaying my head. I felt a tail behind me. Then it hit me—I was a dinosaur!

The realization of what I was made me lose it for a moment. I partially reverted back to the human form, feeling two legs sliding behind me on the ground as if they were paralyzed. But I soon got the dinosaur shape back as I focused on the movement as a whole.

I began to run across the highway, beyond which seemed to be a park of some kind. I only noticed the cars while on the middle of the road, and apparently they saw me, too, judging by the fact that a large truck crashed alongside the road.

I continued to walk up a hill and increased my speed a bit. It seemed a whole lot more efficient than walking on two legs. Nothing seemed able to stop me.

Then, all of a sudden, there was a young woman in front of me walking her dog. I was only barely able to hold still before running into her. She looked up toward me in total disbelief and promptly fainted.

I heard police sirens behind me in the background. I awoke immediately after.

A wide variety of other psychological influences may affect the appearance of your physical body. Of course, most of these are not as dramatic as changing into a different animal. For example, if you're drowsy or tired, you may look rather haggard in the out-of-body state. Likewise, if you feel strong and alert, this may translate as a vibrant and healthy complexion.

In general, the symbolic changes that occur in your second body simply represent psychological preoccupations of the day. They tend to be transient and should not be taken too seriously. For example, just having a bad day or feeling hurt or vulnerable might result in finding yourself with a bandage wrapped around your head.

In fact, what you perceive may not even be a real aspect inside of you, especially if the perception is merely due to fear of what you might perceive. Consequently, if you see your second body as ugly or deformed, do not make too much of it. The same is true when you experience yourself as angelic or anything else of the sort, which might be an uplifting experience but can also find its origin in wishful thinking.

Journal Entry — Friday, March 23, 2007, 5:00 am

I found myself lying in bed out of body last night, with no memory of how I ended up there. I must have gotten lucid very late in the transition process.

In any case, I got out of bed and walked up to the window as usual. On my way there, my own reflection in the mirror next to the bed caught my attention. A black linen mask was tightly wrapped around the upper part of my head, even covering my eyes. Yet, somehow I had no trouble seeing.

I was not sure what to make of it, except that I had seen others in the past with their entire head and face covered in masks of various colors. I left the mirror and walked toward the bedroom window.

I normally jump straight through windows, but for a change, I moved my head slowly through the glass. It felt pretty much as one would expect glass to feel from the inside out. It had a smooth, hard structure.

I moved back and forth for a while until I finally went through completely and landed outside in the front garden...

Journal Entry — Tuesday, August 17, 2004, 5:10 am

Last night, after I left my body, I took some time to observe my nonphysical hands. They looked exactly as they were supposed to look, except for a pinkish hue at the edges.

It was as if my skin was radiating light. This made me curious, and I walked up to the standing mirror in the bedroom to check out the rest of me. Surrounding my head and torso were wisps of dark blue light as well as some of the pinkish colors. I had seen earlier.

It was interesting, but I had no idea what to do with it, so I decided to enter the mirror instead. I soon found myself in the void...

MOVEMENT AND TRANSPORTATION

Moving from one place to another in the out-of-body state is quite similar to ordinary physical reality, at least when inside of your immediate environment. In the majority of instances, you will find yourself walking or running to where you want to go. In general, this mode of transportation poses few problems.

Occasionally, however, projectors report difficulty with movement immediately following separation. You may collapse on the floor, as if you have become paralyzed, or your movement might be extremely heavy and sluggish, as if you are walking through a layer of mud. This is a harmless phenomenon, although it might leave you feeling somewhat vulnerable and exposed.

I suspect that these movement problems are the result of a bleedthrough effect from the physical senses since your physical body is usually entirely paralyzed during projections. There is no muscle tension, which may bleed into the out-of-body state in the form of movement problems or paralysis.

To overcome these problems with movement, it is important not to use force. Your physical body will only send back stronger signals that it is unable to comply, thereby increasing your sense of paralysis in the second body. Instead, do the opposite—try to exercise as little effort as possible as you try to effectuate movement. For example, spin around your axis while simultaneously moving forward as if you were a ballet dancer.

Over time, rather than walking or running, you will want to learn how to fly. This will significantly expand your radius of activity as well as saving on travel time. The act of flying may take a while to learn because it requires overcoming the belief in gravity. The more lucid you are during your experiences, the more difficult it tends to be.

The best way to learn how to fly in the out-of-body state is to realize that you can do so already, even in physical life, provided there is enough distance between you and the ground. So take every opportunity you get to jump out of buildings.

There is no need to worry about hurting yourself. You may land on your head occasionally, but eventually you will be able to maintain a smooth gliding path toward the ground. Once you are able to land softly, establishing continuous flight is relatively easy to accomplish by flaring slightly upward before you touch the ground.

For long-distance locations, and transcontinental travel in particular, it is more efficient to utilize the void to get from one location to another. Reaching an environment can be accomplished directly, or you may wish to fly horizontally in the void for a while before landing. It doesn't matter how long you fly—just make sure to set your intent as you decide to touch ground.

In contrast to flight, moving through objects does not require a great deal of practice. Our belief in the structural properties of matter is not held as strongly as our belief in gravity. If there are any limitations as to the objects one can move through in the out-of-body state, I have not encountered them.

Do keep in mind that if you doubt your ability to move through an object, you will experience difficulty moving through it. Doors and walls may remain solid. To limit any of these problems, focus on anything beyond the obstacle rather than keeping it at the forefront of your mind.

Expect to revert to old habits now and then, bumping your head or, alternatively, falling through the floor when taking the nonphysical aspects of the environment too far. In the end, it is solely a matter of how your consciousness chooses to construct the environment, solid or otherwise.

The level of sensation you will experience during movement through objects varies. If you move through an object quickly, you may feel nothing at all. However, a great deal of detail is possible if you do pay attention, especially when using your fingertips to move through an object. The sensations will generally correspond strongly to the texture of the object, such as whether it is made of wood, glass, concrete, or iron.

One last difficulty associated with transportation that deserves mentioning here is when the environment is completely dark. This may happen immediately after the transition process, but also after you try to enter an environment from the void.

In the majority of instances, darkness does not indicate that you are blind. It just means you are partially in the void. To overcome this situation, try to increase your engagement with the environment, either by feeling your way around or by directly manipulating the environment. You can even try to create light with your second body, although there are some limitations to that approach.

Journal Entry — Wednesday, October 18, 2006, 2:35 am

In my second OBE of the night, I decided to remain inside the house. It was quite dark, which gave me the idea to try creating light with my second body. I opened my palm and pointed it toward the floor, trying to "push out" streaks of light.

Sure enough, streaks of white light illuminated the floor exactly as one would expect a flashlight to do around a two-foot-wide circle of light on the floor.

I walked out of the bedroom and continued to practice lighting up the remainder of the second floor. Everything was pretty much as was to be expected.

The only problem I encountered was related to the brightness of the light. I seemed unable to make it shine as brightly as I wanted and found myself unable to manipulate its intensity. It was as if I needed new batteries.

I tried to focus harder for a while, but it didn't change the brightness. There appeared to be a limitation in the level of luminosity I was able to create with my second body. Unable to come up with any other ideas, I woke up soon after.

SOCIAL INTERACTION AND COMMUNICATION

You will frequently encounter other people in the out-of-body state. It may be tempting to assume these are real people, but in the vast majority of instances, the people you encounter are externalized portions of yourself. They may either reflect relatively stable aspects originating from within your psyche or transient phenomena that come about as a result of your immediate preoccupations.

For example, a social attitude will automatically lead you to encounter people in the out-of-body state. Usually, such interactions hold no significance apart from your desire to interact.

Nonetheless, some of my experiences do suggest that it may be possible to interact with a real person, or at least an aspect of them, either by communication that occurs on a subconscious level or in terms of being able to accurately perceive their appearance, symbolic or otherwise.

For example, a person who is in an excellent mood at the time when you visit them during an OBE may be perceived as having a very healthy complexion and glow to their overall appearance. Conversely, visiting a depressed person tends to lead to an experience in a correspondingly depressing environment.

In other words, similar to how the state of your own psyche may manifest in the out-of-body environment, this may occur with others as well, giving rise to atmospheric changes in the out-of-body environment.

Of course, the idea of atmospheric influences is difficult to validate because in most of these instances, perceived reality finds its origin in the subjective realm to begin with. Worse, communication can be quite cryptic and symbolic in the out-of-body state, making any sort of verification in your interaction with others even more difficult.

Take the following experience:

Journal Entry — Sunday, October 15, 2006, 3:45 am

I briefly fell asleep after the last projection and woke up with energy sensations once again. I quickly flew up into the void with the intent to go as deep as possible into it and try for some meaningful and intelligent communication. I started out with some flight until I felt I had gone far enough. From there, I phased directly into an environment and quickly found myself standing in a large, bright room.

The room had the appearance of a meeting room with several tables and chairs lined up. There was no one there. However, at the end of the room was a door leading into what looked like an office. I made my way there and entered.

The office was only sparsely decorated, bright with neon light, the walls painted white. There were blinds at the left end of the office, and I assumed there was a window behind them. I lifted the blinds but only found a very smooth white wall behind them. It looked more like a projector screen than a wall.

Suddenly, I became aware of someone standing in the doorway. I turned around and saw a disheveled-looking character around sixty years old standing in the doorway. He looked like an old-fashioned professor with an Einsteinian hairdo.

I reasoned that this was the figure with whom I was seeking to communicate. But he did not seem terribly interested in me and appeared instead ready to go about his own business and completely ignore me. I decided to start a conversation.

"Hi," I said.

"Hello," he responded.

"Perhaps we should talk. I'm not dreaming right now—I'm wide awake and alert, so it might be good to take this opportunity."

He looked up at me from the corner of his eye. "Ah, yes. I know you. You're the OBE'er who will write the trilogy."

"I will? Well, I did start to write some, but I only just started. I was not planning on a trilogy."

"So what do you want to know?" he asked, a bit impatient.

I searched for some sort of deep question and then asked, "Why did I come to experience physical life?"

"Lectitude."

"I never hear of that word. What does it mean?"

"Information," he responded absentmindedly.

"I'll have to look it up. The word might not exist."

I then saw a little glint in his eyes, and I promptly woke up.

Note: An Internet search confirmed that the word lectitude does not really exist. It was used here and there in several sermons I found on the Web by religious types, but only as a misspelling of rectitude (i.e., moral uprightness). The only other word that came close is latitude (i.e., freedom from normal *restraints in conduct). Perhaps* lectitude *was a blend of both these words, which is an interesting idea since they revolve around a similar theme yet have opposite meanings. Still, in the end, I find myself unable to really make sense of it.*

Cryptic communication is usually the result of remote representation of language and, as such, is often associated with a lower level of lucidity. However, the symbolic use of language may also represent the rudimentary use of the inner senses during communication—an intermediary step toward full-fledged nonverbal communication.

It is possible, for example, to have a direct knowing of the meaning of the message being communicated, even though the message would be very difficult to decipher on its own. Thus, when faced with cryptic or abstract communication that you do not understand, reach within and then try to open up your perception a little.

You will know you are getting somewhere when you begin to converse in cryptic language yourself rather than being on the receiving end of a message that you do not understand. For example, take the following two instances of cryptic communication in the out-of-body state accompanied by inner sense percepts:

Example 1:

Out-of-Body Character: "Parlez-vous français?"

(Inner sense percept: "Do you know how to speak the proper language in the out-of-body state?")

Me: "Je parle un peu."

(Inner sense percept: "I'm partly able.")

Example 2:

Out-of-Body Character: "Do you think it is true? The Hindu Raising of the Dead?"

(Inner sense percept: "Do you think it is true that there is an afterlife such as proposed in Eastern and religiously inspired writings?")

Me: "I suppose so, but not all [raised] at once."

(Inner sense percept: "I suppose so, but not in any traditional religious [Christian] sense.")

The interesting part about communication with the inner senses is that it suggests that the physical, ordinary use of language is not entirely natural to the out-of-body state. In fact, the same could be said for any attempt in which you try to visit another person in the physical field. This is not always an easy task to accomplish since social interaction has a tendency to open up a field of consciousness that is much wider than the physical field alone.

Journal Entry — Thursday, February 5, 2009, 5:25 am

Last night, I decided to visit John, a fellow projector living in Georgia whom I know from the Internet. It took me a long time to get into the proper condition to project, but eventually the vibrations arrived. I moved my phantom body into a sitting position on the bed until I felt completely detached from the physical and then proceeded to fly out the window into the void.

I continued flying in the void for a while until I got a sense of John. It arrived as hearing music somewhere deep inside of the void ahead of me. The music was faint at first, but as I moved closer, I was able to make out the voice of a man. I was unfamiliar with the melody. It had a country twang to it.

It did not take long for me to reach the source of the sound, and soon I found myself in the back garden of what I assumed to be John's house. It was packed with people.

Near the house, a couple of women and children were playing and chatting—some of them sitting on benches or couches, others standing or moving around. Further into the garden was a round table with six to eight men sitting around it.

I realized that all of this was quite impossible. It was night, and John would be asleep. Everything looked quite curious as well—to have so many people outside at this hour. Dawn had barely arrived.

Instead of trying to clear up any distortions, I decided to go with it and walked up to the table where the men were sitting. One of the men I recognized as John, not because of his appearance, which was different than in real life, but I got the inner sense percept that it was he.

John was unnaturally tall, almost seven feet. It was not at all like real life. He looked a little pale and tired, but he appeared to be in a good mood—jovial with everyone as usual.

It was a friendly group chatting about anything and everything.

I walked up to them and introduced myself. "Hey, John, I decided to come over and pay you a visit," I said.

"Fred! Nice to see you here!"

"You know this doesn't make sense, right? Why are you here in the back garden? I was planning to help you have an OBE. You should be in bed."

"I know. But what can we do? We're all dreaming."

"I don't know, either. How do you get a person to become lucid inside of a dream?"

"Doesn't seem so easy," John said.

Everyone around the table began to chuckle about our dilemma. They understood the problem, but no one had any solution to offer. I could not think of anything, either—not under these circumstances anyway.

"Oh well, forget about becoming lucid then. But I need something to make it worthwhile—perhaps some piece of information, so we can try to validate this visit later on."

John looked pensive as he tried to come up with a solution. Then, one of the other men raised his hand.

"My name is Mark, and I always listen to this song called "Gold Whisper" whenever I feel tense and need to relax." I got a brief percept of a black woman singing the song, although I had no sense of the melody.

"That should do," I said. "At least it's something."

With the formalities and experimentation over, I began to relax a little bit.

"Want me to show you around the house, Fred?" John asked.

"Please, I'd like that," I said.

John got up from his chair, and together we walked into the kitchen, which was located at the back of the house. It looked pretty bland. The colors seemed dead, as if the place had no energy. It was clear to me that it was not his real kitchen as it is in physical life. It was more "energetic"—perhaps representing a lack of nourishment in the emotional realm.

"You're going to have to do something about the kitchen, John," I said.

"Yeah, I know. No one ever spends much time here. It's dead."

"Want me to try to do something about it? I've got an idea."

"Sure, go right ahead."

I waved my hand across the visual scenery of the kitchen, and my vision temporarily blacked out. I could feel myself still standing in the same spot, but I could not see anything. I almost lost it entirely, feeling the pull of my physical body.

I waved my hand again, and the kitchen environment reappeared, but this time it looked entirely different than before. The walls of the kitchen were now covered in large, shiny stones in a variety of bright colors—red, white, yellow.

John laughed. "That looks awful!"

I looked around and laughed as well. "It sure is different. It's a little gaudy, but it did brighten up the place, didn't it?"

"It sure did!" John said. "Come, I'll show you upstairs. It's much better."

We walked up some stairs until we reached the uppermost level of the house. I did not try to memorize every little detail I encountered to validate anything later on. I had already realized that this was his "mental" house.

Eventually, we reached a spacious attic that was clean and well organized. A lot of stuff was lying around, but without disorder. Some of the things lying around were games, such as a foosball table, for example. Some of the other objects I did not recognize.

"You did pretty well for yourself, John," I said. "You've amassed a lot over the years."

"Thanks," John said. "Here, let me show you something."

John walked over to what looked like a rolled-up piece of carpet. It seemed to be something entirely different, though. I got excited, expecting some sort of amazing board game to be revealed once the carpet was unrolled. But my awareness wavered, and I woke up back in bed.

I separated again soon after, and for a moment I thought about going back to see John, but I decided against it. The visit had run its course... *[Continued on p. 217]*

Note: Following the experience, I related the OBE to John. As expected, there was little in terms of physical resemblance, although John did often entertain people in the back garden. The information from Mark did not turn up anything interesting, either. John had a friend named Mark, but he had not seen him in a long time. On a subjective level, however, John felt the experience completely corresponded, including the symbolic nature of the kitchen and the attic. Regrettably, subjective correspondence is difficult to measure.

PARALLEL FIELDS OF CONSCIOUSNESS

The boundaries of time and space are relatively easily transcended in the out-of-body state, opening up the door to time travel, visiting other realities, and exploring distant planets in the universe. Regardless of the degree of reality you attribute to such experiences, you are indeed doing all of these things, from a purely experiential point of view.

However, it seems appropriate to note that a certain level of skepticism is warranted as to the actual significance of such experiences.

It is quite possible that these experiences have nothing to do with physical reality and originate entirely in the mind of the projector.

Nonetheless, even given these disclaimers, some experiences you will encounter in the out-of-body state will give you the distinct impression of having entered a physical reality other than your own. The overall environment is usually similar to your own, including houses, people, cities, homes, roads, and so on. Yet, there are important differences, and you may encounter different societal structures, artifacts, or technologies that do not exist in our world. Some of these worlds seem to have a history of their own, as if they have somehow split off from our own reality, taking a different path as if having entered a parallel reality.

Entering a parallel reality is a fairly common phenomenon in the out-of-body state. Monroe's experiences were a good example in this regard; he had several experiences of this sort before the idea of parallel realities was more widely known.[5] He referred to his experiences as occurring in "Locale III," where he "occupied" the body of a lonely architect.

Monroe describes the architect as "...a rather lonely man...not particularly successful in his field...and not too gregarious." As events unfolded, the architect met a wealthy young woman with two children, resulting in marriage. They lived together for a while, and there were several successes in the architect's professional life. However, things took a turn for the worse when something occurred that alienated his wife. Eventually they separated, and the wife left to live elsewhere. In Monroe's last visit, he found the architect lonely and frustrated.

Monroe was uncertain as to the exact nature of his experiences in Locale III. He considered that they might have originated from a collective memory, a forgotten civilization that may have preceded our own in history. He also mentions the possibility of Locale III perhaps being an antimatter duplicate of our own world, both different and related in some unknown manner. The latter idea is, of course, quite close to modern conceptions of parallel universes.[6]

Interestingly, the existence of parallel worlds has a fairly firm foundation in quantum theory. In particular, the *many-worlds interpretation* of quantum mechanics holds that reality consists of multiple universes where every conceivable possibility is actualized.

For example, if you ever had a moment in your life in which you came close to death, an alternative universe would exist in which that possibility was realized, complete with its own history, present, and future separate from the universe you are now familiar with.

An alternative interpretation of quantum principles would be that parallel realities only exist as possibilities rather than as actual manifested realities. For example, the eminent quantum physicist David Bohm proposes that the universe is in a constant state of flux.[7] In this approach, there is only one universe, which nonetheless exists within a larger field of possibilities with the *potential* to actualize in regular time and space.

Quantum theory aside, keep in mind that even if parallel universes exist as tangible realities, you would still not be able to experience them in an entirely physical-like manner during an OBE. After all, your physical senses are not operational in the out-of-body state, and it would seem difficult to experience parallel universes as an "indigenous" person with a physical body (and brain) at one's disposal.

There are also psychological explanations to consider, which, at the very least, seem to play a role in determining the specific type of environment encountered. For example, certain *psychological parallels* can be drawn between Monroe's experiences in Locale III and his personal life at the time.[8] There is no doubt that similar parallels can be drawn in my own experiences. None of this makes experiences in alternate realities any less intriguing.

Journal Entry — Thursday, April 13, 2006, 4:30 am

I awoke last night following a dream. It seemed like a good opportunity to try for an OBE. In the end, however, it took me more than two hours before high-frequency waves of energy coursed through my body, allowing my body to smoothly slide off into sleep. I flew up into the air a couple of seconds later, holding still in the void.

I was ready to visit the upper rings again, so I moved a bit deeper into the void to get the starscape going. But I was unable to connect and soon found myself back in my body. Luckily, energy sensations were easy to trigger, and I exited for a second time, moving to the void, hoping to connect from there. Once again, however, I ended up back in my body. I wondered what was wrong. I kept being pulled back.

I exited yet again, which was beginning to become more difficult. I got stuck at the hip and had to peel myself out of the physical body. Worse, by the time I was completely detached, my body felt more solid and heavy than usual. It would be difficult to connect inside of the void with such a heavy form. I needed to lighten the load.

I moved backward in an attempt to "leave" the second body in a lighter form. It seemed to be working, and I felt myself peeling out of the second body in a third form. The separation felt a bit artificial, but it did seem to make me feel a little bit less defined.

Taking advantage of the lightness, I once again moved upward into the void. Yet again, I found myself unable to connect with the starscape. I then tried to phase directly to another location, but no shift in awareness occurred. This was getting strange. It should not be this difficult.

I descended back from the void into the bedroom. It looked as though there was not going to be any travel tonight so, standing in the bedroom, I decided on some experimentation instead by rebooting my visual field. There was nothing to clear up in terms of distortions, really, but I had nothing else to do.

I stood in front of the bed and waved my hand across my visual field, with Monique lying in its center, sleeping in bed. Initially, there seemed to be little change except that my vision became blurry at the location of my wife's body.

Then my wife began to move. It was quite unexpected, even though the movement was similar to what I had once seen before, a delicate wiggling type of movement like a butterfly about to emerge from a cocoon. I knew she would soon be out of body like me.

Once the quivering subsided, she got up with ease and walked toward me. I had no expectation that she would be aware of all of this. I did not want to push the issue, so I kept things simple.

"Want to go outside?" I asked.

"Yes," she said.

Without further exchange, we flew out the window. I did not carry her outside, like the last time while we jumped out of the window. She seemed to have no difficulty with movement this time. However, once in front of the house, a large stone stairway descended about a hundred yards toward an equally grand garden.

I decided to pick Monique up and carry her down the stairs. It did not occur to me that the stone stairs were reality distortions. I was too distracted with keeping an eye on Monique. My lucidity must have degraded as soon as we left the house.

Halfway down, still carrying my wife, I turned. The house I had just left behind was now a palace of royal proportions. Seeing the palace felt rather strange, but I still did not sufficiently recognize it as a distortion. Our house isn't a shack, but it's not a palace, either.

Once we reached the bottom of the stairs, an uncontrollable sexual impulse took over, and we began to engage in sex. We did not get very far. I was once again was pulled back into my body. At least I had my lucidity back.

Fully awake, the energy waves hit me yet again. This was the fourth time, and after the last episode, I decided to give the void yet another try. Not surprisingly, I still was unable to connect with the starscape, although I had the feeling that I had moved deeper into the void than before.

Hovering inside of the void, I tried several more times to phase directly to my intended destination, but to no avail. In frustration, I extended my phantom hand into the void, hoping that something could perhaps pull me toward the proper destination instead.

Sure enough, a dark figure started to approach, darker even than the void itself, and grabbed my hand.

I decided to go along with it as I told myself I was hallucinating. Meanwhile, some faint ghostly shapes start to form around me, but nothing readily identifiable. I felt a little nervous but mostly unafraid.

The dark figure then moved below me while still holding my hand. I did not like the possibility of being pulled down and wondered if I should try to get out of his grip. Yet, I decided to stick with it and not react emotionally or otherwise.

I then felt my hand starting to get clawed, as if it was a paw that was holding me. I continued to tell myself this was just a hallucination. Except for a bit of pain, nothing seemed to come of it anyway. After a while, I found myself back in bed once again.

Lying in bed, I open my eyes and saw that it was already light outside. Strangely, I found that my hand was actually hurting a little bit, and I got out of bed to check it out.

I looked at my hand and noticed white claw marks, some of which were even bleeding a little. What had happened out there in the void?! Had I been attacked, with an actual effect on my physical body?!

I looked around and saw our cat and dog lying in bed. At the other end of the room, Monique was standing in the doorway. She was looking at my shocked expression and the claw marks on my hand.

"The cat and dog were fighting while you were sleeping," she said.

It made sense, and I immediately calmed down, amused by the situation. I must have gotten my hand mixed up in the middle of the fight, I told myself. It was only a bleedthrough effect, leading to that clawing sensation in the out-of-body state.

But as Monique left the room, another thought started to dawn on me. Our cat is no longer alive. She died almost two years ago in an accident. And here she was, alive and well!

I quickly looked around, trying to orient myself. This was not my bedroom! It was much smaller than ours, and the furniture was nothing like our own. There were only flimsy cabinets made out of cheap wood.

I almost fell down as I stumbled into the wall behind me. I could not believe it. This was real! I had actually ended up in a different place! Where am I??!!

I now began to get very worried. How was I going to get back? What if this was permanent? What about my real wife? The idea of a quick return seemed impossible. Maybe if I projected again from this place, I could find my way back, but I was obviously not in the right frame of mind at the moment.

I felt homesick. The idea of my real wife being left behind on her own made me nauseous. I needed to find my "other" wife—the only familiar thing out here. At least, she still seemed to be the same person.

I exited the bedroom, ending up in a hallway with stairs leading upstairs. After taking the stairs, I entered a small living room. I did not see any luxury items. In fact, we seemed to be quite poor in this reality.

The layout of the house was also entirely different. Through the window, I noticed a small shack at the back of the house, with a bike in front of it. I had the strong impression that this was the main vehicle of transportation.

Eventually, as I tried to find my way through the house, I saw Monique sitting outside on a small balcony through the window. Seeing her immediately calmed me down. I went outside to join her and now was able to see the surrounding area.

The house seemed to be built on a hill, one of many in the neighborhood. The view from the balcony was actually quite nice. There was a small, picturesque city in a valley below. The feeling was that it was somewhere in Eastern Europe.

I turned to Monique. She was beautiful. I got a strong feeling that our history was quite similar, but with differences as well. We did not have much in any material sense, but despite the poverty we were as happy together here as in the other life.

"Where am I?" I asked.

"Gruchow," she answered.

The answer only reminded me how far I was from home and my real wife. Yet, at the same time, here she was, and I was overwhelmed with a strange mixture of love and loss. Tears began to well up in my eyes.

"What's wrong?" she asked.

For a moment, I considered telling her about my predicament. Perhaps she was familiar with my out-of-body activity in this reality as well. Yet, I decided not to tell her. It was just too strange.

"We came a long way, didn't we?" I heard myself say instead.

She looked straight into my eyes with a beautiful smile that almost broke my heart in two.

"Yes, we did," she said.

The next moment, I found myself back in my bedroom. It was my real bedroom this time. In fact, it took a little while before I was convinced I had actually made it back.

Once I felt reasonably sure, I woke up Monique, who was lying next to me. It took me a while to fully reorient myself back into this reality.

CONCLUDING REMARKS

The physical field is one of the first major fields of consciousness you can expect to encounter, especially following a parasomatic transition. During such a transition, if initiated from the waking state, the physical environment tends to appear as soon as sensory input has sufficiently diminished. However, accurate perception in the physical field is not at all guaranteed. There are no longer any senses to assist in the perception of objects as a singular possibility, and perhaps not even a brain, making it the sole responsibility of consciousness to perceive physical reality in an accurate manner.

In particular, the absence of sensory input opens the door to a variety of different influences that destabilize perception in the out-of-body state. They will quickly lead perception to deviate from ordinary perception, even to the extent that you may enter a dreaming state of consciousness. A number of actions may be taken to prevent this from happening, but doing so requires constant focus and effort, and in most instances, you will eventually end up with a strange mixture of the real and unreal.

Despite all the threats to stable perception in the physical field of consciousness, there are also a number of enhanced abilities that open up as you enter the out-of-body state. Overall, they indicate that perception becomes increasingly flexible and expansive in the absence of sensory input. These abilities appear to be an inherent part of consciousness, including 360-degree perception, x-ray vision, zooming in, bilocation, and inner sense percepts. In fact, they appear to suggest that it may be indeed quite natural for consciousness to be "out" of body.

Yet, we are left with an uncomfortable picture regarding the *objective* reality of anything perceived in the out-of-body state. You will encounter many incidences that are difficult to relegate to the realm of coincidence. At the same time, none of them are convincing on their own, leaving the more critical person who engages in out-of-body activity with a fair amount of doubt.

In fact, the difficulty with accurately constructing physical reality *with* prior knowledge does not bode well for situations in which you are unfamiliar with a particular environment. A more systematic approach appears to be required to move on with some level of confidence. That is, is it at least *possible* to perceive physical reality in the out-of-body state without any prior knowledge? This, of course, touches directly on the topic of veridical perception in the out-of-body state.

Chapter 5
Veridical Perception

THE EVIDENCE

Veridical perception refers to those situations in which your perceptions in the out-of-body state correspond to physical reality without any prior knowledge of the actual physical environment. Robert Monroe, for example, reports quite a few incidences in which he visited people in the out-of-body state and afterward found several "matches" between his experience and what had actually occurred in physical reality.[1]

There are many other such anecdotal reports in the out-of-body literature that give the impression that veridical perception is the norm in the out-of-body state. Even so, scientific approaches rely on more controlled experimentation. They might be willing to consider anecdotal reports, but not without a thorough examination of these accounts. Regrettably, not all of them hold up to close scrutiny.

For example, Susan Blackmore, a parapsychologist, relates a case in which she investigated the claim of a projector traveling back in time and visiting London somewhere in middle of the nineteenth century.[2] He was able to describe his experiences in great detail, including perceiving the exact bends in the river, which allowed him to pinpoint the location he visited. His colleague in London subsequently checked the street that he had visited during the OBE and reported back that he had indeed perceived everything correctly.

On the surface, it appeared to be a perfect match that validated the experience of the projector. However, upon further investigation, Blackmore found that there were only scattered houses in the area in 1840–1860. There were none of the eighteenth-century townhouses that the projector saw during his OBE. Even in present time, there was actually nothing on the street that corresponded to the projector's perceptions. Apparently, something had been lost in the communication between the projector and his colleague.

Yet, there is some evidence for veridical perception in the out-of-body state under controlled scientific conditions. One of the most famous experiments has been carried out by the parapsychologist Charles Tart.[3] Miss Z., who claimed to be able to leave her body, was studied for several nights in a sleep laboratory. During that time, she was asked to try leaving her body and attempting to read a five-digit random number written on a piece of paper that was placed on a high shelf not visible under ordinary circumstances. On the fourth night, Miss Z. reported a fully developed OBE during which she floated high enough to read the number on the shelf. She did so correctly.

While the results of the experiment with Miss Z. are extremely impressive, certain limitations have been mentioned over the years. One of the arguments has been that even though Miss Z. was unable to see the number from her sleeping position, as noted by Blackmore, it is not entirely inconceivable that she might have perceived the target through normal sensory means.[2] This was in fact brought forward by Charles Tart himself in discussing the results of the experimentation, trying to exercise due scientific diligence, and exploring alternative hypotheses. It would have had to involve Miss Z. having used some sort of concealed apparatus such as a mirror attached to a rod in order to read the number on top of the shelf. Alternatively, a flashlight directly pointed at the piece of paper could have reflected the numbers on the plastic casing of a large clock mounted on the wall located above it. Charles Tart considered these possibilities to be unlikely, probably rightfully so.

Perhaps more problematic is the fact that the study with Miss Z. has never been replicated in the last forty years with any other adept projector. For example, several controlled experiments carried out with Monroe have been far less successful.[4]

During one of these experiments, Monroe was to visit the home of Charles Tart and provide an accurate description of the room. However, he perceived people who were not in the room as well as events and activities that did not really occur. Other experiments with Robert Monroe reported some incidences that may have been indicative of veridical perception in the out-of-body state, but the results remained unsatisfactory from any scientific point of view. Charles Tart notes how much of perception often appears to be "...a semi-arbitrary construction, often badly distorted, even in our normal state."[5]

Another series of experiments, by the American Society for Psychical Research, were carried out with the talented subject Ingo Swann, who practices a form of "remote viewing" that resembles the OBE. These experiments involved trying to view a particular object in the out-of-body state and, thereafter, drawing the object on a piece of paper. Some of these trials seemed successful, in which the target object convincingly resembled the drawings made by Ingo Swann.[6] Specifically, post hoc analysis showed that the objects perceived by Ingo Swann resembled the actual physical objects more than would be expected by chance alone as determined by independent raters (1:40.000).[7]

Still, many other controlled experiments did not turn up positive results. For example, one experiment carried out by Charles Tart with "hypnotic virtuosos" was unsuccessful.[4] Likewise, experiments with the proficient projector Keith Harary showed that in the majority of cases, his perceptions in the out-of-body state bore no resemblance at all to the target object.[8] In an overview, Susan Blackmore concludes that if veridical perception seems to occur in the out-of-body state, perception is extremely distorted.[9]

THE CARD TEST

In the summer of 2006, I decided to approach the issue of veridical perception in a far more systematic fashion than I had ever done before. I was already quite aware that perception in the out-of-body state was nowhere near as clear-cut as is often suggested in most of the popular literature. However, I did believe that veridical perception was possible in one way or another.

For my first set of trials, I decided to follow a method suggested by Robert Bruce—the card test.[10] You place a playing card somewhere without looking at it and then try to perceive it correctly in the out-of-body state. Initially, I decided to place my playing card downstairs in the kitchen area.

To make sure no self-deception crept in, I set up some strict rules for the experiment. I decided beforehand that each time I made a "call," it could only be either a hit or a miss. There was no possibility for any backtracking on results, such as that it may have been partially correct or that there was some form of correspondence on a symbolic or subjective level.

In addition, I decided that I could make a call on the basis of anything I had perceived in the out-of-body state, even if it was distorted. For example, if I perceived something only remotely resembling an ace of hearts, I could make that call, even though I perceived it as different. Of course, if I did not make a call due to not having enough information or anything else, it would not be included in any of the results.

With this setup, I felt fairly optimistic that I would be able to obtain a significant result. Of course, the lack of any of these kinds of controlled experiments in most of the literature should have given me pause right then and there. I will report my attempts here in their entirety, which will illustrate the difficulties involved with veridical perception in the out-of-body state, especially under controlled, non-spontaneous conditions.

Journal Entry — Sunday, July 23, 2006, 3:10 am

Last night, I finally had a chance to detach from the physical. Once energy sensations had intensified sufficiently, I immediately separated and got out of bed.

I quickly noticed a cabinet against the wall in the bedroom that did not belong there. But I had an experiment to do, so I didn't let my attention linger on it. Once I was downstairs, I would try to clear up any distortions that remained.

I made my way to the bedroom door. Standing in front of it, I could just see myself getting stuck while trying to go through. I was a little bit nervous about messing things up. So instead of moving through it, I simply grabbed the handle and opened the door.

Beyond the door, it was very dark. I had to feel my way going down the stairs. I hoped I would be able to see something once I got downstairs. I had made sure to leave the light on. But when I reached the bottom of the stairs, I still could not see. I got frustrated and promptly woke up before I even made it into the kitchen.

Journal Entry — Friday, July 28, 2006, 2:00 am

I tried to continue the experiment last night. I had already been moving in and out of the hypnagogic sleep stage for a while when eventually the energy sensations hit me. I relaxed into them and then detached fully from the physical. But something was not quite right. There was another person lying in bed between my wife and myself.

Almost immediately, as soon as I noticed him, he tried to convince me not to do the experiment. Might it be dangerous to go out there? Why not do something else more interesting? Who knows what the outcome of the experiment will be anyway? Why even try?

It did not take me long to figure out that the character was an aspect of myself. He represented all my reservations about the experiment. Still, I was surprised by all the objections. I did not realize I had that many.

Monique had woken up by this time. Of course, she had not really awoken, but I did not question the situation. I just wanted to get the experiment done.

"How do we get rid of him?" I asked her. There was no answer.

I then tried to block the person out of my mind, ignoring his very presence. He disappeared into thin air soon after. I was initially surprised that it worked so well, but before I had even moved to go downstairs, I heard a loud knocking on the front door.

Now I was getting a little mad. I rushed downstairs to throw any potential intruders out of the house. Once downstairs, I opened the front door. I did not expect to see what I did. There was an entire carnival going on outside! There were inviting-looking stands all across the neighborhood with vendors offering games, food, and toys. It certainly looked like a lot more fun than doing an experiment.

I must have lost lucidity soon after. I vaguely remember trying to buy a hamburger somewhere. I even remember seeing a dancing elephant. No playing card anywhere to be seen, however.

Journal Entry — Wednesday, August 2, 2006, 4:40 am

After my last two failed attempts, I moved the experiment to the second floor, in a small room next to the bedroom. It should be easier to reach, I thought. The same night, I had another OBE.

The OBE occurred fairly late at night. I had woken up and stayed awake for a while until the energy sensations came. Once they did, I rolled out of body, landing on the floor beside the bed.

I had some problems getting up and walking. I felt too heavy, so I move on all fours. Once at the door, I tried to move my head through it. But the door behaved like a trampoline, pushing my head back as I pushed into it.

Luckily, after a while, the heaviness disappeared, and I got up. This time, rather than trying to move through the door, I opened it in the conventional manner and walked into the hallway.

It was dark, even though I had left the light on in the hallway. Still, I knew that card was in the room immediately to my left. I made my way there, but almost immediately a dark humanoid shape came rushing toward me as if trying to block my way.

I waited until it was near. Then, I quickly jumped aside and shoved it as hard as I could into the wall.

I could hear the figure falling on the floor behind me, but I did not look back. I was determined to get a view of the card.

Once inside the room, it was a lot lighter. But there was nothing there that resembled a card. I had left the card on a table, but the entire table was filled with clutter—mostly a bunch of paperwork, notes, and pencils.

I waved my hand across the table in front of me to clear up the distortions, but very little changed. So I went through the papers instead. Maybe I could find some clue that had something to do with the playing card.

I soon came across a print. It was a picture of a knight sitting on a horse. It reminded me of Don Quixote. The print then began to shift, and a bunch of letters appeared. One of these was the letter "K." In my mind, this translated as the card being a jack. In any case, I made the call that the card would be a jack.

I continued to wave my hand several times over the print, trying to get the color of the card. Soon, some colorful spots of red and yellow began to appear on the print. I decided it was either hearts or diamonds.

I then tried to determine the suit using the same hand movement. The print shifted yet again, and I got a vague impression of a diamond. I woke up soon after and made the call "jack of diamonds." This was incorrect. It was the three of hearts.

Journal Entry — Friday, August 4, 2006, 3:05 am

I woke up from a dream last night with buzzing vibrations across my body. I moved out of bed fairly easily, stood beside the bed, and started to walk toward the door. Again, the door failed to move, as if it were made of soft rubber. I stepped back, pulled myself together, and then was able to pass through it.

The hallway was fairly dark, as usual, but there was some light in the room where I had left the card. The light was rather dim, not as it was in reality, but I could see. I turned to the table, but except for a deck of playing cards, it was empty.

Before going to bed, I had indeed left the deck of playing cards on the table, and this corresponded with reality. However, there was no upturned card lying beside it.

I made a large sweeping movement with both my arms across my entire visual field, trying to update my perception.

Now there was a card lying on the table next to the deck of cards. However, it did not look like a regular playing card. It was an illustration that looked like some kind of cartoon figure.

This was obviously wrong, so I once again updated my perception with several sweeping movements. It made the environment quite fluid. I saw a bunch of different symbols in a short period of time. I also simultaneously zoomed in to the card as if it were only a couple of inches away from my face.

During all of this, I saw a seven on one corner of the card and a few red diamonds elsewhere on the card. There were small pictures of a jack, a queen, and a king, in both black and red, near the center of the card. It was difficult to make up my mind, but eventually I decided on the seven of diamonds.

After I found myself back in bed, I got up and checked the card in the other room. On the table lay the ace of spades. Again, I had made the wrong call.

Journal Entry — Friday, August 11, 2006, 1:30 am

Last night, as usual, after separating from the physical, I made my way to the other room. I have been getting a little frustrated, but I wanted to try the card test once more before moving on to other things.

This time, I moved through the bedroom without any difficulty and found myself in the hallway. Then, just as I was about to walk into the room, I tripped on something and fell straight to the floor.

On my knees, I eventually made it into the room where I had placed the card. It was completely dark in the room, however, and I was unable to see anything. I awoke soon after.

Following these failed attempts, I felt quite disappointed with the results. Of course, I should have known better. The externalization of the inner psyche into the environment, as well as remote perception, leads even a known environment to deviate from ordinary perception. It was unrealistic to think this would not also apply when trying to perceive an unknown. In fact, it was a lot worse.

Ordinarily, while in the out-of-body state, there is not a great deal of pressure to perform. During controlled experimentation, there is much more pressure, which increases environmental instability to a great extent. It does not take much for even fleeting thoughts and worries to manifest.

For example, my wish to do more exciting things manifested as carnivals in the neighborhood. Likewise, the slightest worry about reaching the target object manifested as obstacles inside of the environment. It made me feel like a knight chasing windmills, which, of course, eventually manifested inside of the environment as well.

It was not until a year later that I decided on a new experiment.

REACH OUT AND TOUCH

After taking a break, I came up with an experiment that I hoped would circumvent some of the difficulties I had been experiencing. What if I tried to identify the target object by sensing it with my hands rather than by looking at it? It seemed like a neat way to conduct an experiment specific to the out-of-body state. After all, a pair of phantom hands would be required to identify the target object. It would certainly not be the typical ESP experiment.

For the sensing experiment, I decided to use five wooden blocks as my target objects, each of them with a different number of nails attached (see Figure 6.1). Next, I found a box with a lid on it that was big enough to fit one of the wooden blocks in.

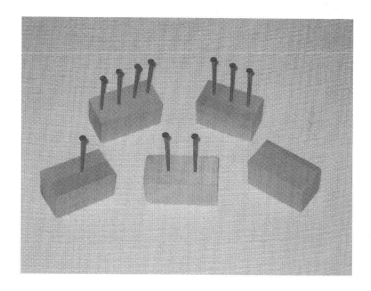

Figure 6.1. Target Objects of Tactile Verification Experiment

Unlike with the card test, I asked my wife to randomly place one of the wooden blocks inside. The box itself was placed on the nightstand next to the bed. I did not have to go far to feel inside. I only had to roll over and stretch out my arm.

Journal Entry — Thursday, September 20, 2007, 2:10 am

Last night before going to bed, I asked my wife to place one of the wooden blocks in the box on the nightstand next to the bed. I also decided beforehand to combine the experiment with trying to perform the healing "experiment" for my wife [pp. 144–149].

I never fell asleep before the vibrations started. I tossed and turned for a while and eventually managed to detach from the physical. I sat up in bed and felt for the nightstand.

My hand quickly found the corner of the glass top of the nightstand. It indeed felt like glass. I then moved my hand a couple of inches further and located the box.

After I moved my hand through the box, I felt several nails almost immediately. I started counting with my fingers from left to right. This was a bit more difficult than I had assumed since I could feel myself starting to wake up.

Still, I was able to keep my focus on the nails. I counted at least four of them. There may have been more. I decided that there were four nails inside the box... *[Continued on p. 146]*

Note: I did not look in the box until the next morning. There was only one nail in the wooden block.

Journal Entry — Sunday, September 23, 2007, 3:15 am

Last night I decided to go for an OBE again. I had been under the weather from a stubborn chest cold, but I estimated that I would still be able to induce an OBE. Immediately after the experiment, I would then turn to Monique.

After a couple of dreams, I finally woke up, induced the energy sensations, and rolled over to the nightstand to check inside the box. For some reason, it was fairly light in the room, and I was tempted to try to see what was inside of the box, but I pushed my hands through the sides anyway. There was nothing there.

I then lifted the lid of the box with my nonphysical hands and looked inside. There really was nothing inside. I briefly wondered whether my wife was playing a joke on me.

I thought I would go about it in a different way and check the closet on the other side of the room, where the other wooden blocks with nails were kept. If I could figure out which one was missing, I could then deduce which one had been placed in the box.

I got up and walked to the closet. Meanwhile, my wife had gotten up and was on her way to the bathroom. I was careful not to bump into her. She did not seem to notice me.

When I reached the closet, I opened the door and tried to determine which of the blocks was missing. It seemed like a simple task, but it wasn't, especially with all the clutter in the closet. It was quite dark inside the closet as well, and I could not see. I eventually located the wooden blocks with my hands.

I began to feel and memorize which blocks were there. The wooden block with no nail was there. Then I felt for the wooden block with one nail, followed by the wooden block with two nails. I was almost there but got confused by the time I was looking for the block with three nails. My vision and mind clouded. It might have been either the wooden block with three or four nails that was missing, but I was not sure about anything anymore. I made no attempt to guess... [Continued on p. 146]

Note: I found a wooden block with three nails in the box the next day.

Journal Entry — Monday, October 1, 2007, 1:50 am

I made one last attempt with the wooden blocks last night. There was too much on my mind with my wife having surgery before long. This time, I lined up all the wooden blocks in the closet and asked my wife to remove one of them. My plan was to move to the closet and try to figure out the missing block, as I had done in my previous attempt.

Later that night, I easily detached and made my way to the closet. I had no trouble feeling my way to the closet door. Once there, I opened the closet, unable to see anything at all.

I quickly detected a wooden block with no nail in it on the right side. This caught me a bit off guard since I had placed the blocks in ascending order from left to right. The wooden block with no nails should have been on the left side.

I assumed I was somehow mixing up left and right and decided to continue counting. This seemed to work for a while. I first felt the block with one nail and, beyond that one, the block with two nails. But then, as I moved on the next, I felt a wooden block with four nails.

Under normal circumstances, this would have led me to assume that the wooden block with three nails had been removed. However, one of the nails on the block with four nails was much shorter than any of the others, as if it had pierced deeper into the wood (see Figure 6.2). I could have interpreted it as either a block with three or four nails.

I hesitated for a moment and then decided it had four nails. I surmised that the wooden block with three nails was the one that must therefore have been removed by my wife. However, the next day, I found out that it was the wooden block with four nails that was missing.

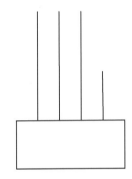

Figure 6.2. Wooden Block with Three-and-a-Half Nails

SIMPLE COLORS

A couple of months after I had abandoned my last series of experiments, I decided on yet another setup. The target object itself was kept simple, involving the perception of a single color. However, I also matched each color with a particular shape and printed the name of each color underneath it (see Figure 6.3).

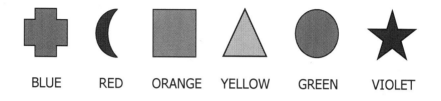

BLUE   RED   ORANGE   YELLOW   GREEN   VIOLET

Figure 6.3. Target Objects with Different Colors, Shapes, and Text

The main purpose of the different shapes and corresponding text printed underneath them was to alert me to the presence of environmental instability. For example, if I were to reach the target object and then perceive the color yellow, yet without it being in the form of a triangle, I would know that something about my perception was not quite right, especially if the printed text underneath the shape was wrong as well. In contrast, if I were to perceive the color green, and the corresponding shape and word were correct as well, I would know that the level of distortion was relatively low.

In addition to the target object itself, I also decided to keep track of the *overall* level of instability in the out-of-body environment. This could provide further information about whether or not I would make a call regarding a particular target object. For example, if I could not even perceive the known environment correctly, it seemed unlikely that I would be able to perceive the unknown target object correctly.

I wrote up a simple scale for this purpose, based on my experiences up to that point with environmental and mental stability. I termed it the *Mental and Environmental Stability Scale* (MESS) (see Appendix 1). Higher scores indicate more environmental instability and lower levels of lucidity. The scale is rated according to the environment and one's mental state around the time that perception of the target object occurs.

The target object itself was placed on a footstool in the downstairs hallway. The location was not ideal, given my previous difficulties in reaching the target object, but I felt more confident this time. Each night before going to sleep, I asked my wife to place one of the printed color sheets on a stool located in the hallway downstairs. In terms of veridical perception, I was not at all sure this setup was going to work, but at the time it seemed worthwhile to try.

Journal Entry — Tuesday, January 1, 2008, 6:05 am

I had a brief OBE last night. I'm not sure whether I projected from the waking state. My lucidity was not as high as I preferred it to be. Remembering the verification experiment, however, I made my way downstairs. I did not bother moving through the bedroom door but instead simply opened it.

I initially had to feel my way down the stairs. It was pitch-dark. However, halfway down the stairs, it began to get lighter, and I could see into the hallway. This made sense since I had made sure to leave the light on in the hallway.

I quickly noticed that all the furniture in the hallway was in disarray. The footstool, on top of which my wife had placed the target object, was lying on its side in the middle of the hallway. Cabinet tables, normally on either side of the footstool, were not in their usual location. Papers were strewn all over the floor.

I looked around, trying to find the target object. There was a small object on the floor where the footstool should have been. It was a flower or, more accurately, a flower made of paper. The paper itself had a purple hue, although it was a bit ambiguous, going toward pink.

It could be a bad representation of the target, I thought. If it did indeed represent the target, the corresponding shape would have to be a star. But I could not be sure.

I tried to update my perception, waving my hand across my visual field, hoping to see it more clearly. This time, the flower took on a more circular shape with an orange hue. It was now made of layered pieces of paper in the form of petals surrounding its center.

What made it confusing, however, was that each layer of petals had a different color, corresponding to the colors I had included in my experiment. I knew it may not have been a wise decision, but I decided to go with my first impression, which was purple and starlike.

Once I was back in body, I checked the target downstairs. It was red and moon shaped. I should not have made the call, given the distortions along the way. It's difficult to stay neutral in all of this.

MESS score: 6
Result: Negative

Journal Entry — Friday, January 4, 2008, 5:40 am

After waking up in the middle of the night, I felt as though I would be able to project. I only needed to slightly touch on the borderline of sleep, and the energy sensations started. Then, immediately after separation, I tensed my nonphysical muscles a little bit. Energy sensations began to run up my spine, and I felt reenergized, which heightened my level of lucidity.

I proceeded to go downstairs. It remained very dark, even as I made it down the stairs and into the hallway. However, once I concentrated on seeing light, I was able to detect some yellow flares in the darkness, which quickly transformed into a fully lit hallway, as it should have been.

Most of the environment was as it was supposed to be, except that the footstool was missing. Instead, it had been replaced by a small cabinet with an orange block note on top of it. The color of the block note was quite clear, but it was nothing like what the target was supposed to look like.

There were a couple of unintelligible scribbles on the top piece of paper. I picked up the block note and flipped through it. Two of the pieces of paper had drawings on them. They looked like children's drawings—two cartoon-like figures that were drawn in pink.

I awoke soon after, not sure what to make of the experience. The block note was rectangular in shape, which corresponded to the color orange. However, the MESS level was quite high, and I did not want to make the wrong call, as I had done in the previous OBE. I eventually decided not to make any call at all.

The next morning, I found out that the real target object was green.

MESS score: 5
Result: None

Journal Entry — Sunday, April 20, 2008, 2:50 am

I decided on one last verification attempt last night, as it is becoming more apparent that the entire setup is too complicated. I detached from the physical body in the early morning. Vibrations were light.

I walked out of the bedroom, keeping my mind as calm and neutral as possible. It remained that way as I looked from the stairs into the hallway downstairs. It was a bit too dark, however, and I decided to increase the lighting with a few hand strokes across my visual field.

After a few strokes, light began to appear, and I could see more clearly. Finally, everything looked as it was supposed to be, and I quickly walked up to the footstool on which my wife had placed the target. To my dismay, it was not the target object.

On the stool was a tarot card. It was the Death card, illustrated by an image of the Grim Reaper. I began to feel fear, and the environment began to shift. There was movement behind the front door. I looked through the glass, and there was an outline of the Grim Reaper, waiting to come indoors.

My fear was then replaced with anger at having allowed the environment to go into disarray. I made an obscene gesture at the figure behind the door, turned my back to it, and once again focused on the footstool.

The card was still there, but I replaced it quickly with a stroke of my hand. The color yellow appeared with the letters "YELLOW" written underneath. The shape came close to being a triangle. I awoke immediately after.

Lying in bed, I reviewed the experience, as usual. While there were some distortions and impossible events, I did eventually end up seeing the target object clearer than at any other time. I decided to call the color yellow. The next morning, I went downstairs and found the color blue.

MESS Level: 5
Result: Negative

The third attempt to identify a color in the out-of-body state was also my last. In retrospect, the entire notion of using "error detection" was probably far too ambitious. I could barely even perceive a single color, let alone being able to perceive its corresponding shape. I felt quite disillusioned at the prospect of ever being able to find proof of veridical perception.

In the meantime, I came to learn quite a bit about the various threats to environmental stability. For example, although I was not aware of the connection at the time, the manifestation of the Death card in conjunction with doing a verification experiment made a great deal of sense. In my mind, veridical perception in the out-of-body state was intimately linked to the continuity of consciousness, which, if possible, provided indirect proof of its survival following physical death. So in a sense, in my mind, it was as much an experiment about veridical perception as it was an experiment about death—an issue that took on greater importance due to my wife's illness the year before.

FEELING THE WAY AGAIN

In 2010, I began to consider one last series of experiments. So far, results had been negative, and I was quite ready to conclude that veridical perception in the physical field was not possible, at least not in any controlled manner. Yet, I felt the issue deserved one last chance. It would be my final experiment—the clincher.

Before setting up the experiment, I went over my notes, trying to find potential explanations for my failures to date. Of course, the problem of environmental stability stood out the most. I had attempted to solve it the last time by having some sort of feedback mechanism to establish whether or not I perceived the object correctly, but the complexity of the experiment had only led to more distortions.

Yet, the idea behind it still seemed sound. That is, if the larger known environment is full of distortions, I could not expect to perceive the target object correctly. So I decided to continue using the MESS to guide my decisions by rating the level of mental and environmental stability, while using an otherwise simple setup for the experiment.

Going over my notes, I surmised that the tactile experiments involving the wooden blocks with the nails, even though unsuccessful, had shown the greatest promise. I also identified one other potential explanation for my lack of results with the wooden blocks. Each time, I had *counted* the nails in sequence, which may easily have led to hallucinating nails that were not there. For example, if I count to three, memory dictates that four comes next, which will consequently make that number appear simply by expectation. So I decided that the number of nails should be sensed, preferably all at once, *after* which the count is made.

Figure 6.4. Nightstand with Box

Again, I asked my wife to place one of the wooden blocks inside a box on my nightstand. I used some tape to secure the lid, just in case I got nonphysical movements mixed up with physical ones. This seemed unlikely, but it was an easy-to-implement control that I had not thought of before. The only other difference was that I used a different box than the previous time. The old box I had been using was pretty unsightly, so she gave me a box with mirrored glass on the top and sides, which matched the nightstand nicely (see Figure 6.4).

Journal Entry — Monday, May 3, 2010, 1:55 am

I made a renewed effort last night to determine whether verifiable perception is possible in the out-of-body state using the box and nails. I spent a while tossing in bed before a brief burst of energy sensations finally hit me. I could sense that they would not last long, so I had to hurry.

I quickly separated from my body and reached with my arm toward the nightstand, touching the glass on the side of the mirrored nightstand. I then carefully felt my way upward to the top. Nothing was out of the ordinary yet, and I wanted to keep it that way.

Once my hand reached the top, I felt the side of the box and gently pushed my hand through the solid surface. There were quite a few nails, which I grasped all at once.

My immediate impression was three or four nails, but I had to wiggle my fingertips on top of the nails to make a final decision. There were four of them.

I was back in body immediately after I had felt the nails, and the next morning I opened the box. There were indeed four nails—the same amount that I had felt during the OBE. It was a pleasant change from the failures of the past, but it is obviously too soon to draw any conclusions.

Note: The next morning, while in my body, I replicated the movement of feeling the nails with the box lid open. Surprisingly, except for having to open the lid from a slightly different angle, the sensation of touching the nails was identical in every way. I could not tell the difference.

MESS Level: 1
Result: Positive
Cumulative Probability: 0.2

Journal Entry — Monday, May 17, 2010, 3:10 am

I made another attempt last night to find out how many nails there were inside the box on the nightstand. I felt good about the results of the previous attempt, especially since they corresponded with such a low MESS level, but I tried not to make too much of it. It was still a long way off from any statistically significant result.

I transitioned into the out-of-body state after lying in bed for a few hours. Eventually, I was able to trigger energy sensations fairly deep into the hypnagogic stage of sleep. I felt a bit drowsy, but I easily separated and remembered my purpose.

Lying on my right side as usual, I lifted my arm and felt my way around the nightstand. My hand soon hit the corner of the box. I slid my fingers along the edges and felt a little crack, which I knew was not really there. Not wanting to get distracted, I paid no further attention to it. Instead, I pushed my hand through the side of the box and felt for the wooden block with the nails. It was there.

I wrapped my fingers around the nails near the base of the wood. There seemed to be three nails. However, as I moved my fingers toward the top end of the nails, further from the wooden base, there were only two nails. In other words, the third nail was fused together with the second nail (see Figure 6.5).

This threw me for a loop. Were there two or three nails? I decided to try again, pulled my hand out of the box, and then immediately pushed it back in again. I felt exactly the same thing. Apparently, the distortion was quite stable. I then awoke without being able to project again.

Going over the experience in my mind, I tried to come to a decision as to how many nails there really were in the box. My mind had felt a bit clouded during the experience, and there was some distortion when I sensed a nonexistent "crack" in the box. It might have been unwise to make a call.

Yet, I had come across this situation before. That time, I had felt three regular nails and a fourth short, crooked nail. If this situation was the same, underestimating the number of nails was the best course of action.

I tied the knot and settled on there being two nails inside the box. Next, I removed the tape from the box and placed my hand inside. There were indeed two nails. I had difficulty getting to sleep afterward, unable to get the thought of fused nails and blending possibilities out of my mind.

MESS Level: 4
Result: Positive
Cumulative Probability: 0.04

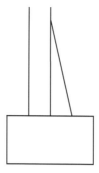

Figure 6.5. Perceptual Blending

Journal Entry — Monday, May 24, 2009, 4:55 am

Last night, I tried to touch on the vibrations for several hours from the waking state. It was difficult to get into the right state, however, and eventually I had to move fairly deep into a semi-lucid hypnagogic stage of sleep to get some energy sensations going. Once they did, I separated without problems, even though my mind felt a little clouded.

I quickly noticed that I was lying further away from the box than usual. Rather than stretching my arm, I had to lift my entire body toward the nightstand, and as I did, I ended up in a bit of an awkward, unbalanced position. I had to place my right hand on the nightstand to keep my balance while my left hand felt along the edge of the box. It felt as if it were wooden, not glass.

I pushed my hand through the box. I only felt the nails for a brief moment—three-and-a-half nails, to be exact. Again, one of the nails was fused with another. I immediately began to doubt.

However, I barely had time to think it over. The hand that kept me balanced fell straight through the nightstand, bringing me, the box, and everything else on the nightstand with it. I ended up on the floor in a mess of broken glass and what looked like a ruined box.

The piece of wood with nails had fallen out of the box and now looked like a clump of nails—as if they had been mangled in the fall. Sitting down, I picked it up to get a closer look. However, as I looked at it, the nails began to move in and out of the wood as if dancing in front of my eyes. One moment there were three sticking out, another there were two, or one. Eventually it settled into two wooden nails sticking out of the wood.

I then noticed some movement on top of the bed. My wife, who had woken up, leaned over the edge to see the mess I had made. For a brief moment, I wondered whether I had really woken up or whether I was still in the out-of-body state, but I soon surmised I was still out of body.

"Did you put a wooden block with two nails in the box?" I asked Monique.

"No," she said with a smile. I did not ask for any further information. I felt confused enough already.

I got on my feet and felt as though the OBE would soon be ending. I reacted by tensing my abdomen and upper body, which induced energy sensations and helped me prolong the experience.

I decided that I had had enough of nails for the night and walked up to the window to go outside. Once there, I hesitated about jumping down into the garden. My second body felt very heavy, as if it were made of actual matter. I turned and looked at my wife, who watched me from the bed.

"Do you feel like going outside?" I asked. "We'll have to go through the front door downstairs, I think." She nodded, and soon we both quietly walked downstairs and out through the front door. The opening in the door seemed a bit wider than usual.

It was raining outside. I knew this was probably not really the case, as it had been sunny all day. But I barely noticed the discrepancy as my lucidity began to waver again. Once outside, we both tried to levitate for a while. The heaviness was still there. We were only able to get a foot off the ground.

My lucidity only degraded more over time. At one point, a middle-aged, somewhat overweight lady came over with two cats she seemed to be taking for a walk. One of the cats stared straight at me with red eyes. The cat looked unusual, and its eyes spooked me a little bit. Next, a car came up the driveway and then reversed. Luckily, before I fell into a dreaming state, I woke up.

Once back in body, I noticed that the muscles in my abdomen and shoulders were aching. I had tensed a little bit too tightly during the OBE. But it did not seem too serious, and I went over the experience in my mind to decide whether or not I should make a call about the wooden block.

I decided there was simply too much confusion throughout the experience. The MESS level was too high. I opened the box for real, and it contained a wooden block with three nails. My initial impression had not been too far off after all.

MESS level: 6
Result: None
Cumulative Probability: unchanged

Note: A week and a half later, my wife's son moved into the house with us while he waited for another place to open up. He brought his two cats with him, both quite spooky Abyssinian cats. One of the cats has red fur. They looked quite similar to the cats that the woman in the OBE had been walking. I knew beforehand that he might be moving in, even though it was not entirely clear at that point. I never considered the cats moving in as well. Even after they moved in, I only noticed the link with this experience a few days later when I was rereading it.

Journal Entry — Friday, July 16, 2010, 5:10 am

It's been a while since my last OBE, but last night I was able to complete the transition with some very mild energy sensations. I immediately reached out for the box.

The distance between the nightstand seemed a little too short, and although there was some confusion, I eventually felt the box. Then, a number of possibilities went through my head as I pushed my hand through to guess how many nails were in the block of wood. I tried to suppress these thoughts, and once I felt inside the box, I detected two nails.

I then decided to take a brief tour in the void. I rose up in the air with fairly little body awareness. At first, the void was a little bit murky or cloudy, as if my eyes were out of focus, but then it opened up completely. The sky above me was pitch-black, interspersed with pinpoints of white lights. Just as I reached it, however, I found myself back in bed, still detached from the physical.

I decided to check the box a second time. I once again pushed my hand through, but this time it was filled with junk. There were loose, broken nails in there and pieces of wood, as well as a lot of other junk I recognized. I awoke soon after.

I hesitated to make a call. On my second attempt, things were clearly in disarray, but that only occurred later in the projection. There was some instability in the beginning, but otherwise my perception of the two nails was clear.

What bothered me more was that the fact that several possibilities went through my head at the time I pushed my hand through the box. Eventually, however, because of the relatively good environmental stability at the time I perceived it, I decided to make the call that there were two nails in the box.

It was the wrong decision. There were actually four nails in the box.

MESS level: 3
Result: Negative
Cumulative Probability: 0.096

Journal Entry — Monday, August 2, 2010, 8:20 am

I had a low-powered OBE this morning. My mind was a bit cloudy, and I lost quite a bit of lucidity in the course of the transition process, but I remembered to reach out for the box. Although my mind was cloudy, there were no telltale signs of environmental instability in the wider environment.

Inside the box, I initially clearly felt three nails but then noticed another nail wrapped around the third nail. This extra nail was attached to a second wooden block that had two nails in it. So there were two wooden blocks in the box, each with a different number of nails in them (three versus two).

However, the wooden block with the two nails felt out of place, as if it was an insignificant, unreal add-on. I decided to trust the percept and made the call that there were three nails in the box. This turned out to be correct! The results are now significant, with a probability smaller than .05!

MESS level: 4
Result: Positive
Cumulative Probability: 0.0256

Journal Entry — Saturday, November 20, 2010, 7:15 am

I've had another long hiatus in OBE activity, as work has almost entirely taken over. Apparently, my inability to get any "lift-off" in an OBE from a couple of months ago has come true for real. The household has been a lot busier as well with everyone moving in.

Last night's OBE came more or less accidentally. I was sleeping more lightly than usual, and after a period of moving in and out of sleep, the idea of an OBE occurred to me.

Initially, I entered the void, as I decided to visit a deceased family friend. I never actually got to meet him and only heard his voice. It did not feel like a direct contact—more like listening to a monologue or a prerecorded tape without any sentience behind it. He was talking about soccer—his favorite sport.

After a while, I ended up back in bed, but I was able to induce energy sensations again. I decided to do the experiment. The box was still there, untouched for the last three or four months.

To make sure the environment was stable, I initially reached for the bottom of the nightstand. There, I got an odd sensation. A force seemed to push my hand away from the wall, like a magnetic field of some kind with opposite polarities.

The sensation was surprising, but I did not let it distract me. I lifted my hand to the top of the nightstand to feel for the box. There, I pushed my left hand through the side of the box and immediately felt the wooden box with three nails in it.

As a double check, I then pushed my right hand through the box and wrapped my fingers around the nails. The sensation was a bit less clear, and as I began to doubt, I detected a fourth nail. It felt pretty unconvincing, however, in comparison to my first impression. I awoke soon after.

For a while, I contemplated the different sensations, but I had gotten the clearest sensation when I felt three nails. Environmental *stability was quite good as well, except for the unusual magnetic sensation. I'm not sure where it originated from except that there is a power plug on the wall not far from where I had placed my hand. In either case, I made the call for there being three nails, which turned out to be correct when I checked the real box.*

As an aside, while writing this and looking at my other entries, I noticed that there was the same number of nails in the box during the previous experiment, three months ago. I later asked my wife whether she had purposely put the target object with three nails there again or whether she had simply forgotten to change it. She did not remember, as it was three months ago. In either case, I do not believe it makes any difference. I had no idea what to expect either way.

MESS level: 3
Result: Positive
Cumulative Probability: 0.0064

It is difficult to say why this last set of experiments was more successful than the others. Perhaps the most important factor was that task-related demands and worries about the project were kept to a minimum. I no longer cared a great deal about the outcome. This attitude might have kept environmental stability under control more so than before.

One last observation I hesitate to mention is that for this last series of experiments, I used a different box than before. It was covered with mirrored glass. It was also rather curious that, in one of the experiences, I perceived a (nonexistent) crack in the box exactly at the joint between the mirrored panels of the box. Beyond this, I have no idea about the significance of mirrored glass in these types of experiments.

INFLUENCING THE PHYSICAL WORLD

In 2007, in the course of my experimentation, I also became a reluctant participant in a different kind of "experiment." My wife was diagnosed with thyroid cancer. Thyroid cancer has a very good prognosis, and luckily, our family physician caught it very early on, but it was still a shock to both of us, and it required immediate treatment.

The radiology exam indicated the presence of two nodules in the right lobe of the thyroid, one large nodule measuring 2.2 cm x 1.3 cm x 1.3 cm at the lower pole, and a smaller nodule measuring 4 mm x 3 mm x 3 mm. A subsequent biopsy revealed papillary carcinoma, and the proposed treatment involved surgical removal of the entire thyroid followed by radioactive iodine treatment.

On top of all this, at around the same time, one of our pugs, named Amber, was diagnosed with encephalitis leading to brain swelling and epileptic seizures. She was diagnosed and treated at a university teaching hospital. We even went so far as to track her condition with some costly MRI scans. The prognosis for Amber was bad. There was no real cure.

During all of this, I began considering doing something in the out-of-body state in hopes that it might have a real-life physical effect. Monroe, for example, relates an account of pinching someone in the out-of-body state, which coincided with a real physical effect on the person.[11] I was quite skeptical, however. There are many more accounts in which projectors fail to exert an effect on the physical world.[12] Yet, given the seriousness of the situation, I decided it was worth a try.

Journal Entry — Saturday, September 15, 2007, 3:40 am

After some hiatus in my OBE activity, I finally got to project again. This was triggered by several things, the first one being my wife's illness. I wanted to at least try something, despite feeling rather skeptical about it. I also wanted to start my verification experiments again, the urgency of which only increased with the bad news about my wife. And finally, there was Amber as well, who had had several epileptic seizures in the last month. She has been responding well to medication, although she has often become nauseous lately while lying in bed with us.

Last night, Amber kept me awake for several hours. She was breathing heavily and panting. I tried to keep an eye on her as I drifted in and out of sleep. Not surprisingly, at some point, the energy sensations came.

I moved upward slightly, floating above my body. I turned in the air, hovering above Amber and my wife, and looked at the outline of my hands. I knew that healing of this type was usually done with the hands; people claimed some sort of energy was involved. I doubted any real energy would be involved, but perhaps the symbolism of the act would matter.

I concentrated, and after a couple of seconds, a small white band of light appeared around my hands. I had hoped for something more dramatic, but it was all I had in me. At least the light was sufficiently bright to see my wife and Amber lying below me.

I was not quite sure what to do, but with both of them being ill, I decided on a group session and began to rotate above them as streaks of white light came from my hands and lighted up their bodies. The light was not particularly intense, but I felt good about doing at least something.

I continued to rotate for a while, now and then touching my wife and Amber with my hands. After a while, I awoke to a calm bedroom. Both my wife and Amber were in a deep and restful sleep.

Journal Entry — Thursday, September 20, 2007, 2:10 am

[Continued from p. 128] ...After having completed the verification experiment, I turned my attention to my wife. I had to feel my way toward her on the bed and asked for outside help this time.

It did not take long for something to happen. A humanoid shape made of light appeared, hovering above the bed. As soon as I noticed it, a strong current of energy sensations rushed through me.

The humanoid was not terribly bright. Its shape was mostly made up of small white stars interspersed throughout the 3D blackness, but its effect was strong in the flow of energy sensations I felt.

Feeling "charged up," I continued to do the light thing with my hands, holding them above my wife's neck. This seemed to wake her up after a while, and she asked what was happening. I told her it was nothing and to go back to sleep. Soon after, I awoke. My wife was soundly asleep.

Journal Entry — Sunday, September 23, 2007, 3:15 am

[Continued from p. 129] ...I then focused on my wife. She had returned from the bathroom. I concentrated, and my hands lit up with white light—more so than usual. I then proceeded to hold my hands above my wife's body at a distance of around one foot.

I then noticed something that I had not seen before. There were two seemingly highly concentrated dots of light that moved along her body as I moved my hands. They looked like the dots of light produced by laser beams. They clearly originated from my hands, even though they could only be seen once they hit their target.

I moved my hands toward her neck area, and the dots followed my movement. One dot was red, and the other was yellow. I tried to keep the dots as close as possible to her thyroid, just above the collarbone.

I did this for more than a minute until I got worried that doing it for too long might actually have an adverse effect. The idea of a laser was a bit discomforting. I decided to stop the entire session, feeling a little bit silly about the whole thing, and then proceeded to wake up.

I had a few more projections after these that focused on my wife and Amber. After my wife's operation to remove her thyroid, we waited for the results of the pathology examination, which involved an examination of the cancerous nodules in the thyroid. I did not think about any validation at this point, not expecting to ever find out whether my efforts had any effect.

However, the results of the pathology examination came with a few surprises. Unlike in the radiology report, there was mention of only one cancerous nodule in the pathology report, without any spreading elsewhere. It was good news, but it got me a little suspicious as well, so I compared the initial results of the radiology examination with those from the pathology examination. There was indeed a second nodule mentioned in the original radiology examination, while there was no mention of it in the pathology exam.

In addition, the larger nodule in the pathology examination was much smaller than was reported in the radiology exam. It mentioned "a "non-encapsulated, white, rubbery nodule measuring 1.1 cm x 0.8 cm x 0.5 cm extending into the isthmus." If I were to calculate the volume of the nodule as if it were a rectangular box, which is as far as my math skills go, the total volume was only 12% of the original nodule. It seemed like a very significant reduction in size as compared to the original size. Was it possible that the nodule had shrunk? And if so, what caused it?

I asked my wife to ask her specialists for an explanation regarding the reduction in size of the larger nodule. We did not pursue the question of the absence of any reference to the smaller nodule in the pathology report. Validating my OBE activity was still not very much at the forefront of my mind. There were more important questions to ask, such as about the radioactive treatment that was still in store.

The first physician—an ear, nose and throat specialist—suggested that the procedure used during the radiology examination may lead a nodule to "stretch out" when they measure it and that it would therefore seem smaller in the pathology examination. This answer was unsatisfactory to me since, as far as I know, the volume of an object does not change when it is stretched.

The second physician, the actual surgeon who performed the operation, was quite surprised. He said it might be the result of the use of formaldehyde in the pathology exam, which can lead to some shrinkage. However, he added that it did not explain the amount of reduction and that he should perhaps review the files of some of his other patients and look for any potential discrepancies in the radiology and pathology exams. He did not have a real answer, however.

The third, an endocrinologist, who was quite knowledgeable in this area, reacted to the formaldehyde explanation by saying that this is often the standard answer if questions arise surrounding any discrepancies between the radiology and pathology examinations. He agreed that formaldehyde could lead to a small reduction in size, but that it did not apply in this particular case. The shrinkage was too significant, he said. He added that such large reductions are not entirely unheard of, but they occur only rarely, and there is no known medical explanation.

In sum, there was no obvious materialistic explanation for the reduction in the size of the larger nodule. There may be one, but despite asking three specialists, there was no apparent conventional explanation. Of course, none of this proves that my out-of-body activity was responsible for the reduction in size of the larger nodule and the disappearance of the other one. There may very well be a conventional explanation. For example, it later occurred to me that a biopsy may have these effects, although this still did not explain the disappearance of the second nodule.

In the end, the whole affair had a positive outcome. The endocrinologist decided that radioactive iodine treatment was now unnecessary, due to the small size of the nodule and the fact that there was no cancer elsewhere. The only regret we had was not to have had another radiology exam right before the operation. If we had, perhaps part of the thyroid might have been saved.

Finally, regarding Amber—my frequent partner in crime in the out-of-body state—she passed away two years after being diagnosed. This period of time was quite a bit longer than the veterinarians had expected her to survive. Again, whether my out-of-body activity had anything to do with it is impossible to say. I do not have sufficient knowledge about her disease to make any sort of judgment in this area. She is still very much missed.

THE BOTTOM LINE

OBE adepts have so far failed to convincingly prove the existence of veridical perception in the out-of-body state. While a few successful experiments have been reported in the scientific literature, these results do not seem to replicate very well. Not surprisingly, veridical perception in the out-of-body state has remained contentious. Indeed, my own initial experiments are largely consistent with the scientific literature on the subject. Without prior knowledge, little or nothing of what is perceived during the out-of-body state corresponds to ordinary perception. This seems to be consistent with the view that, for the most part, perception in the out-of-body state is an "arbitrary" construction.

In retrospect, I should not have been too surprised. As we saw earlier, even *with* previous knowledge, reconstructing physical reality without sensory data is no small feat. These difficulties only seem to increase when trying to perceive an environment without prior knowledge. Task-related demands, and performance anxiety in particular, interferes quite strongly with the overall stability of the out-of-body environment. Even the slightest uncontrolled emotional conflict or doubt has the tendency to manifest inside of the OBE environment.

Despite all these difficulties, I did obtain some promising results in my last set of trials trying to determine the number of nails in a wooden block placed inside of a box hidden from view. The multinomial probability of that outcome was close to 1 in 150. Is this proof of veridical perception in the out-of-body state? Not by any scientific standard, which requires more trials, a more controlled setup, and replication across different studies.

Still, I consider the results as reflecting fairly decent odds, making me believe that that veridical perception might be provable under certain circumstances. In the end, however, taken altogether, my series of experiments show that *if* veridical perception is possible in the out-of-body state, it is clearly not a simple, straightforward matter. The reasons can only be speculated upon.

The most important difficulty clearly lies in the high level of environmental instability that characterizes the out-of-body state, which is caused by the mind of the projector interfering with accurate perception. For example, the notion of "overlay errors" has been introduced in research on extrasensory perception and remote viewing, in which the observer produces "noise" that interferes with the accurate perception of a target object.[13]

The term *overlay error* may be a bit of a misnomer, since it presumes that there is a separate world out there being "overlaid." However, if there is no fixed, separate world out there, nothing can ever be really distorted or overlaid. Rather, you *construct* your perception of reality in discordance with objective reality. Doing so does not automatically imply a "distortion."

In either case, it is remarkably easy to construct perceptions that are discordant with ordinary physical reality. The slightest expectancy, or any sort of guesswork, on either a conscious or subconscious level will produce a perception that has no direct link to objective reality. Many of these different influences have been discussed previously as threats to the stable reconstruction of physical reality. However, the current set of experiments also highlights another potential influence that renders veridical perception in the out-of-body state a difficult task.

The phenomenon is best described as *perceptual blending*, in which distinct perceptual categories fuse together as one category. For example, during one of the tasks, when attempting to perceive a single color, I perceived a multicolored flower that incorporated all the colors I could possibly perceive. Similar phenomena occurred later on, such as when I perceived a nail welded together with a nonexistent third nail.

If we were to speculate on the exact causes of perceptual blending, we might characterize the phenomenon as the result of a greater degree of competition among perceptual possibilities. That is, when different possibilities compete for "actualization," sometimes neither one wins or loses. The end result is a blended object with multiple possibilities combining in a creative and novel manner.

In fact, perception itself, as we experience it in physical reality, might also be the result of competition between possibilities. What we experience as different perceptual categories might simply be different blends of the same underlying field of possibility or wave of potential, where such separate categories do not really exist.

Interestingly, perceptual blending is the opposite of a "lack of fusion" that has been reported in remote viewing research. Here, the person attempts to perceive a distant target through extrasensory means, but without leaving the body.[14] One of the frequent distortions during these experiments is the perception of disjointed parts of a particular target object that fail to form a complete whole. For example, the incident in which I perceived a lot of junk in the box, consisting of broken nails, pieces of wood, and so forth, suggests a lack of fusion.

To illustrate the trappings of verifiable perception, we only need to look at the many illusions that easily occur during ordinary perception. For example, I experienced quite a bit of difficulty producing the picture of the wooden blocks with nails included in the present chapter, which initially did not accurately represent the number of nails. Instead, in trying to capture the image, I created an unintended perceptual illusion (see Figure 6.6). In the current context, it was a rather ironic occurrence that showed that even ordinary perception cannot always be relied upon.

So where do all these experiments leave the pragmatic projector? Should the physical field of consciousness simply be left alone because accurate perception appears to be virtually impossible? It might be wise not to jump to conclusions too quickly. After all, if veridical perception is possible in the out-of-body state, it should at least be *theoretically* possible to perceive the entire environment correctly. And in fact, this may occur more often than the current series of experiments suggests since, under ordinary circumstances, there are far fewer task-related demands interfering with perception. In that sense, it should perhaps not be too surprising that the best anecdotal evidence often occurs under spontaneous circumstances, rather than in the context of an experiment.

Figure 6.6. Perceptual Illusion of Target Objects

There is also another important factor to consider. The degree of mental and environmental stability seems directly related to the likelihood that veridical perception occurs in the out-of-body state. For example, in a study by Smith and Irwin, participants were asked to perceive two targets in another room while out of body.[15] In addition, participants were administered an "OBE-ness" questionnaire that produced a score reflecting the extent that their experience was *like* an OBE. The results of that study indicated that the likelihood of verifiable perception was very strongly related to the level of "OBE-ness." The more participants felt that their experience was like a real OBE, the more likely they were to perceive the target correctly.

I strongly suspect that the "OBE-ness" questionnaire indirectly measures level of mental and environmental stability. After all, an OBE will feel more real when the environment and the state of mind of the projector correspond to physical reality. Future experiments may wish to control for environmental and mental stability in the statistical analysis of data. The removal of random error may make veridical perception in the out-of-body state a great deal easier to detect and prove. The MESS scale (see Appendix I) could be useful in such an endeavor, with a few adaptations, depending on the task.

Finally, what are the theoretical implications of the limits of veridical perception in the out-of-body state? Does it mean you are "merely" having a paranormal experience, while not really out of the body? In my opinion, this question starts out on the wrong footing since it fails to take into account the constructed nature of perception. Consciousness is wherever it constructs itself to be; as such, it is never really anywhere to begin with.

Clearly, however, it does not appear to be very natural for consciousness to reconstruct physical reality accurately, at least not in the absence of sensory input. This obviously makes a lot of sense since why else would we need a physical body? Indeed, all these difficulties with perception may simply represent a natural push outward toward another field of consciousness altogether. This brings us to the *personal field of consciousness*.

PART THREE

The Human Spectrum of Consciousness

Chapter 6
The Personal Field of Consciousness

THE PERSONAL FIELD

As we have seen, the out-of-body state and the environments encountered are subject to psychological influences. Many of these influences are often already apparent inside of the physical field. They originate from an area of consciousness where the inner psyche of the projector plays a decisive role in the type of environment encountered—the *personal field of consciousness*. Monroe, who initially referred to it as Locale II, described it as follows:

> "...a state of being where that which we label thought is the wellspring of existence. It is the vital creative force that produces energy, assembles "matter" into form, and provides channels of perception and communication. I suspect that the self or soul in Locale II is no more than an organized vortex or warp in this fundamental. As you think, so you are."[1]

The personal field is the repository of one's fears, dreams, hopes, ideas, motivations, expectations, tendencies, impulses, intents, memories, representations, models of the world, personal symbols, and everything else associated with what it means to be human. Yet, when inside of your own personal field, the out-of-body environment will generally still present itself as ordinary landscapes, parks, houses, cities, and people commonly encountered in physical reality. In other words, your inner psyche is *objectified* as actual events, people, landscapes, and objects in the environment. The environment is subjective, but it will nonetheless appear to you as a physical-like, objective environment as if it exists apart from you.

In traditional approaches, the personal field is often considered to be an early encounter with astral environments—an area of consciousness similar in appearance to the physical world, but without having any real physical counterpart. Others have referred to these environments as *nonconsensual environments* to emphasize the relatively private nature of the field.[2]

My own preference is for the term *personal field of consciousness* since environments in the personal field may not always be entirely nonconsensual. Shared dreaming, for example, in which people have almost identical dreams, is mentioned as a possibility in some of the popular scientific-based literature.[3] It is also not inconceivable that one person may enter the subjective reality of another during an OBE, such as is usually the case during atmospheric influences.

In general, however, during an OBE, when fully immersed inside your own personal field of consciousness, there is no interacting with anything that has an independent existence outside of you, nor is there any relationship with the physical field. You will be inside a world of your own making that is largely cut off from any other influences. Indeed, the subjective nature of the personal field can make experiences in the personal field often appear dreamlike, even if perceived under conditions of high lucidity.

For example, Monroe describes the chaotic level of focus 22—an area of consciousness with people engaged in all manner of hallucinatory and dreamlike activities who are oblivious to the wider reality surrounding them. Others report on an area of consciousness heavily populated by dreaming minds wandering across "...a confusing mismatch of cities, landscapes, peoples and times, all of which appear to be in a constant state of flux."[4] Not surprisingly, Monroe reportedly had some with difficulty drawing the line between dreams and his early experiences in Locale II.[5]

A relatively straightforward way to understand your own personal field is to transpose the mental architecture of your own psyche onto it. From top to bottom, we can identify the most transient aspects of the psyche, which includes an ongoing flow of thoughts, feelings, and expectations. This is then followed by more permanent layers of fears and emotions. Beyond that, more stable structures consisting of your beliefs system and personal symbols may be encountered, as well as a reservoir of memories and life experiences. Even further out, if you were to reach beyond the known parts of the psyche, you may encounter aspects of yourself you did not even know existed. For example, some have suggested the existence of probable selves, past selves, and future selves that may also be encountered in altered states of consciousness.[6] Yet others claim to have met with their own "soul," consisting of a conglomerate of reincarnational selves.[7]

Keep in mind that these divisions in consciousness are rather arbitrary since the different fields of consciousness, as well as different subfields of consciousness that be identified inside each one, continuously merge and intertwine. In fact, you can never entirely escape the personal field of consciousness, regardless of where your main focus lies. For example, the personal field of consciousness is not only responsible for "distortions" in the physical field; it allows for accurate perception as well. It provides you with an *impression* of physical reality—a picture that "floats out there" to provide you with the illusion of existing in a three-dimensional reality.

While entrenched in the personal field, the manner in which the out-of-body environment will manifest around you is generally in accordance with the particular aspects of your mind that it represents. For example, transient aspects of the psyche that revolve around your immediate thoughts and emotions tend to occur as relatively isolated events with a high degree of mobility and fluidity inside of the environment. In contrast, more structural aspects of your psyche, such as belief systems and moods, tend to lead to the manifestation of entire landscapes and worlds. For example, persistent pessimistic aspects of your own psyche may manifest as a brooding landscape devoid of color and filled with dreariness.

Of course, none of this implies that *everything* you will encounter in the personal field is psychologically meaningful. Often, mere expectation or intent is already enough to make complex and detailed environments appear. For example, flying over any sort of typical forest or city does not automatically imply that your perceptions have any symbolic meaning. Rather, the scenery is created on the spot, borrowing on your own memories and ideas of what a city or forest might look like. As such, the personal field also functions as a fantastic realm of the imagination—an inherent part of both the human psyche and perception itself. You can therefore create any environment you want and engage in whatever activity you want, if you know how to control the personal field.

ENTRY INTO THE PERSONAL FIELD

It is not difficult to enter the personal field. You will often end up there automatically without effort, even if you originally start out in the physical field. In effect, you will often find it quite difficult to remain inside the physical field for a prolonged period of time. Like an invisible force, the personal field will pull you toward it, whether you like it or not. It represents a mode of consciousness that is far more natural to the out-of-body state than any other.

Leaving the physical field behind also often represents a point at which you might lose lucidity and revert to a dreaming state of consciousness. However, as you become more familiar with leaving the physical field, it will become easier to maintain lucidity, especially if you control your entry into the personal field. For example, passing through a door or window in the physical, while simultaneously *intending* to enter a different environment, will generally ensure that you end up in the personal field with lucidity.

"Rebooting" the environment with a stroke of your hand across your visual field is also good method for entering the personal field (see p.

86). If your efforts are not successful initially, such as when part of the environment is still reminiscent of the physical world, you can execute multiple hand strokes in quick succession until the environment conforms to your intent. Make sure to remain detached and to stabilize the environment immediately afterward. Otherwise, you run the risk of entering a non-lucid state.

You can also enter the personal field directly from the void. You might want to make more of an "inward turn" when engaging with an environment, as if you were moving into your mind. None of this is absolutely necessary, however. Even if you are moving outward into the void, you are still quite likely to end up in the personal field of consciousness. It exercises a much stronger pull than any other field of consciousness, often even overriding your conscious intent.

If you use the void to enter the personal field, keep in mind that it is very easy to create a remote replica of the void in the process. Rather than actually arriving at your intended destination, you would enter a symbolic version of the void. For example, you may find yourself inside a water world or a dark river, both of which are common symbolic representations of the void, not unlike the river Styx, which the Egyptians believed needed to be crossed in order to reach the afterlife following death. In these circumstances, you have not yet arrived at your intended destination.

UTILIZING THE PERSONAL FIELD

Even though the personal field is largely a subjective realm, it would be a mistake to underestimate its potential utility. It provides you with a rare three-dimensional glimpse into your own mind. In a sense, it is quite real since, after all, the constructs of your mind are real. Still, this does not mean that everything you encounter in the personal field is an accurate reflection of your mind. For example, if you fear yourself, you might encounter exactly that which you fear. The fears themselves are unfounded and unreal, but they are nonetheless given full expression in the personal field. So whatever you do, never give away your power to the environment. There can be only one captain at the helm of your own psyche. It is very important to claim that role.

Journal Entry — 1997, date and time unknown

I found myself in the void last night. I'm not sure how I ended up there. I had no memory of having left my body. But it was an opportunity, and I immediately began to fly, even though I was a little fearful about where I might end up. It is still difficult to enter an astral environment not knowing what to expect beforehand.

After flying horizontally for a while, I decided to make my descent. I soon found ground under my feet, and almost immediately the environment appeared. I found myself inside a large, dimly lit hall. It looked a bit like a gymnasium, but it was too dark to make out any details. Worse, there was a shadow moving near the walls on the other side of the hall. There was something there, I was sure, but I could not identify it.

I moved toward the center of the gymnasium, where it was lighter. Again I noticed movement near the walls. This time, I caught a glimpse of what was lurking in the shadows. It was an animal—a black panther. I instantly knew what it represented. It was a representation of the entire astral realm. I was not sure why it would be a black panther, but the percept was clear.

I sensed a possibility. Maybe I could let go of my fears once and for all. I had been afraid so many times as I've moved into these out-of-body environments. What if I simply lay down here in the middle of the gymnasium and surrendered to what I knew to be only a symbol? The idea seemed harmless enough, so I lay down on the floor, entirely sure that I would not be harmed.

With my decision, the panther reacted immediately. It came out of the shadows, moving slowly toward me in a circular pattern—a typical predator movement. Then the panther came even closer until it stood right above me, straddling me, staring coldly into my eyes.

The beast was massive, and I could feel its nonhuman strength better than I could ever have imagined. Still, I was not afraid. I felt pretty good about "facing up" to my fears. Besides, what could possibly go wrong?

Then it lunged, mouth wide open, straight for my throat! I barely had time to react. I turned my face away from its jaw as I lifted up my arms to protect myself. It was already too late. Its jaws were already on my neck, its teeth breaking the skin, as it held me down tightly to make its kill. I panicked. This was not supposed to happen! I tried to wake up but was unable to do so. It held me down. I was going to be ravaged.

I frantically tried to push it away, without success. I was no match for its strength. I knew I had made a terrible mistake. Surrendering to a wild animal? I could just as well have jumped into a lion's den like a real loon.

This last thought triggered another percept. I had to refuse the experience.

I took a deep breath and then yelled at the top of my lungs: "NOOOO!!"

Suddenly, the panther backed off, curiously turning its head like a dog trying to understand, except that its eyes remained cold, like those of a wild animal.

I yelled out again: "NO!"

This time it worked. It came off me, moving backward, not in any great hurry to obey. It then turned and, without looking back, retreated quietly to the shadows of the wall. Only then was I able to force myself to awaken, still shaking in my real bed with the entire experience.

Note: I later looked up the symbolic meaning of a black panther in dreams. To my surprise, it is indeed often understood as a symbol of astral travel—a totem of death and darkness as well as a guardian to challenge the person into reclaiming his or her personal power.

While seemingly negative experiences may occur now and then in the personal field, this is by no means the norm. Of course, a certain amount of emotional off-loading may occur during your initial visits, and you might surprise yourself with some of the baggage you carry. However, none of this has to get out of hand if you do not give your power away to the environment. In fact, so-called negative experiences can be of great benefit, allowing you to overcome any limitations, false beliefs, or fears you have imposed on yourself. And if you are able to learn from your experiences, you will also be able to take a more proactive approach toward the personal field and use it to your advantage.

Housecleaning

In my own out-of-body activities, the resolution of personal limitations, or *housecleaning,* as I have come to refer to it, started out largely unintended. Often, after having entered an out-of-body environment, I would unintentionally be faced with a particular problem or issue that needed to be solved. On occasion, a voice coming from an unknown place guided me through it.

For example, in one particularly frequent scenario, I found myself standing on top of a platform with a muddy lake filled with alligators below me. If I wanted to get any further, my understanding was that I had to jump into the lake and swim to the other side. So I jumped, over and over again, avoiding the alligators as I swam across, until the entire experience became trivial. I still avoided the alligators, of course, but they became much less threatening over time, even diminishing in size.

Experiences such as these are like virtual reality *simulations,* the purpose of which is to overcome personal limitations and fears. In this particular case, the scenario was entirely geared toward overcoming my fear of entering the out-of-body state itself, symbolically represented by me jumping into a lake crawling with alligators. As I jumped in over and over again, I found that I could handle myself and avoid any potentially traumatic experience.

Interestingly, many modern psychological interventions for specific phobias and other psychological disorders use the same kinds of exposure techniques. During exposure, the person is slowly and gradually confronted with feared objects, activities, or situations. The purpose is to habituate to the object of fear until it no longer provokes a negative emotional response.

More recently, some psychologists have begun to use virtual reality environments to treat psychological problems. For example, a person with a fear of flying would be immersed in a virtual airport environment, enter a plane, and sit down in a seat as if it were really happening. It is not difficult to see how the out-of-body state has positive applications as well, allowing for an even higher level of immersion, this time controlled by your own consciousness rather than by expensive equipment. Despite the high level of immersion, a graded approach is still possible by slowly increasing the level of difficulty according to your intent. Jumping into a lake with alligators, for example, might not always be a good idea.

There is also another reason that projections into consciousness seem to have a beneficial effect on the resolution of fears and limitations. The out-of-body state, including during dreaming, is a highly fluid state of consciousness in which the introduction of alternative possibilities has a highly beneficial effect as old patterns are shaken up and replaced. Of course, the opposite is true as well, in that new possibilities are easily invented to confirm and reinvent preexisting dysfunctional behavioral patterns. Nonetheless, the natural impetus in the out-of-body state appears to lean toward the dissolution of limiting beliefs and emotions.

Setting Intent

Housecleaning is most effectively carried out with a controlled entry into an out-of-body environment, which includes setting an intent as to what you wish to accomplish. This can be a generalized intent (e.g., "I want to enter an environment that teaches me something new"), a semi-specific intent (e.g., "I want to enter an environment that helps me to overcome any limiting aspects of my own psyche"), or a very specific intent (e.g., "I want to overcome my fear of spiders").

My personal preference is to use a generalized intent, especially of the type "I want to experience something that is beneficial for me" or "I want to experience something that I need to know right now." Such phrasing has the benefit of leaving the experience open ended while at the same time keeping at bay a great deal of interference from your own psyche. You are in effect relying on your own nonconscious total self to decide what is best for you. In contrast, a specific intent tends to bring along a lot of expectations generated by the superficial mind, including mistaken ideas about how a particular problem needs to be solved.

For example, if you have anger issues and expect to enter some sort of scenario in which your temper will be tested, do not be surprised if the actual solution is something entirely different. For example, you might be guided to the root of that anger only to discover that the problem was not about anger at all, but rather another emotion underlying it (e.g., hurt, shame, guilt). In that sense, there is some sort of "higher intelligence" operating inside of the personal field. With an open-minded intent, you are likely to be guided exactly where you need to be.

When you do use a specific intent, which can be useful at times, depending on the situation, try to initially "limit" yourself to relatively minor issues or problems in order to build up some confidence. Once you become comfortable with that, you will also often find yourself in the position to do some *mindscaping*, which involves the direct manipulation of out-of-body environments. You are in effect treating the externalized and seemingly objective environment as the subjective and symbolic environment it really is.

Journal Entry — Saturday, October 27, 2007, 3:50 am

I recently purchased the biography of the now-deceased Monroe written by Ronald Russell. I have only skimmed it so far, but it has renewed my interest, and I decided to try to contact Monroe in the out-of-body state. I had met him before on occasion, but I wanted to give it another try.

Conditions were excellent. The energy sensations were slow to arrive, but once they did, they remained for a prolonged period of time. It gave me the leeway I needed to reach out further than usual even while still feeling myself lying in bed.

I set my intent and then reached out.

A bright flash soon followed. It lit up the entire environment, temporarily blinding me. I was still in my bedroom immediately afterward, but something had changed. There were several letters lying at the foot of the bed. There was no doubt in my mind how they had gotten there. My intent had worked.

One of my goals had been to find out the original title of the manuscript of Ultimate Journey. *I had recently heard that it was different from the published title, and rather than try to find out what it was through regular means, I thought it would be an interesting way to get some validation if I could obtain the answer from Monroe himself.*

Excitedly, I began to read one of the letters. For a while, the text appeared to be written in Spanish, which I don't know how to read. There was also an accompanying picture with three entangled gorillas that soon captured my attention, leading to a zooming-in effect that clouded my awareness.

One of the gorillas held two smaller gorillas, giving the impression of a family. I then noticed a piece of English text, apparently in reference to the picture, that started with "The three...." It reminded me a bit of the three wise monkeys embodying the proverbial principle of "see no evil, hear no evil, speak no evil."

I did not get much further with this letter. Even if it did contain the answer to my validation attempt, I could make no sense of it. So instead, I began to read the other letters lying on the bed. They were quite a bit easier to read, as they were completely in English.

I read through them quickly, not trying to memorize the details. I remember kindness and warmth. In one of the letters, Monroe expressed his willingness to help me. I was not sure how he would help me since he was not in the room. I figured I'd better get "out there" so that he could.

I walked up to the window and stared into the darkness to help distract me from my surroundings. Again, there was a bright flash. I no longer was surprised at how effective the transition was. It really did feel like an outside influence. I'm not that good at navigating consciousness. I was swept from one environment to another. In each environment, there was something for me to "work out."

One environment stood out. It was at an underground metro station. Usually, the characters I meet are chatterboxes. There, none of them wanted to talk to me. They were actually quite rude, either ignoring me or looking at me with annoyance. It was much as you would expect real people to react if you were to approach them in an actual metro station. The environment disappeared as soon as I had noticed this, as if that were the purpose to begin with.

The pace was very fast. I never stayed long in each of the environments I encountered, nor were any of the "issues" particularly complicated, as if I had already dealt with them. Meanwhile, during all these encounters and environments, the presence of Monroe could be felt in the background, until eventually I heard his voice asking me to reach for focus 27.

There was no bright flash this time. Instead, I heard him say, "Focus on my voice." The next moment, I was listening to a guided, seemingly prerecorded session on how to reach focus 27.

"Wow, it's exactly as it is on the focus 27 tapes of the Monroe Institute!" I thought to myself.

Only now, as I'm writing this, I realize that no focus 27 Hemi Sync tapes exist—or, at least, the Monroe Institute has never released them. In any case, it did not take long before I began to perceive a glowing orange light ahead of me. I seemed to have made it.

Then, suddenly I felt myself sink. I felt a little uncomfortable at first but then decided to trust the process. It did not feel as though I had much choice anyway. The process had been set in motion.

Once I touched ground, what I encountered was not what I expected from focus 27, if that was what it was. I found myself in a putrid, abandoned swimming pool overgrown with weeds and crawling with all kinds of critters. There were insects, spiders, small alligators, and many other nasty life forms I could not even identify.

I spend some time avoiding the critters. None of them were large, but I did not want them crawling into my pants or onto me. Luckily, the water level was only ankle deep. I managed to keep them off me fairly easily. But why on earth had I ended up here?

In the midst of deciding what to do next, I saw Monroe standing at the edge of the swimming pool. I was not sure how long he had been there. I did not waste any time.

"What is this place? I had expected something different from focus 27."

"We need to get rid of the parasites first—the ones attached to you," he said calmly.

Now I was concerned. "What are they?"

"Addictions, just addictions related to physical life. Whether it's substance abuse or whether it's a psychological addiction to an idea. It's really all the same. Everyone has them."

I looked at the repulsive critters crawling at my feet. The disgust on my face must have shown. Monroe looked amused by my reaction.

"This here is not much," he said. "Some people only get into it ankle deep. If you look carefully at my life, you'll find that I had quite a few myself."

I was unconvinced as to the normalcy of the situation. I wanted to get rid of them as soon as possible and immediately began to concentrate on my surroundings.

I'm not quite sure why it worked, but the environment began to clear up just by concentrating on it. The parasites dissolved into thin air, the rot and weeds disappeared, and the swimming pool filled up with clear blue water. And then, as if to finalize the act, families with children came out of nowhere, jumping in the pool and having fun.

Happy with the result, I walked up to Monroe. But before I got close to him, I was thrust back into bed. I did not have a chance to ask about the manuscript.

Mindscaping

Mindscaping is quite similar to housecleaning, but it involves a more detached stance toward the environment. During mindscaping, rather than acting as a participant in the environment, you try to change the environment directly, either by simply concentrating on the changes you want to make or by rebooting parts of the environment. Essentially, you are sculpting and recreating the environment around you.

In order to mindscape, you want to ensure that you enter an environment that represents a particular aspect of your psyche. This requires a semi-specific intent relating to that aspect of your mind you want to delve into. If you want get really specific, you can also hold an intent regarding the manner in which the environment will be represented, for example, a landscape or city, house, or garden. Again, my own preference is to leave it open, thereby minimizing interference.

Once the intent has been set, and after you have entered the environment, your first order of business is to assess the overall health of the environment. Your immediate reaction to the environment provides the best clues as to the meaning of the environment, so try not to overintellectualize your assessment of the environment. Your gut feeling is probably the correct one.

For example, if a desert landscape makes you feel empty and lonely, the environment probably means just that, namely, that a part of you feels empty and lonely inside. In contrast, if you feel very comfortable inside such an environment, such as when you associate deserts with a contemplative, peaceful, or even spiritual state of mind, you can safely assume that the environment reflects just that.

In general, anything that appears out of balance, chaotic, or brooding should alert you to make some changes to the environment. For example, a festering pond in an otherwise clean environment is a good candidate for a cleanup. Dead trees and bushes may need replacing. Hoodlums and thugs need to be removed. Before you start looking for a shovel, however, realize that you do not need physical-based methods to change the environment. You are not gardening—you are *mindscaping*.

An effective method for mindscaping is to reboot parts of the environment with the hand-stroke method. Alternatively, you may simply concentrate on a particular aspect of the environment in order to effectuate a change. While doing so, maintain a relatively open mind about any changes that will occur in the environment. You don't want to be involved in every little detail of your environment, acting as a tyrant of your own mind. Initially, it is often more about simply creating the right conditions, removing anything cancerous, and providing room for new seeds to grow. Like any garden, the mind is a living thing that sometimes needs to be left alone to flourish.

Long-standing, recurring issues tend to manifest as relatively stable semipermanent structures in the personal field. For example, a common recurrence in my own personal field is encountering a cage filled with birds. Often, the environment is luscious and green, and the entire habitat is thriving, sometimes a little bit too much, with barely any metal wiring to keep the birds enclosed. The birds are in excellent shape, vibrant in colors and diversity, often nesting and multiplying. On some occasions, however, I find the birds neglected, sick, and depressed, and the larger environment in a state of decay.

Eventually, it became quite clear to me what this environment represented. Whenever I felt overwhelmed in daily life, unable to keep up, or letting things slide, I found the birds and habitat in a neglected state. Conversely, if I felt on top of things and able to take on even more tasks and projects, the entire environment would be thriving.

Semipermanent structures like these can often be traced back to events in your own childhood. For example, the "bird environment" originates from a period in my childhood during which I kept and bred a variety of exotic birds. It required a great deal of discipline to ensure that they were always well cared for. I managed to do so, and the birds were never neglected, but an awareness of the consequences of not taking care of them was always present. These days, the responsibilities and duties have changed, but the symbol in my personal field has not.

One of the trappings of the personal field is that the environment can sometimes reinforce preexisting beliefs if taken too literally, or perhaps sometimes not literally enough. For example, a belief in the duality of good and evil may confront you with environments reinforcing that belief, in which you find yourself slaying an endless deluge of monsters and demons, never entirely losing or winning. Of course, therein also lies the lesson, but it can be difficult to see if you are too attached to your own beliefs, mistaking them for reality itself.

Recognizing the subjective nature of the personal field, and making changes where needed, appears to have a beneficial effect on both your state of mind and your experience in physical life. Of course, keep in mind that the physical world and the personal field do not move apart. It does not suffice to change the environment through mindscaping, while neglecting the physical state of affairs it represents. Reinforcement in physical life is required.

For example, if you spend time on changing a dead, gloomy environment and you find yourself waking up the next morning with more energy than usual, *do* something with that energy to make it last. The opposite may be true as well; efforts in physical life to overcome a particular problem may require some sort of positive nightly activity as reinforcement.

Home Base

Inside the personal field, it is also possible to create environments as part of a creative endeavor. This is not just some fanciful enterprise. For example, it is quite beneficial to build a *home base*—a comfortable way station from which you can delve deeper into the void.

If you decide to lay claim to your own empty piece of "land," try to create an environment where you feel safe. You might want to build your dream house at a favorite location isolated from the rest of the world. Alternatively, you might prefer to take up residence in a penthouse in the city. It can be anything at all, ranging from a simple platform in the void to an entire world that you call your own. Just make sure that easy reaccess to the void is always possible, such as through a dark window or anything else that convincingly serves as a portal.

You do not necessarily have to build your home base from scratch. Imagination is quite powerful in the out-of-body state, and as such you can also simply enter a fairly random environment and let yourself be surprised by the outcome. In fact, do not be surprised if you already have a "second life" out there.

Journal Entry — Sunday, October 15, 2006, 2:00 pm

As usual, the energy sensations hit me after the first sleep cycle of the night. I immediately flew up into the void, attempting to gain some speed. Meanwhile, I reflected on my goal for the night. I decided to simply go as far as I could.

However, it was difficult to keep a sense of movement going. No real change in consciousness occurred. Nonetheless, I managed to keep some semblance of movement going by enjoying the melody of a song I was hearing around me. It sounded familiar, and I told myself to listen to the song again in ordinary life.

After a while, the lack of real movement made me worry about waking up prematurely. It was time to enter an environment. I mentally pushed into the immediate darkness surrounding me, without having any idea beforehand where I would end up. Before I knew it, I found myself standing next to a swimming pool.

The pool was part of a house. It was an indoor pool with a large glass roof above it. The pool itself was surrounded by many light bulbs that shone into clear blue water. Stairs led to separate rooms located on higher platforms.

The place looked pretty upscale and artistic. In fact, the entire house seemed to be floating in midair without anything solid to hold it up. There were barely any walls or ceilings. It seemed to be an open home surrounded by windows and glass, looking out into the void. The airy space gave it an indoor and outdoor feeling at the same time.

The swimming pool was in the lowest area of the house, and multiple interconnected platforms made up the different sections of the house. Some areas were divided by curtains and tapestries, providing a bit more privacy than other areas, but still very accessible and open. The thought occurred to me that everything was exactly to my tastes.

Then it hit me. I knew this place! I once had a very elaborate dream about this place and remembered writing a long journal entry describing the entire layout of the house. This was my place!

Excitedly, I walked toward a staircase on one side of the pool that led to an elevated area of the house. But before I got there, a small blue card lying on a corner table grabbed my attention. It was a Post-it note—the same kind that I use at work to write reminders to myself. I picked it up and began reading.

The note was an old reminder to work on a specific issue. In fact, I now remembered several dreams in which I had already dealt with that issue. They had all started from this house. I could sense how easy it was to start a dream from this place. I could have easily restarted and relived the previous dreams right then and there.

I shook off the encroaching dream before it started. I wanted to explore further. I walked up the stairs onto the upper platform. From there, I could see all the way to the other end of the house with no walls to block my view.

There were lights of different shapes and sizes all over the house. I liked the overall lighting scheme, especially with the entire structure being surrounded by the darkness of the void, but I wanted some areas a little brighter. I focused on one area of the house and mentally increased the luminance a little. The lights responded, and even though I did not manage to get them up as much as I wanted, things got quite a bit brighter.

I then looked into the void through the glass walls, reminding myself to practice moving from in and out of the void one day. It would be interesting to see what the house looked like from the outside. I imagined it to be like a surreal Daliesque structure—a brightly lit multilevel house suspended in midair and utter darkness. I awoke after this.

Note: I later found out that the song I heard during this experience was entirely new and did not (yet) exist in physical life, nor had I ever written a journal entry about the dream house.

DISINHIBITION

Another utility of the personal field lies in its potential for leisure, fun, and games. For example, sexual escapades inside of the personal field rank pretty high for many projectors. Likewise, many engage in adventure and thrill-seeking experiences such as flying across landscapes, cities, and seascapes. Alternatively, you might prefer power-related activities such as trying to levitate in front of large crowds and impressing other people.

My best advice regarding these activities is to do whatever you like, drop what is no longer enjoyable, and overcome whatever turns out to be limiting to you. The latter may be the case if you find yourself engaging in activities that go against your conscious will.

Not uncommonly, *disinhibition* occurs in the out-of-body state, meaning that you may engage in acts that not only go against social conventions but also against your own volition. The most prominent type of disinhibition you can expect to encounter revolves around sexuality, while aggression comes in a close second. Certain motivations and wishes will take over, and despite your best intentions, you will find them very difficult to resist. Characteristically, these behaviors are excessive and blown out of proportion.

When disinhibition occurs, the environment quickly shifts to include the object of your fear or desire, which pulls you more deeply into the personal field. Sometimes, a mere stray thought may already be sufficient for the nymph or knight of your dreams to appear. If that was your intent, there is nothing wrong with it, but if it goes against your conscious will, there might be a problem.

The important thing to keep in mind is that the source of disinhibitory behaviors or emotions always lies inside of your own psyche. There is no "outside" influence. Rather, disinhibition in the out-of-body state comes about due to an insufficient level of awareness of your own thoughts and emotional patterns in ordinary life, especially those of an automatic nature.

For example, a highly sexually active person, entirely by conscious choice and within the realm of his or her intent, is unlikely to experience any uncontrolled sexual impulses. He or she may be very sexually active in the out-of-body state, but it won't be experienced in the form of disinhibition. Conversely, if you are unaware of your own sexual desires, they might come to haunt you in the out-of-body state. They will tend to take on a life of their own exactly because you have insufficiently claimed them as yours.

Unclaimed or insufficiently recognized aspects exist in all of us, and as such, you can expect to occasionally return to the body with reddened cheeks. Keep in mind, however, that most disinhibitory acts are blown out of proportion, sometimes merely resulting from unrecognized stray thoughts and impulses, and as such, do not represent the totality of you. In addition, for the vast majority of us, there is not some sort of dark, bestial Freudian unconscious waiting to raise its ugly head as soon as you find yourself out of body. For some, a lack of integration in the personal psyche may lead to more disinhibitory behaviors than in others, but it is a rather neutral phenomenon to begin with, not solely defined by what is dark and negative.

For example, you may also experience disinhibition in the form of uncontrollable emotional outbursts, such as finding yourself sobbing on the floor all of a sudden. You might also experience something that might be impolitely referred to as "religious hysteria." Monroe, for example, relates the experience of unwillingly arching his back and exposing his belly to "the father."[1] This type of disinhibition is often a side effect of unknowingly associating the out-of-body state with authoritarian-based spirituality or religion.

Whatever disinhibitory types of behavior or emotion you experience, they hold the opportunity to increase your self-knowledge. So do not berate yourself for having them, especially not when you are still young, which puts you at a disadvantage compared to those who have had the benefit of time for their personal identity to become more aware and integrated.

Journal Entry — Thursday, February 13, 1992, time unknown

I had a short but strange OBE last night. I had awoken in the middle of the night and managed to fly away pretty quickly, soon finding myself above the city. I flew along over the buildings for a while until I lost my way, unable to recognize surroundings. I tried to orient myself and find some landmarks. My eye fell on a church far below me. I did not recognize it but suddenly experienced a strange urge to go there. I flew down, and once in front of its doors, I experienced a sudden, uncontrollable burst of emotion combined with a sudden urge to pray. I even fell to my knees and began to cry. There was no sense to any of this except for an overwhelming urge to pray. I was dumbfounded with my own behavior when I awoke soon after. I thought I was not religious anymore. Apparently, there were still some remnants left.

ASPECTS, PROBABLE SELVES, AND HIGHER SELVES

Common Aspects

Just like the out-of-body landscape itself, many of the people you will meet in the out-of-body state will be reflections of particular aspects of your own psyche. They usually present themselves as relatively well-rounded personalities but nonetheless only represent a facet of your own psyche. These may include aspects that are wise, dumb, wild, guiding, noble, aggressive, sexual, loving, paranoid, fearful, and more.

The appearance of characters encountered in the out-of-body state often directly relates to the aspect of your psyche they represent. For example, if you ever meet a person in uniform in the out-of-body state, there is a good chance that he or she represents the more authoritarian aspects of your own psyche—parts of your psyche that you feel you have to obey. Likewise, the manner in which aspects behave is also often in accordance with the portion of your psyche they represent. For example, aspects that are not very talkative could potentially represent under-expressed aspects of your personality. Others may be chatterboxes, sometimes annoyingly so.

Keep in mind that certain aspects give out really bad advice and information or may even behave in a manipulative and destructive manner. In the same way that aspects of your psyche can sometimes take on a life on their own, so do some of these characters, acting as if they exist independent of you or even working against you. Indeed, some of the more negative aspects may appear to know you better than you know yourself and may be able to push hot buttons and find weak spots with amazing ease.

For example, if you regularly berate your self in ordinary life, ignoring or downplaying your positive attributes, meeting the aspect that represents this part of yourself will be quite unpleasant. Such aspects might appropriately be referred to as *tricksters*. This is especially the case if you are insufficiently aware of your own inner dialogue in ordinary life, in which case the information may come across as extremely revealing or insightful.

Even so, an encounter with a trickster is not necessarily bad because it holds the potential to raise your awareness with respect to ongoing issues in your psyche. Not surprisingly, some traditions even refer to tricksters as messengers or imitators of the gods—an essential conduit to enlightenment.[8]

Certain clues in the appearance of tricksters usually give them away, although it is difficult to state any general rules. For example, a heavily tattooed aspect dressed in black might be an indication of a negative aspect for one projector, while it may represent freedom or rebellion for another. It all depends on your personal symbols. Over time, after having been tricked a few times and getting to know yourself better as a result, it will become easier to recognize and differentiate your different aspects.

In any case, the vast majority of aspects represent rather mundane facets of your own personality—mere tendencies and traits that find an outlet as externalized characters seemingly existing outside of you. It is important not to exaggerate their importance. You also want to focus on the many others that represent the more positive aspects of your own psyche, such as your hopes, dreams, strengths, love, and depth.

An interesting philosophical issue is whether or not these characters in the out-of-body state are conscious and sentient. After all, if they represent aspects of our own consciousness, are they not automatically endowed with awareness and consciousness, at least at some level? Some argue that such characters do indeed have a rudimentary level of consciousness and therefore deserve to be treated with a certain level of respect. It has even been argued that when a person overcomes a certain aspect, this aspect will detach from the person, yet continue to exist "elsewhere," separate from its original creator, as a sentient being.[9]

Whatever the case may be, it probably doesn't hurt to treat the constructs of your own mind with a little bit of respect. After all, how you behave in the personal field does reflect how you interact with yourself, including anything you would like not to be there. This is not to say you should give free rein to aspects that try to limit your expression. However, literally trying to beat certain aspects out of you might also not always be the best way to go. You would only be hurting yourself.

In particular, traumatized aspects need additional care, and here, a compassionate approach is quite appropriate. Even so, when it comes to the out-of-body state, you will have to be in a position to provide the compassion. Moreover, if in daily life your mind does not respond well to compassion, your aspects won't, either.

The out-of-body state is very honest. There is no hiding from yourself. Therefore, avoiding the potential to be overwhelmed in the personal field is your first order of business. It is only through your leadership that change can come about, and if your sense of self is not strong enough, everything else suffers. Over time, with a strong self, a compassionate approach becomes more feasible and effective.

Probable, Past, and Future Selves

Probable, past, and future selves are like common aspects, but they represent those aspects of you that *could be* there, *might have* been there, or *might be* there in the future. They are more remotely related to your own psyche than common aspects.

Not infrequently, entry into a psychological past or future is accompanied by transitional phenomena that are out of the ordinary. The reason likely lies in the fact that these aspects are indeed further removed from your psyche than common aspects, and as such, a greater amount of psychological distance must be traversed to reach them.

When encountering these aspects, you are often dealing with *potential* states of being that are non-actualized, but which nonetheless might become part of you, or could have been. On some occasions, you may find future selves and their environment to become actualized into physical reality, sometimes quite strikingly so.

Meeting up with past selves can also be used to come to terms with events that occurred in the past, especially if they affect you in some negative way in the present. How you relate to your past selves in the out-of-body state will affect your present, often in the form of a revitalized appreciation of your own history and identity.

Likewise, in the case of probable and future selves, you might learn about talents you did not know you had and then make a conscious choice to develop them in physical life.

Journal Entry — Monday, January 21, 2008, 4:50 am

I thought I had awoken the middle of the night but soon figured out I was lying in the bed of my childhood bedroom. I only considered it to be a mild distortion and assumed I was now in the out-of-body state, so I went through my usual routine and made my way downstairs.

Once in the hallway, however, I noticed that things were not quite right. The bedroom was located on the opposite side from where I usually make my way downstairs. The hallway was different as well, albeit familiar. I really was in the house I grew up in as a child.

I went down the stairs, not sure what to expect. It was daytime, and everything felt eerily familiar. It was exactly as I remembered.

Downstairs, I made my way to the back of the house and looked at the bookcase there. I had always enjoyed picking up a book from there and reading something new. I did the same thing now, randomly picking up one of the books off the shelf. As I did so, I noticed my father coming out of the kitchen. He looked much younger than in actuality.

"You can have that one if you want," he said, pointing at the book I was holding. "Perhaps you can use it for your homework."

I looked at him in surprise for having made this strange remark. It's been ages since I've done homework.

"How old are you?" I asked him.

"Why? I'm forty-four."

"Forty-four?! That would make me what?"

Now it was my father's turn to look at me strangely. In the next moment, my mother entered the house.

"What are you doing here!?" she asked. "I thought I just saw you outside."

"Me?" I said.

I looked out the window into the back garden just in time to see a boy of around eleven going into the house. Only moments later, the door opened. It was me!

I looked slightly different than I remember myself looking. The boy looked better somehow—more at ease and healthier.

I immediately walked up to him. I embraced him and wished him well.

I awoke soon after.

Note: I was unable to calculate my age during the experience itself, but calculating it afterward revealed that the age of the boy (around twelve years old) was consistent with the age of my father.

Occasionally, rather than meeting up with another self, you might temporarily *become* another self. Often, when this occurs, the different worlds collide, and except for the knowledge that it means something, you will frequently be at a loss as to the significance of the experience. One such puzzling experience is the following:

Journal Entry — Monday, September 4, 2006, 3:05 am

I felt the energy sensations in the middle of the night and immediately mentally reached for the 3D blackness. Nothing happened for a while until it started to get lighter and lighter, as if I were caught in the headlights of an approaching car. Then, all of a sudden, I found myself transported into the back garden of the house where I grew up.

Excitedly, I ran to the front of the house to check if there was something to do. But no one was there except for a bunch of kids riding their bikes on the street. It was a familiar scene. It's the route my class used to take to get to the gym.

With nothing else to do, I flew over them. They seemed to enjoy it, but I soon found myself bored again. I decided to check out the town center and see what was there.

On my way, I came across another group of kids riding their bikes. This time, as I was swooping over them, something strange happened. They quite literally aged in front of my eyes, becoming decades older.

Then, the next moment, the entire environment shifted, and I found myself in a different location. I was still in the same town but in a different area. Monique was standing right next to me.

"What's going on? What are we doing here?" I asked, trying to get my bearings.

"You don't remember?" she asked.

"No," I said, "I don't remember anything."

She sighed. "You have been like this for days—disoriented and forgetful, ever since you went to the dentist a couple of days ago. We're on our way to see the doctor now."

"I went to the dentist?"

"Yes, the dentist," she said, matter-of-factly.

I began to remember now. Yes. There was a dentist. I went a couple of days earlier and had trouble with my memory immediately after.

"So we're headed to the doctor now?"

"Yes," she said, patiently this time.

I looked around and noticed that we were indeed on the street leading to the doctor's office. It was the same office building where I had gone to see the dentist, a similar setup as in my childhood.

"But what are we doing in my old hometown? Don't we live in Canada?"

Monique looked at me with a sweet smile but didn't say anything. I was not sure whether it was the kind of smile you give a confused person or whether she was hiding something from me. I did have the faint memory that we had lived in the town for a while or were perhaps visiting.

Along the way, we came to a store, and Monique went in to buy something. I followed her inside, trying to ask more questions.

"What year is it?" I asked.

"2057," she said. This time she said it with a mischievous smile, as if fully aware of my situation. I grabbed a newspaper from the stand in the store and looked at the date and year. The year did not correspond to what Monique just told me.

It was an almost impossible year for us to still be alive.

"2073!" I yelled out loud.

Some heads in the store turned toward me. The store owner looked at me as if I had lost my mind. I had to give him a somewhat plausible reason for my outburst.

"Nothing ever changes in this town, does it? I just came back after having been gone for many years. And now, decades later, still nothing has changed."

"You come from here?" he asked.

"Yeah, I grew up here."

This seemed to satisfy the store owner. He grumbled something and went back to work.

I turned back to Monique. "Well, you still look amazing in 2073. You're as beautiful as ever. Still, none of this makes any sense. The dates are all wrong."

"We have to go," she said.

"Yeah, the dentist...umm...doctor," I responded. "But if it's 2073, then what were the last 60 years like? Did I have a lot of OBEs? Did it get me anywhere? Did I accomplish anything with it? Or was it all a waste of time?"

Again, she smiled at me mysteriously but did not respond. I gave up, and we continued our way silently to the doctor's office.

We arrived at the office shortly afterward. Nothing much changed there either, except that there were now arcade games of some kind for the kids, to keep them occupied. We barely had to wait. The doctor soon invited me into his office. He looked like my childhood physician.

Once inside his office, there was a chair of some kind. It looked quite strange to me, with a lot of technological equipment that I did not recognize.

"I have to sit in that?" I asked. It looked quite odd to me.

"How are you doing?" the doctor asked, ignoring my question.

I thought it better to not tell him I was having an OBE right now. It would not sound right. "Well, apparently I have memory problems. I don't remember much from the past few days. Perhaps it was the anesthesia from the dentist?"

"Could be," he said. "You must have been going through a lot, then, in the last couple of days."

"Not too bad," I said. "Just a little confused, that's all."

I sat down into the odd-looking chair. As soon as I did, I felt a slight vibration and awoke.

Guides and Higher Selves

Guides and higher selves are often given special status in the out-of-body literature as independent entities that exist apart from the projector. They are typically believed to function as "helpers" that assist both the living and the dead. In most instances, however, you are having an encounter with an aspect of yourself rather than any sort of independent entity. They do not exist entirely apart from you. This does not diminish the value of such encounters. Guiding aspects are usually wiser and more intelligent than you are on any conscious level.

Journal Entry — Wednesday, May 12, 2004, 7:15 am
I woke up in the morning from a light sleep after a couple of vivid dreams. In the last dream, I was traveling on a train and reached a hotel where some sort of action was going on that involved dogs. I don't remember a whole lot about it except for waking up with my real dogs moving around in the bed. Their activity must have seeped into the dream.

Once I awoke, I allowed myself to fall back asleep, and without any memory of the transitioning, I found myself near the hotel of the previous dream again. I had no intention of continuing the dream, however, and instead stared into the dark sky above me to go elsewhere. I could still feel the dogs moving in the bed but was able to block them out and solidify my presence in the environment.

There were a lot of stars above me, and the view looked very inviting, so I flew upward with the intent of finding some of the multicolored planets I had seen before. It felt pretty artificial, however, as if was a "fake" phenomenon. I had difficulty maintaining momentum and eventually decided to enter an environment.

It was the same environment I had just left. I felt a little angry and frustrated. Then I noticed it was not quite the same environment—there were many similarities, but everything now glowed with a beautiful purple light.

I looked upward. There was a wispy indigo hue lighting up the sky. I recognized it almost immediately. I had seen it before. That time, someone identifying himself as a "guide" had soon appeared.

I turned around and saw someone walking up to me. He was wearing a white Indian tunic top, white pants that looked like pajama bottoms, and sandals. Quite frankly, the guru outfit turned me off.

"So what do I do now?" I asked rather abruptly. "Why is it that I can't seem to get anywhere? And why are you wearing that outfit?"

He smiled a little, walked straight past me, and then said, "An Indian cult has a hold on your mind." His answer took me by surprise. I had not expected an intelligent reply.

I ran after him, and as soon as I caught up with him, a wall of mist appeared, with another world that lay behind it. We both walked through the mist and, at the other end, found ourselves standing at the corner of a busy crossroad in a foreign city.

I was immediately struck by the unfamiliar look of the city. It was not like any city I knew. In many ways, it was like a modern Western city, but at the same, it had a strong oriental and Indian feel to it due to the numerous teahouses, restaurants, and gift shops lining the streets. It felt to me like the best of both the Western and Eastern worlds.

I then noticed the "guide" once again walking away from me, veering down the street to my left.

"Will I see you again?" I yelled after him.

"Yes," he said calmly, without looking back. I woke up not long after.

Similar to the notion of guidance in the out-of-body state is the idea of "higher selves." In the literature, higher selves are often considered to be intimately connected with the person's soul, sometimes even responsible for your physical existence to begin with. Likewise, some view higher selves as consisting of a conglomeration of reincarnational selves, which nonetheless form a coherent whole as the essence of you.[6] They are often considered to exist relatively independent of the projector. Interestingly, however, the term *higher self* automatically locates it inside of the personal field of consciousness. After all, it is *your* higher self. Nonetheless, higher selves do fall outside of the boundaries of the known psyche. They are entirely different from how you ordinarily view yourself. Experiences in this area tend to be profound.

Journal Entry — 1994, time and date unknown

I had another OBE last night. I flew up into the void as soon as I left my body. But I did not get very far. I tried to move horizontally through the void, but found myself unable to pick up any speed.

Worse, I was intermittently aware of lying in bed in exactly the same position as I was floating in the void—on my side, with my hand in an awkward position near my chest.

I felt exposed. I did not want to linger in this darkness for too long out of fear of what I might attract. Yet, I did not want to return back to my body, either. I called out for my soul to help to me, unsure if anything would respond. But then something happened that I was unprepared for.

I could say here that I simply felt a hand touching my hand, moving it into a different, more relaxed position, but it was so much more. When I felt the touch, the most intense wave of love flowed inside of me. The sensation was beyond imagination. I did not even know anything like that existed.

Then, just as suddenly as it had arrived, it was gone, and I awoke. To my surprise, my physical arm had moved into a more relaxed position as well.

Journal Entry — Friday, May 23, 2003, time unknown

I had been working during the evening before finally going to bed, including listening to audio-recorded Nazi speeches. I was doing research for a book on reasoning, including the use of rhetoric in politics.

By the time I retreated to bed, I shook off the energy of the speeches and decided to try for an OBE. My intent was to access my total self, or soul. It did not occur to me that this might not be such a great idea right after listening to Nazi speeches.

I do not remember exiting my physical body. I simply found myself outside in the garden, in front of the house. Then, I heard a loud noise roaring in the sky above me. An airplane approached the spot where I was standing. It was huge—the size of a Boeing 747. It was aimed for the street and what looked like a crash landing.

It flew straight past me, only a couple of feet above the ground, and then crashed around three hundred feet further down the street. It ripped through the streets, engulfing the entire neighborhood in flames. I was happy that none of this was real.

I ran toward the area of impact, more out of curiosity than anything else. I had no idea what it represented. There was little at the crash site I recognized. Light and fire danced around the entire area, and the location of the impact was just a huge crater.

I then glimpsed a different kind of light at the center of the crater. It seemed to be in the form of a shape, a rotating disk that emanated bright white light. As I got closer, I saw that it was not a disk. Rather, it was a rotating swastika!

I tried to determine in which direction it was rotating, as the symbol of the swastika actually originates from Indian religions and represents well-being and good luck. The Nazis had turned this symbol backward. After a while, I did notice it rotating in the proper direction, and I relaxed a bit.

Then, with a roaring voice, it spoke: "ARE YOU READY FOR A NEW WORLD?! ARE YOU READY?"

I was dumbfounded. The words were incredibly charged, not unlike the speeches I had listened to earlier. But before I could react, the light continued, and it spoke these words:

If you need me, call me. No matter where you are, no matter how far. Just call my name. I'll be there in a hurry. On that you can depend and never worry...

I recognized the song! It seemed completely on target, even though I would never have been able to reproduce it under ordinary circumstances. But none of this mattered anymore. I was quickly swept off my feet as the music began to swell and the song reached the chorus. I found myself singing and dancing along. It was a reunion of joy and bliss unlike anything I had ever experienced before.

The disk now became a source of blinding light, filling up the area of what was previously the site of the plane crash. I laughed about how it took such a huge symbol of a jumbo jet crashing down to earth to harness all this energy, coming down to me, able to shatter my world apart.

As I sang along, I noticed something else in the white light, behind or inside of the disk—the silhouettes of other people, looking outward at me. They were difficult to see. The light was too blinding. I awoke back in bed soon after the song ended, exhilarated.

I looked up the song afterward. A burst of energy sensations went through me when I listened to it. It had indeed been on target, and in more ways than one.

An encounter with your higher self is almost always uplifting and inspirational. It tends to go far beyond what you know yourself to be. Even so, your higher self is a part of you, and encounters are still influenced by your own personal symbols and even daily preoccupations. Yet, none of this changes the value of such experiences, especially since the depth of the inner self is currently unknown. The term *soul* is often not at all inappropriate.

As far as guides and other helpers, I do not wish to exclude the possibility of being able to interact with something that exists apart from you in the out-of-body state. Perhaps I indeed did so in some of these experiences. It is impossible to tell. However, even seasoned projectors, when delving deeply into this area, often find that guidance in the out-of-body state originates from somewhere deep within, albeit often in the context of reincarnational or future selves, which adds yet another layer to the issue.[7]

Overall, for lack of any conclusive evidence, the simplest and straightforward explanation is that these experiences do relate to the inner psyche, and as such, form part of the personal field of consciousness. But of course, invoking Occam's razor, which is to select the hypothesis that makes the fewest new assumptions, does not automatically make it true. We are, after all, only scratching the surface, and perhaps a hard-headed scientific approach to these phenomena is not always the right one, or the only one.

Journal Entry — Wednesday, January 3, 2007, 5:10 am

Last night, I once again decided to explore the idea of guidance in the out-of-body state. It was my third OBE of the night, with little of significance to report during the first two. By the third, however, things got more interesting.

I began by exiting my body and heading to the window in the bedroom that leads to the front of the house and the street. Suddenly,

I heard a hysterical laugh coming from the bed. I held still and listened carefully. I did not want to make things worse by looking.

After a while, I could detect another, more realistic sound underlying the laughter. It was the dog snoring.

I shrugged. No wonder the out-of-body state is so scary. All these distortions do not help a bit.

I continued my quest and dove through the window. I aimed a little bit too low, however, and exited the house through the wall underneath the window. This distracted me a bit. I ended up in front of the house, but there was no street. It had been replaced by a large green field.

I decided to clear up the distortions and wiped my hand across my entire visual field as if washing a window. With each stroke, the environment changed a little bit. Trees and bushes changed shape and were repositioned where they belonged until eventually even the asphalt street reappeared.

After a while, there were still many things that didn't fit, but two people in the distance caught my attention, reminding me of my intent. I now wondered whether there were not any distortions at all. I might have "accidentally" arrived exactly where I needed to be.

I walked up ahead, wondering which of the two people I would approach. But as I came closer, they split up, with one of them walking away from me and the other taking a seat on a small terrace in front of a building. She was female, around 45 years old, looking quite busy and efficient. I decided to ask her.

"Hi, I'm looking for guidance."

She looked up, watched me intently, and then asked, "Are you sure? Do you think it's time?"

The question caught me off guard. I had questions prepared in my mind, but I did not expect to have to answer any questions myself. Was I ready? How would I know?

"Uh...I don't know," I stammered.

She then looked down at some papers and went through them as if to study my case. Then, without looking up at me, still going through the papers, she said: "You're still waiting for those papers from the government? That's okay. Just let them process it for two months. No harm in waiting two months more."

For some reason, her words made sense at the time. It did feel as if I was waiting for some official business or formality to conclude.

I left her alone, which seemed like the appropriate thing to do with respect to the issue she had brought up. Meanwhile, I took in the surroundings.

The building was a restaurant of some kind, or perhaps a type of community building where people gather. The guide seemed right at home, and she went inside as if going back to work, still looking quite busy.

Slowly, people began to fill up the tables on the terrace outside. I recognized some of the people from real life, but others I did not recognize. The ones I did recognize were all scientists I knew.

Strangely, many of them were scarred or injured in some way. One person seemed to walk with a limp from a burn across the entire side of his body. Others had scars on their faces. Yet, no one seemed bothered by their injuries. Most had healed long ago, and all of the people seemed to be in a normal, even jovial, mood.

I chatted for a while with some people sitting at a table, trying to get an idea of the kind of people on the terrace and what this was all about. It was like a gathering of a bunch of colleagues at a conference who were having a relaxing lunch in between the many presentations of their latest work. I relaxed a little bit too much, and the dialogue is now forgotten.

Then, some street musicians appeared, playing tunes alongside the terrace, perhaps organized for the group I was with. I couldn't be sure. But the music was clearly directed at us.

The quality of the music was quite awful. It reminded me of a self-organized performance at a psychiatric institution or a home for the aged, where talent did not matter much. It was difficult to appreciate the melody. And yet, we, the entire group of scientists on the terrace, were expected to sing along.

I felt a little offended with the entire setup. I could never let myself go to the extent of singing along to a tune of such bad quality. If this was guidance, I would go my own way, as I had done all along. I've come a long way in doing so. I opted not to sing along.

Apparently, practically all of the people on the terrace felt the same way. After all, many of them were intelligent, cultivated people in daily life, and all of them were well educated. None of them would easily "let go" by singing along with such a simple tune.

Meanwhile, I needed some answers as to the meaning of it all, so I walked inside to look for the guide whom I suspected had organized all of this. I found her inside in one of the offices. She still looked busy, but I was adamant this time.

"What is this place? Who are these people?! What do they have to do with me?"

She spoke calmly. "Apart from the fact that you like them...they are all damaged."

Again, she left me at a loss for words. She did not have to explain to me that the damage was not physical. I did not know what to say. It did not occur to me to ask whether I was "damaged" as well.

I went outside. The terrace had completely emptied by now. For a while, I stood there, not sure what to do. I told myself it was probably time to wake up, but then I noticed a new wave of people taking their seats on the terrace. None of them appeared to be "damaged" like the previous group.

I recognized one of the people sitting at the table as my mentor and colleague from my workplace, a scientist as well.

I walked up to the table. "Hey, how are you?"

"Hi, how's it going?"

I was not sure how to respond. In the out-of-body state, it is often a bit awkward to engage in small talk with people you know in real life, while ignoring the elephant in the room.

"We'll see each other soon, I suppose," I said eventually.

"Yes, you're back at work already?"

"Not until next week. Still some holidays left." I answered. "Anyway, I have to go now. It's time to wake up. I have to write down what I experienced here before I forget."

He looked at me as if I had said something very strange, so I decided to elaborate, just to see if there was any reaction.

"We're both asleep," I told him. "Except that I'm lucid and wide-awake."

I waited for a reaction for a while, and after a brief silence, his response was as expected. "Yeah, right," he said with a smile, as if I had been joking.

"Yeah, right," I responded in kind. "Anyway, I have to run. See you soon!"

FEAR AND NEGATIVE EXPERIENCES

Subjectivity reigns supreme in the personal field of consciousness, and no matter how you look at it, expectancies do matter, including those revolving around a fear of the unknown—an empty void easily filled up with all manner of frightful fantasies. Consequently, it is not uncommon for projectors to sometimes find themselves confronted with less than ideal environments. In fact, the influence of the personal field can already be felt during the transition process in the form of hearing loud, screaming voices, seeing threatening imagery, or having a strong sense of impending doom.

The form of these illusions and hallucinations is largely culturally defined. For example, in the last couple of decades, perceiving alien boogeymen crouching near your bed has become more popular. This may even be followed by abduction experiences and medical experiments if you simultaneously slip into a semi-lucid state of awareness. You will have entered your own subjective reality in these instances; it is not an objective reality. These occurrences are the result of your own fears of venturing into the unknown. If there were no fear, you would not experience any of these manifestations.

Nonetheless, there are many similarities across cultures, and there is also a more objective influence that can make these experiences more likely to occur. Specifically, the onset of energy sensations, if triggered in very close proximity to the waking state, often coincides with a substantial increase in arousal. This is a survival response with a long-established evolutionary history, and it cannot really be controlled except by not exacerbating the situation with fearful thoughts.

However, if you keep your mind as relaxed as possible, not react too much, and maintain some sense of detachment, any illusions accompanying the increase in arousal will be kept to a minimum. In fact, over time you may actually begin to appreciate the heightened sense of arousal and eeriness associated with the onset of energy sensations, since as much as these sensations are associated with fear, they are also associated with a dazzling and spine-chilling sense of power and aliveness. The energy is extremely vital once you have worked your way through the associated layer of terror and toxicity.

Interestingly, most esoteric disciplines also mention the existence of this natural fear barrier. They typically refer to it as the "dweller on the threshold," where an entity guards the crossover point between waking and dreaming reality. If you wish to overcome your fears, however, you should understand that it is not a literal event. Any sense of doom or an evil presence during the transition process is a primal protective response to avert the possibility of imminent death. The key is to not react too strongly and to keep your thoughts and emotions under control when moving through such a collective memory.

Do not worry that these hallucinations will somehow leave you in a terrible out-of-body environment once you exit. If you remain focused on the task at hand, everything will actually be quite calm as soon as you reach the end of the transition process, quite contrary to what you might have experienced just one second before its completion. The reason lies in the fact that the heightened sense of physical arousal will have disappeared as soon as the transition process is completed. In the words of Oliver Fox, as quoted by Carrington:

> "Often two or three attempts were required before I could generate sufficient will-power to carry me through. It was as though I were rushing to insanity and death; but once the little door had clicked behind me, I enjoyed a mental clarity far surpassing that of earth-life. And the fear was gone....Leaving the body was then as easy as getting out of bed...."[9]

It should be noted that a heightened sense of arousal and the possibility of accompanying hallucinations are not present during each transition. They are more common in highly lucid transitions initiated straight from the waking state, rather than those in which you stumble your way into the out-of-body state from a more clouded state of consciousness. If you do experience hallucinations, however, try to avoid interpreting them as real, as if you were really in danger or under some sort of attack. Over time, it will become quite clear that these hallucinatory phenomena are only fearful attempts of your own mind to try to explain something it does not yet understand. They will eventually disappear from your transitions. Meanwhile, you will have to push through any fear, no matter how bad it may feel, if you truly want to get anywhere.

Journal Entry — 1992, time and date unknown

Last night before sleep, I tried to repeat the imagination exercise, visualizing myself inside the cockpit of a spaceship, sitting at the controls and letting myself be guided by the artificial intelligence onboard. The purpose was to see if it had any effect on my ability to get in the right state to project. For example, one of the details included imagining myself pressing a red button in the cockpit in hopes that it would trigger the energy sensations.

In terms of inducing energy sensations, I never had much success with this particular method. Neither did I last night, but it did have an unexpected effect on the transition into the out-of-body state.

While lying in bed, I had done the imagination exercises for a while before I finally gave up and let myself drift off to sleep. Apparently, this drifting off toward sleep was all that was needed because as soon as I did so, I was hit by the vibrations. But there was a whole lot more going on this time.

As I felt the vibrations, red lights flashed all around me, and there was the sound of a blaring alarm. It was almost as if I were actually inside the cockpit of a spaceship except that I could still feel myself lying in bed. This was totally different from the transition phenomena I usually experience.

I felt terribly afraid but decided to push on anyway, intensifying the vibrations as I allowed myself to fall into them. As the vibrations intensified, so did the hallucinations. The alarms got louder, and the flickering of red light intensified. Worse, I now got a clear warning from a computer voice yelling out:

"DO NOT LEAVE YOUR BODY! YOU WILL DIE! DO NOT LEAVE YOUR BODY! YOU WILL DIE! DO NOT LEAVE YOUR BODY! YOU WILL DIE!"

I hesitated. Perhaps I should break off the attempt? What if the warning was real? But it was all too obvious. Clearly, this was my own fear talking to me. It was just a different manifestation of the same fear barrier I had experienced so many times before. The only difference was that the fear had finally clearly formulated itself.

Cursing to myself, I mustered all the courage I could and pushed through the fear. I allowed the energy sensations to intensify, which further increased the hallucinations until the vibrations reached their peak. Then, suddenly, as usual, everything was quiet. I rolled over, and there was no sign of any of the hallucinations I had experienced just a few moments before. I felt free and fearless...

Immediately after having established the out-of-body state, the environment will generally be quite stable, at least initially. I have only rarely had negative encounters in close proximity to my bedroom, and when they have occurred, they have generally been no more than minor nuisances. The out-of-body environment is not *that* thought responsive, especially when your level of lucidity is high.

Also remember that a certain level of engagement is required for any sort of manifestations to occur. You can be quite fearful in the out-of-body state, and yet nothing will manifest as long as you do not engage with the environment. In a sense, this is like ignoring everything around you, sometimes quite literally, by turning your back on a certain manifestation.

If you use this approach, you will have to be able to *truly* ignore. It does not suffice, for example, to turn your back on a manifestation while still worrying about what may happen behind you. If you are not able to truly ignore, you are better off dealing directly with the environment.

The most effective approach here is refusing to accept the environment and briefly envisioning what you *do* want to perceive. For example, when faced with a boogeyman, envision him looking innocent and nonthreatening. This will generally lead to an immediate response from the environment. Likewise, you can use the hand-swiping technique to deal with anything bothersome that comes your way. It is not that hard to turn a person into a toad while in the out-of-body state.

Finally, do not purposely delve into danger just for the thrill of it, especially not anything of a collective nature. You *will* get more than you can handle. Remember, there is nothing out there looking for you unless you look for it or invite it into your own field. But if you do ever find yourself in an iron grip as a result of having made some wrong choices and you are not even able to force yourself to awaken, remember that you can leave your *second* body at any time. There is nothing out there that can hold you. You are a projector of consciousness, after all—slippery like an eel.

LANDMARKS AND HORIZONS

Some have argued that the personal field is a "training ground" in preparation for the real thing that comes afterward once you have graduated from it.[2] It may not be quite as clear-cut as that because the personal field permeates all other areas of consciousness. Nonetheless, certain landmarks and horizons become increasingly evident after prolonged activity in the personal field. They often indicate a certain progression in your out-of-body activity.

At its most basic level, the personal field of consciousness deals with the polar opposites of pain and pleasure. Not surprisingly, then, the resolution of these opposites in the out-of-body state is one of the landmarks you can expect to come across. Of course, this is not some sort of sadomasochistic endeavor. It is about the transcendence of these polar opposites.

None of this makes you enlightened, and life continues as usual, including the experience of pain and pleasure, idiosyncrasies, and personal limitations, but I suspect that prolonged activity inside of the personal field does change something quite fundamental in the deep recesses of the personal psyche. Or perhaps it is the other way around.

Journal Entry — Friday, May 26, 2006, 5:00 am

After a couple of sleep cycles, I woke up and was relaxed enough to fall asleep again while maintaining a semblance of wakefulness. I then tried to move upward into the void, but I did not get enough lift, so instead I took a sharp turn and flew through the bedroom window.

Outside, I did not find myself in the usual environment. I was standing in front of a house, but it was not my own. It looked more like a mixture of my real-life home and the house of my grandparents. Strangely, even though it was not cold, there was melting ice on every surface I encountered. It was a peculiar scene because the garden itself was in full bloom. It looked surreal.

I wasn't sure what the melting ice was about except that I remember having had a few non-lucid dreams in the same environment. In one of them, I was told that winter was on its way. Perhaps that winter had passed now?

I started to walk around, taking in the scene. The entire place was well decorated, organized into separate sections divided by pathways, with boulders placed here and there. The atmosphere was charged, as if there was magic in the air. After a while of moving through the garden, almost bumping my head on an overhanging wooden beam at one point, I came across a small veranda.

There was a seagull there on the ground, staring straight at me. It came with a sudden, rather abstract percept as to what it represented. It represented a "core" inside of me, something related to my out-of-body activity.

I tried to approach it, but the seagull did not seem to allow it. Each time I took a step forward, it moved back a couple of feet. Then, as I moved away, it moved a little closer to me. It wanted something from me, but I was not sure what. It did not want to be approached, yet it tried to stay close to me.

I grabbed a pebble and threw it in front of the bird, seeing if it would accept the "gift." But it pushed the object away with its beak as if to say it was not relevant. Then it occurred to me, why was this seagull here on the ground to begin with? It did not seem hurt, and it should be soaring in the skies instead.

I looked up, expecting to see a blue sky, but there was none. Instead, there was a huge white dome all around me. I was not really outside at all, but rather enclosed in some sort of artificial environment. I woke up soon after.

Note: After the experience, I looked up the symbolic meaning of the seagull in shamanistic traditions. There appeared to be relatively little consensus except for its ability to travel vast distances.

Journal Entry — Thursday, June 1, 2006, 2:15 am

While practicing last night, already at the borderline of sleep, I suddenly felt a jolt of joy go through my mind and body. I have no idea where it came from. It was just simply joy. I immediately lost all sense of the physical environment.

I continued to hold onto the joy. It felt like a thread in my mind that was able to carry me elsewhere. I felt myself moving upward, not so much physically but mentally along this thread of joy. As I did, the joy intensified until blinding, white light filled my entire vision. The joy became bliss.

Before I knew it, I was riding huge waves of endless bliss. I could barely contain myself. I was in ecstasy. It was simply everywhere—a never-ending, blinding wave of love, bliss, and rapture.

I kept riding these waves of bliss, submerging myself deeper and deeper into it. It was so good, it made me cry out in pain. The hurt intensified. Excruciating, awful, terrible hurt. But it felt so good. I yelled out in pain and ecstasy. Never before had I experienced something with so much joy and pain. It was the same thing.

Then everything stopped. I abruptly found myself on a small island, standing on a beach with tears streaming down my face. I had a body suddenly, out of nowhere. How did I get here?

I looked toward the sea in front of me. There was something on the horizon. It was a tsunami sixty feet high roaring toward me, casting its shadow over me. There was nowhere to go. I stood frozen, the last thought before I awoke being "Oh...My...God."

Chapter 7

Collective Fields of
Consciousness

COLLECTIVE FIELDS OF CONSCIOUSNESS

One of the great attractions of the out-of-body state is its promise to provide you with a glimpse of immortality. Both esoteric and popular literature speak of visitations to otherworldly environments located in some nonphysical dimension. Religious and spiritual connotations tend to be strong in many of these interpretations, not unlike the traditional notions of heaven, hell, and purgatory.

Even those who actively avoid religious interpretations still propose some sort of psychological hierarchy that differentiates between the types of environments that may be encountered. Robert Monroe, for example, identifies so-called "belief system territories" that are organized according to the principle of "...like attracts like."[1] Following death, an individual is believed to take residence in an environment that resonates with him or her on a psychological level.

For example, if you have a strong belief in hell and you feel deserving of being in such a place, you may find yourself ending up there with others who hold similar beliefs. Likewise, a Catholic may end up in Heaven, a Buddhist in Nirvana, a Norseman in Valhalla, and so on. Those with secular beliefs would find themselves attracted to different kinds of environments, but still, the environment would always correspond to their most firmly held belief system or psychological tendencies.

The similarities between the near-death experience and the OBE give some credence to the view that the out-of-body state is related to death. The initial stages of the experience are remarkably similar, both often involving a sensation of leaving the body and subsequently being located elsewhere. In fact, some have suggested that the OBE may very well be responsible for the human concept of an immortal soul.[2]

We might take that further, in that the OBE might even be responsible for the birth of many religions. There are indeed references to these types of experiences, such as, for example, Jacob's perception of the ladder to heaven and angels following his flight from his brother Esau in the Book of Genesis. The Jewish philosopher Philo later offered an interpretation of the angels as representing souls descending to and ascending from their bodies.[3]

Regardless of the potential continuity of consciousness after death, it seems warranted to be critical of accounts describing what exactly such an afterlife entails. It is easy to see how afterlife environments can be confused with environments in the personal field of consciousness. This confusion could easily give rise to the intricate and detailed descriptions of afterlife environments seemingly occupied by the deceased but in reality originating solely from the mind and belief system of the projector.

Even if we accord some sort of reality to these experiences, subjective and psychological influences clearly play a role. During both OBEs and near-death experiences, for example, perceptions vary in accordance with the individual's religious beliefs and psychological makeup. The brevity of these experiences does not help, either, easily giving rise to misinterpretation and inaccurate conclusions. For example, void experiences during either an OBE or the near-death experience lead some to mistakenly fear that what awaits them following death is eternal nonexistence.[5] Of course, the void is black, but otherwise it is entirely neutral.

Apart from misinterpretations, there are also many inconsistencies in accounts of the afterlife. For example, in the case of Robert Monroe, it is quite unclear how to distinguish focus 27 from the belief system territories (see pp. 22–24). According to Monroe, both are an artificial synthesis created by human minds, yet focus 27 is considered more stable and objective. In fact, the entire notion of focus 27 is in conflict with the earlier writings of Monroe in which he claims that the illusions imposed by time and space ultimately disappear on the "outer edges." Would the physicality of focus 27 located at the outer edge of human consciousness not be expected to disappear as well?

Reading most of the popular out-of-body literature, one is often left to wonder whether or not all these experiences exist solely in the mind of the projector. Nonetheless, the idea of nonphysical dimensions has a long history in the out-of-body literature, and many projectors would swear to the reality of their experiences. Even if it is recognized that it is possible to fabricate experiences in the out-of-body state, it is argued that these experiences can be distinguished from those encountered in the personal field.

Perhaps it would indeed be a mistake to dismiss all notions of an afterlife on the basis of the presence of psychological influences alone. After all, the presence of psychological influences does not necessarily imply that perception in the out-of-body state lies *solely* in the eye of the beholder. Similar influences are present when it comes to any attempt to perceive physical reality in the out-of-body state, yet veridical perception may still be possible there.

Most crucially, however, there is currently no evidence that consciousness is produced by the brain. Its survival following death is just as logical a possibility as anything else. So while we may take issue with the interpretations, touching on something in the out-of-body state relating to the continuity of consciousness after death is not at all unlikely. Evidence may be difficult to come by, but the issue can nonetheless be explored and speculated upon.

Journal Entry — Sunday, March 9, 2008, 10:00 am

After a break in my out-of-body activity, I decided to kick-start the process again. It took a while. The entire night had been filled with vivid dreams and frequent wake-ups, but it was not until the morning that I was finally able to project.

The transition was smooth. The process never ceases to amaze me—feeling the covers and mattress of the bed without any interruption in these sensations, and yet something surely changed that allows me to fly up into the air.

I flew over downtown Montreal for a while, enjoying flight in between the skyscrapers. The sun shone brightly in the sky, even though it was still quite low on the horizon, as would be expected at this time of year and day. It was light everywhere, as it had snowed the night before. The white snow reflected the sunlight in every possible direction.

It occurred to me that the sun might be a good target to make my exit from the physical field. I flew directly toward it, gaining speed as I did so. Before I knew it, I was engulfed in a flash of bright light, followed by complete darkness and silence. I seemed to have arrived at the void, except that everything around me was a deep indigo. It felt difficult to move.

I stretched both my arms sideways, and it was not long before two invisible helpers grabbed them. I'm not sure of the sequence of events that followed or even if there was any, but I soon found myself "deposited" in what looked like a public cafeteria area of sorts.

To my left, a line of about forty people waited to be served by what appeared to be two female cashiers. It was an odd scene, however, as I could see no money being paid for the food.

I closely observed the people in the queue. Many of them looked disoriented, unsure of why they were even there. Others seemed unresponsive and oblivious to their surroundings. Yet others, completely without awareness, were lying on their backs passed out on the tables, even though still holding a spot in the line.

I then got an inner percept of what was going on. These people had all died recently, and their mental state was in disarray due to the shock of the transition. That was all the information I received through the percept. I wanted to know more, but I wasn't going to wait in line. I *didn't have the time.*

I cut in line and walked straight up to one of the "cashiers." She saw me coming, and just as I was about to speak, she said: "You're going to have to wait in line."

"I know, but I'm not dead. I'm just visiting, and I'd like to learn more about this place."

She looked at me quizzically for a moment and then pointed to an open door behind me.

"Go there," she said. "There might be someone to help you."

She immediately focused back on her work, so I turned and made my way to the door. Behind it was a large warehouse filled with pallets, boxes, and other supplies. Whatever it was, it looked like an environment used to support the "cafeteria."

I went further into the warehouse and, to my surprise, saw Monique standing near the wall.

"What are you doing here? You should be lying in bed next to me," I said.

She seemed unresponsive as well, and I gave her a closer look. Her eyes had a blank stare. It occurred to me that she might be dreaming and not lucid enough to respond properly.

Another person walked by, and I immediately stopped him. "Is there someone in charge here? There must be someone around who is responsible for the care of all these people."

The man pointed toward a small room a couple of feet away.

I nudged Monique to come with me, and we both entered the room. There, two men were conversing. I had no difficulty identifying the one in charge. He had a peculiar look, almost otherworldly, with a black beard, heavy eyebrows, and deeply sunken eye sockets. He had no eyes.

I walked straight up to him. I had a lot of questions to ask before I awakened prematurely.

"Why is everyone so disoriented here?"

He responded without pause. "They all just recently died," he said. "It's confusing for them. I'm here to keep an eye on things."

I ignored the pun, not sure if it was intended. "Can you see that I'm not dead and am lucid?" I asked.

"Yes, I can."

I pointed at Monique: "What about her?"
"She's dreaming."
With the reminder about lying in bed, I quickly lost my focus and woke up back in bed with Monique next to me.

Note: Monique and I got up shortly afterward. I asked her whether she remembered any dreams. She told me she had an unpleasant dream in which she watched the faces of several dead people who died with their mouths open. This had bothered her. She had thought to herself in the dream how she did not want to die with her mouth open.

PROBING BEYOND THE PERSONAL FIELD

Barrier Zones

One of the arguments in favor of the existence of collective environments might be that they can be quite difficult to reach. The personal field exerts a strong pull, at least for this projector, and any attempt to move out of it can be difficult to accomplish. Typically, you will enter an environment that contains all manner of obstacles preventing you from reaching your destination. Some have referred to these environments as *barrier zones.*[4]

Barrier zones are often related to any psychological reservations you might have associated with your intent to reach a certain destination. For example, if you have doubts about the existence of a certain environment or you feel fearful about getting lost, you are quite likely to end up in an environment reflecting those concerns. It is only once you resolve those issues, especially any fears associated with the topic of death, that you will be able to reach your intended destination.

Journal Entry — Sunday, April 16, 2006, 4:05 am

Last night I found myself awake in bed following one sleep cycle. My body was quite ready to go back to sleep. Beside me, however, Monique was tossing about in bed, so I waited a couple of minutes for her to settle. Then, as soon as I relaxed, the energy sensations started. I immediately detached and flew up in the air.

I had some difficulty staying focused. Perhaps Monique was still moving in bed. In either case, I had to exit at least two more times after being pulled back. Eventually, however, I was able to remain in the void and set the intent to reach a collective environment while feeling for ground under my feet.

After I touched ground in the void, I had difficulty seeing anything. I spent some time on my knees until I reached an edge of sorts. It felt like the edge of a swimming pool, and I wondered how I had anticipated such a thing.

Why was it so difficult to get anywhere you really wanted to be? It happened each time I was trying to get further "out there." Then, suddenly, as my frustration built, I was able to see.

For a brief moment, I thought I had reached my intended destination, but as I looked around, my hopes were quickly quashed. Everything was cold, desolate, and covered with snow. Trees were cut off at the trunk and were just stumps. It was exactly how I felt.

Not far from where I stood was a shoreline that was partially frozen. I had little hope of ever getting across this cold sea, but my instinct was to get as far as I could by walking down a small stretch of land extending further out into the sea. As I did, the ice surrounding it began to break up. The sea got quite a bit wilder. High waves bounced against the small stretch of land.

I looked back toward the mainland behind me. To my shock, the sea had already engulfed the stretch of land I had just been standing on. My return route was cut off. Worse, it looked as though the remaining piece of land where I stood would soon be swallowed up as well.

I decided against waking up and instead tried to fly upward. I succeeded in getting some liftoff, but the freezing water was still too close for comfort. Still, I managed to fly away back to the mainland as the last remaining piece of land underneath me disappeared into the sea.

Once back on the mainland, the environment quickly started to morph. The whole seascape disappeared from view, and I soon found myself standing in front of a building. Two security guards stood in front of the door, which was locked. It was a repetition of a scene I had encountered before, except this time it was in a different format.

I lied to the guards that I was there on official business. The guards seemed unimpressed, but they walked over to a small office to check whether my name was on the list of visitors. I woke up before getting an answer.

Journal Entry — Monday, November 6, 2006, 4:30 am

I felt fairly awake and energized before bedtime and decided to project. Yet, even though there were frequent wake-ups throughout the night, there were none of the usual energy sensations. Eventually, however, without any memory of how I got there, I found myself lying in bed completely detached from any physical senses—lucid and alert.

For a while, I hovered in the bedroom, rolling around in the air, until I decided to try and visit focus 27. I reasoned that I probably had to move fairly deep into the void first, and with that last thought, I began to move through the darkness. I moved upward for a while but quickly lost momentum, and without willing it, I felt ground under my feet.

A barren, gloomy environment appeared around me with a dark sky, as if a thunderstorm could develop at any moment. In front of me, a fetid, swamplike lake stretched to the horizon. The only solid piece of land was a small island of muddy soil under my feet.

The entire scene seemed familiar enough, and I realized the whole thing was a huge self-created psychological barrier preventing me from getting to my destination. It was exactly how I had been feeling about the void lately—overwhelmed by its scope, its endlessness, and sometimes even its desolateness.

I made an attempt to fly across the swamp, even though I was not sure if this was a good idea. I fell straight into the muddy water below me. Worse, there was movement underneath the surface of the water not too far from my location. I made a halfhearted attempt to swim back to the island, but it was too late. A huge, vile insect rose up from the swamp.

The creature was grotesque. It looked like a giant beetle, more than four feet tall, standing on its hind legs, while its front legs sliced wildly through the air. Its mouth, a gaping hole in the middle of its head, opened and closed rapidly. It was a real bottom feeder, the kind you associate with scavenging the dead.

I stood transfixed, unable to move. Then it came rushing toward me, shouting loudly, "I am a flesh eater!"

I needed no further encouragement. I cut off all my emanations and focused back on the safety of my bedroom. One second later, my mind shifted, and I found myself back in the bottom section of the void. I had made it back safely. The sudden shift had made me lose my focus, however, and I began to drift off into dreaming consciousness... *[Continued on p. 285].*

Identifying Markers in Navigation

We can speculate on why it is so difficult to leave the personal field behind. Why, for example, not simply create a fake mind replica of whatever "otherworldly" environment the projector intends to project to? Yet, a strong intent to venture beyond the personal field does not appear to have these effects, and the projector is often instead faced with insurmountable distances and obstacles.

However, it is possible to be successful in reaching your intended destination. In these instances, arrival at your destination is typically preceded by inner sense percepts, help from the outside, or sounds and music emanating from a source deep inside of the void, which suggests some sort of qualitative difference between personal and collective environments.

Journal Entry — Monday, November 6, 2006, 4:30 am

[Continued from p. 286] *...I moved deeply into the void this time. Then, at what felt like some midpoint, I heard a faint melody originating from somewhere even deeper inside of the void. It was a simple, pleasant melody.*

I honed in on it, and with several twists and turns, the volume increased. Just before I reached the source, the melody was loud and clear as I came to a sudden halt.

I was standing in the living room of a house that was unfamiliar to me. It was rather dark to begin with, and looking outside of the window, I could still recognize the void from which I had come. It would be easy to get back to it from here.

Not far from me, a middle-aged man was sitting on chair, quietly staring out of the window. I wondered whether it only appeared to be night to him or whether he experienced it like the void, as I did.

Further down, there was another room that was separated by an open doorway from the living room. Inside of it, a woman was doing some chores. It looked as if the man and woman were a couple living together in this house. It did not seem anything like focus 27, however.

Neither had yet noticed me, so as calmly as I could, I posed the question in my mind, hoping they would understand me and not be startled.

"Hello, I'm looking for the Park," I said. The Park was the hub of focus 27, according to Monroe, a way station to ease trauma for the deceased.

They both looked up in my direction. They actually seemed to understand what I had meant by The Park. The answer was not favorable, however.

"It's all fantasy," the man said. "You could just as well go to the movies." I was about to answer him, but his wife was one step ahead of me.

"You don't know that for sure. Perhaps he'll be able to find it," she said in my defense, and then added, "You never know."

"Sure," the man said, unwilling to continue the conversation. He turned away to once again stare out the window into the darkness.

It took me a moment before the significance of what the man had said hit me. Here I was, with someone who believed there was no such thing as the Park. It was all just a fairy tale to him. And this was exactly how I felt, or at least it was representative of my reservations. Clearly, I had stumbled upon this couple for a reason. If I wanted to get to the Park, I had to temporarily suspend any disbelief.

Without hesitation, I flew out the window into the darkness, and following a sharp flash of light, a bright, sunny scene opened up in front of me. A smooth carpet of bright green grass stretched out before me. Next to me was a small canal or waterway with clear blue water. A stone pathway led deeper into the garden toward some buildings. It was quite beautiful. The stones had a pinkish hue as if emanating light somehow, and the Park itself was beautifully designed, with varying elevations and borders with flowers and small trees.

There were several people around. They all seemed to be busy with daily affairs or just relaxing on one of the many benches along the stone pathways stretching into the garden. None seemed to be particularly out of place except for two men dressed in military clothing from a long time ago, complete with helmet, mail armor, and swords.

I walked up to the soldiers with the intent to strike up a conversation. But strangely, as soon as I got within ten feet of them, my vision seemed to blur, and I could no longer see them clearly. It actually felt as if I was about to be thrown out of the entire environment. I turned my attention away from the pair of soldiers and decided to walk along the stone path leading up to a large building.

Soon, I reached the entrance of the building. Again, everything was beautifully decorated, completely in tune with the outside garden. The floor was made of marble tiles in the same hue as the stone paths in the garden. Bright green cedar trees leading up to main entrance were lined up in a tasteful fashion, delineating a clear path to a lobby inside the building.

Inside, on both sides of the lobby, reception desks were lined up against the walls, with friendly looking women behind them ready to serve anyone seeking help. It was quite crowded. In the middle of the lobby, a man, like the concierge of a hotel, was directing people to the appropriate location. He seemed like a good candidate to ask for some more information.

I walked up to him. "Hi, I'm new here. Can you help me?"

"Of course, come with me. You have just arrived?"

I realized he understood having "just arrived" differently than I, but I answered affirmatively. He treated me like a real newcomer.

The concierge walked up to one of the reception desks as I followed close behind. He briefly talked to one of the receptionists behind the desk and then turned back toward me.

"What is your name?"

I gave him my name, and the receptionist responded by handing the concierge a file. He then walked up to some sort of computer or machine a couple of feet away to type in some information from the file. I moved closer and began to read the form he was typing from.

At the top of the paper was my name. Right below, I was able to see different categories with a number next to each. I quickly realized that these were grades for how I had lived my life. This was exciting and unexpected!

I began to memorize as much of the information as I could. Apparently, I had not done too badly. Most of them were eights and nines on scale of one to ten. One of the highest scores was in the category "purpose." One low score stood out—a three. The category next to it was "world view." I was not quite sure what to make of it.

I continued to read the second half of the paper, ignoring the remainder of the categories. I had already experienced several zooming-in effects while reading, and if I was not careful, the environment around me would dissolve. Yet, I still managed to read three separate dates at the bottom of the page.

The first one was my birth date. I ignored the middle one, not sure what it signified, and went straight for the last one—the date of my death. It was difficult to read by this time, especially the last number, but I could make out that the year of death ranged somewhere between 2056 and 2059. That would make me 85 to 88 at the time of my death.

"Not bad," I said out loud.

The concierge briefly glanced up from the computer and gave a friendly nod. He seemed to assume I was commenting on the life review.

"I'm not dead, by the way," I said, attempting to clarify.

The concierge looked up again, this time with a surprised look. Then, he got serious and looked at me intently as if to get a closer look. His face cleared after a while.

"You got me. I didn't realize."

"And I'm lucid, too. I will be able to remember the dates," I said.

The concierge laughed. "Okay, no need to rub it in. It's not the first time this has happened."

At that point, I suddenly lost my entire focus and awoke.

Interestingly, this experience was quite closely aligned with popular ideas on both belief system territories (i.e., "the disbelieving couple") and the idea of the Park as a way station designed to ease the trauma and shock of physical death (i.e., "the reception area"). It even included a life review and the date of my future death.

Still, there is no real proof here. The experience might very well have originated from my own psyche. For example, the couple's attitudes were quite similar to my own—rather conflicted. Likewise, my experience of the Park could have merely been due to expectancies once I suspended disbelief. Hence, it remains entirely inconclusive from any sort of scientific perspective.

Another issue is the overwhelming presence of sociocultural influences, for example, the presence of hotels, lobbies, computers, and other paraphernalia. Even if we were to believe that these experiences have some sort of reality, surely they can be no more than symbolic and metaphorical, which may make them informative and significant, but not stable and permanent.

Indeed, the role of symbology and metaphor has been increasingly recognized in the out-of-body experience, in which experiences cannot always be taken literally.[5] Rather, it is proposed that during an out-of-body experience or any other state of consciousness, you are immersed in a wider energy field carrying information and knowledge, the form in which it is perceived determined by the symbols and metaphors that your consciousness utilizes.

Journal Entry — Sunday, May 13, 2007, 4:45 am

Last night, I moved in and out of sleep several times, each time partially moving out of body. My lucidity was mediocre throughout. However, I eventually managed to move out fully with the intent to explore some new territory. It was not ideal. I soon became entranced by metal pipes reaching into the void above me. It looked like normal water piping, possibly made of copper. It was difficult to tell since the piping was painted white.

I began to climb the pipes, which was not too hard to do since plenty of piping ran horizontally. It gave me the foothold I needed to climb up fast. I did not give the meaning of the piping too much thought, which seemed entirely in line with my intent. I was still trying to explore new territory.

I continued to move up until I noticed a different layer in the overall structure. The pipes were much wider now, almost twice as thick. It did not take long before I came upon another layer even wider than the previous one.

I understood the general idea now. The higher I moved up, the thicker the piping became, and the closer I came to the source. I continued to climb until the pipes were so wide that I could barely wrap my hands around them.

I looked around and now noticed a lot of light bulbs suspended in the air. It was a bit confusing since I could discern no ceiling they might have been attached to. There were hundreds, many of them powered up and emanating light. Others had not been turned on yet for some reason.

Not far away, I then noticed a wall with two music boxes sitting on a ledge. I had no idea why they were there, but I picked up one of them. I turned it on by winding up the springs. An angelic type of music came from the box. It was pretty. Soon after, I woke up.

DIFFERENTIATING THE PERSONAL FROM THE COLLECTIVE

Is there any difference between personal and collective fields of consciousness? Is one more real than the other, even if perhaps symbolic and metaphorical? I do not claim to have any definitive answers, but we can have a closer look at some the distinctions that have been proposed by various projectors:

- Level of awareness is much higher in collective fields.
- The environments in collective fields are more stable and solid.
- Events that you do not expect occur in collective fields.
- Individuals have minds of their own.
- Everything is just different.

Level of awareness is much higher in collective fields

It is frequently claimed that collective fields of consciousness coincide with a "higher awareness" than the personal field. It is only when you raise your awareness sufficiently that you will be able to perceive anything real that exists outside of yourself.

However, it is often unclear what is meant by *higher awareness*. In most instances, the argument is circular, where higher awareness is synonymous with perceiving a real "astral" environment.

If higher awareness were understood as a higher level of mental clarity and lucidity, perhaps the argument could be made that it is relevant to collective fields of consciousness. For example, level of lucidity does appear to be associated with accurate perception in the physical field. It stands to reason that similar processes would apply to accurate perception in other fields of consciousness.

Even so, a high level of lucidity may also be experienced in the personal field, and as such, it is not intrinsic to any sort of collective field of consciousness. Hence, even though a high level of lucidity may possibly facilitate more accurate perception, it does not really differentiate between the personal and collective.

Collective fields are more stable and solid

Another claim is that the environments in collective fields are more stable and solid than those in the personal field. The reason often mentioned is that collective fields of consciousness are created by more than one individual. Consequently, the environment is more stable and less likely to change in response to individual thoughts.

Again, the problem with this argument is that environments in the personal field can be as stable and solid as those in the collective field, given a sufficient level of expectation and belief. Conversely, an environment that appears to be collective in nature does not always behave in a stable and solid manner.

It deserves to be noted, however, that some environments can be extremely convincing in terms of their solidity and stability. There is a strong sense of something external supporting your perception. Yet, again, none of this truly differentiates the personal from the collective.

Journal Entry — Wednesday, May 28, 2008, 4:15 am

It had been two hours since the last OBE, and I decided to give my grandfather another visit. During a previous visit, I had found him gardening near a small farmhouse, as he liked to do when alive. We had barely talked and instead just hugged.

I had considerable difficulty reaching him the last time, so I decided to move deeper into the void this time. Also, to avoid interference as much as possible, I refrained from imagining the environment I had found him in earlier.

It was not long before I began to discern moving geometric shapes below me. They were building up incredibly fast—initially white beams of energy that soon took the shape of a rectangle. There were a few other rectangles forming in other places as well. I had no idea what they signified, but I descended straight into the square below me.

As I did, I immediately found myself in a building that corresponded exactly to the shape of the square I had honed in on. The building itself was empty. Nothing was there except for a maroon-colored wooden door that led outdoors.

I opened the door and stepped outside. I felt a chill. It was cold outside. I had been in winterlike environments before, but only rarely with such strong physical sensations. I was barefoot, standing on moist, cold earth, with the soles of my feet close to the freezing point. The experience was extremely vivid.

I bent over and grabbed some of the sand off the ground, running it through my fingers. It was some kind of black mud like that of an almost dried-up riverbed. I was fascinated with the physical-like sensation of it all.

I stood up and looked around. It was a stark environment—rocky and barren. There was some green here and there, though—some moss and small shrubs. It was not an unattractive environment. It resembled alpine tundra.

I could not see very far from where I stood, so I moved a little further up toward a rocky ridge located not too far away. Once up there, I could see for miles—a mountainous environment with rocky slopes everywhere around me. A few miles ahead in the distance, I could even see an animal. It looked like a grizzly bear, but it was a lot larger.

I thought about exploring further, but the combination of wildlife and strong physical sensations did not appeal to me. There was little doubt in my mind that I would be able to experience some very realistic pain here. I decided against trying to find my grandfather and awoke soon after.

Events that you do not expect occur in collective fields

Another proposed difference between the personal and collective is that not everything you encounter in collective fields can be explained by your expectations. In contrast, events in the personal field will always follow your expectations.

However, unexpected events also occur in the personal field. Remember, environments in the out-of-body state do not solely stem from immediate and easily identifiable thoughts. There are many nonconscious influences as well. Hence, it is not quite as simple as saying that something occurred that went against your expectations and that therefore it must be real.

Yet, psychological explanations can also be taken too far. It does not really suffice to relegate every unexpected event to a nonconscious "black box" in your own mind. This would merely be an attempt to explain away one unknown with another unknown. And you will sometimes be at a complete loss to explain certain events.

Overall, then, unexpected events in the out-of-body state should carry some weight in determining whether or not your experience extends beyond the personal, even though the determination is never entirely conclusive. I suspect that the debate on psychological influences in the out-of-body state is likely to continue.

Journal Entry — Thursday, February 5, 2009, 5:25 am

[Continued from p. 109] ...I moved through the void for a while and randomly touched ground somewhere. The environment appeared immediately, and I found myself in a large public area—an underground transportation hub of some kind. It was busy, with lots people moving about.

I watched people coming and going for a while before noticing something unusual. None of them seemed to see me. There was not even a glance, as you would normally do to keep from running into other people. I seemed to be invisible.

I wondered where I had ended up. It was not a physical environment I recognized, and even though I had landed randomly somewhere, the intent had been to enter a nonphysical environment.

After a while, I finally caught a glance from someone coming in my direction. It was a young woman. Unlike the other people, she did seem to notice me.

"Hey, you can see me?" I asked. She was a bit taken aback with the question but then quickly composed herself.

"Yes, you are dead. That's why no one else can see you."

"Not really," I responded. "Look at me a bit more closely."

She seemed a little annoyed and made a reluctant effort to look at me more closely. Her eyes widened for a split second, and then she suddenly put on a friendly face as an image was superimposed on her torso, while her real torso behind it became a blur. It was the image of a perfect naked model's body.

I was not at all in a sexual frame of mind when this occurred—quite the opposite. She was fairly plain looking, and there was the distinct impression that she had created the image, superimposing it on her real body. This was odd. I had never before experienced another character so clearly manipulating my perception in this manner. Some tricksters might be deceiving now and then, but not by actually manipulating my perception.

"Thank you for the invitation, but I'm already with someone," I responded in the friendliest manner I could think of.

My rejection did not go down well. She looked pretty upset and ran off toward a bathroom door not far from where we stood. I felt bad that she had taken my response so badly. I ran after her to explain.

I entered the bathroom. To my right was a piece of transparent plastic separating one part of the bathroom from the other, as there was some sort of construction going on. Behind it, the girl stood staring straight at me.

I got a very uncomfortable feeling. There was something very wrong. Then all of a sudden, I was jumped from all sides by three ghoulish, crazy-looking people who were clawing and pulling at me. I tried to get back to the door, but I was unable to move with all three of them hanging onto me. I had to take a different approach.

I emptied my mind and then tried to ignore the environment around me. I was surprised that I was able to do so, with all the clawing happening at the same time, but I somehow managed. Soon, with a single-minded focus, the darkness of the void began to envelop me as the environment and crazy people faded from view.

I continued to hover in the void for a while, as it was difficult to get back in touch with my physical senses. Eventually, however, the physical world began to fade in, and I made it back to my body. For a few minutes, waves of energy passed through me until I calmed down. Afterward, I promised myself that this was the last time I would ever enter a bathroom in the out-of-body state.

Individuals have minds of their own

Closely related to the idea of unexpected events occurring in the out-of-body state is the argument that you will meet individuals who have minds of their own. For example, if you were to ask a person in the out-of-body state whether or not he or she was aware and conscious, the answer would almost always be affirmative. People may also behave quite independently, acting against your conscious will and expectations.

As is true with unexpected events, this argument should hold up from the point of view that it is consistent with how we approach physical reality. We generally do not treat the people we meet in ordinary life as if they do not exist. However, none of this excludes the possibility of psychological influences in the out-of-body state, especially since corroborating evidence is quite difficult to come by.

For example, it seems relatively simple to verify an encounter with an individual in the out-of-body state. It would only require a name and address, which can be later checked in physical reality. However, as we have seen earlier, simple verification tasks are quite difficult to carry out successfully.

You can engage in those types of experiments, but you will often find that the information obtained is incorrect or otherwise unverifiable. Still, you may sometimes get unexpected hits, which, albeit often circumstantial and anecdotal, will give you pause as far as dismissing anything prematurely.

Journal Entry — Monday, December 29, 2003, time unknown

I had a short experience last night. I was not even planning to write it down until I found out that it had meaning.

The experience consisted of me waking up in the middle of the night while staring straight into the void. This was unusual and abrupt, especially once I saw a hand reaching toward my face.

It was a bit disturbing since the skin on the hand and the arm attached to it looked rather decrepit, almost as if in a state of decay. There were lots of brown age spots and blue veins.

I did not have time to react, however, and before I knew it, the hand softly stroked my face. Then, just as suddenly as it had appeared, it completely disappeared from view.

"Okay, whatever," I thought to myself and quickly went back to sleep.

Later that day, I heard from my parents that my grandmother had passed away.

Note: I had not been in contact with my grandmother for years, ever since I moved from Europe to Canada. In the last year, I got the occasional update from my parents and knew she was ill with a bad prognosis. Apart from that, we had lost touch, and she was not on my mind. Apparently, she might have felt differently. She died in the late morning, which made it the middle of the night for me, due to the time difference.

Everything is just different

Yet another argument for the independent reality of environments encountered in the out-of-body state is that everything just *feels* different there. It is very different from a dream or lucid dream.

On the surface, this argument seems quite unconvincing. It lacks precision. Yet, it also highlights that what makes anything real or unreal is sometimes difficult to identify. So what might be happening here?

Frequently, when it comes to experiences in the personal field, there is a sense of intimacy with the environment—a feeling of the environment belonging to you rather than just happening to you. This feeling of closeness to the environment is often lacking in collective fields, making it difficult to claim personal ownership.

The lack of personal intimacy in collective fields is sometimes further enhanced by a foreign background energy emanating from the environment. It may manifest as music coming from the environment or everything seeming more alive in some way, such as with colors more vivid than usual. Whatever form it takes, there is the distinct impression of an external energy supporting your perceptions.

In fact, it is possible to get a glimpse of this background energy underlying perception. For example, right before you enter an environment from the void, if you slow down the process, you may perceive abstract geometrical patterns providing the building blocks for your eventual perceptions.

I realize this is all quite unsatisfactory from a critical or skeptical point of view. It is difficult to be precise about a hypothetical underlying energy informing our perceptions. Nonetheless, it is something that has been present in my experiences, and it seems important to report here.

Journal Entry — Tuesday, April 11, 2006, 3:30 am

I awoke with energy sensations and immediately exited my physical body. I flew upward into the darkness but was unable to gain any speed and soon found myself back in my body. However, I was still buzzing, and it was easy to separate again.

This time, I did not try to fly through the darkness, instead holding still as soon as I separated. I looked into a dark sky. There was nothing there until a slight shift in my awareness took place, as if I were raising my head above water.

Several stars and points of light began to appear around me. I knew better than to try to chase them, and instead I decided to phase to my destination directly. I moved inward and kept my destination firmly in mind—a nonphysical location that would be "far out there."

My awareness shifted immediately, and before I knew it, I found myself in a different environment. In fact, I had landed right on top of a palm tree on a beach!

A deep blue sea was located not far from me. The setting felt exotic and foreign. It was beautiful. It felt as though I had entered the painting of a surrealist artist.

Scattered across the beach were other palm trees. They looked marvelous, out of this world. They were not like any palm trees I had ever seen before. Thick, curved branches shaped in the most sensual forms extended from the main trunk.

I heard music, or something I can only describe as music. I did not actually hear it in the ordinary sense of the word. It was more like an energy that moved through the entire place. It made the environment very energetic and alive. This truly seemed like a real place.

While looking inland, I allowed the music to move "through" me. It had a curious effect. People began to appear, none of whom I had noticed before. It felt as though I had blotted them out earlier, and only now, feeling the full energy of the place, was I able to perceive them.

They seemed to be going about their own business, even though I had little idea of what that "business" entailed. A sense of anticipation arose inside of me. I suddenly "knew" that someone was going to appear to help me.

I looked down from my palm tree, and a couple of feet away stood a man looking straight at me. He had a somewhat stocky build and was around fifty years of age. I smiled at him, and he smiled back. It felt as though we already knew each other.

"Welcome to [garbled sound]," he said.

I was unable to understand the last part of the sentence, as if my mind was interfering, causing the information to be all mixed up. But he continued loud and clear.

"I am here to assist you and show you around."

I jumped down from my palm tree, and soon we were both heading toward a road located not far from the beach. We walked quietly for a while, moving further inland down the road. There were trees all around us and a few small cabins scattered here and there along the road. There was little conversation as we continued to move further inland.

A few moments later, we arrived at a small house made of wood. It looked like a small shop and had several items displayed on the porch. I was not sure what the shop was selling. It seemed like a typical "along the road" type of gift store.

A woman came out of the house. She walked up to me, holding a coffee cup. The purpose of the cup became clear to me when she brought it close to my face.

It was a "magic cup," and by holding it close to my face, writing would appear on the cup with something of value for the person.

After she finished her routine, she looked at the cup while moving slightly away from me.

"He can't be read," she said to my companion. "His face does not show anything."

Her answer surprised me. I did not understand. Did she just tell me the writing on the cup, or did she tell me there was no writing on the cup?

I awoke soon after.

EXPLORING AFTERLIFE ENVIRONMENTS

One approach to exploring life after death is to treat it as a "working hypothesis" as a basis for further research. This approach sets the stage for a relatively open-ended exploration without completely handicapping you. Some sort of intent or expectation will always be required, which includes considering the possibility. Without intent, your "cup" will remain empty.

Common Vistas

When you do decide to explore afterlife environments, there are certain types of experiences you can expect to come across. In particular, it is not uncommon to encounter other people wandering in darkness without any particular destination. The environment is quite reminiscent of an area of consciousness that Monroe labeled *focus 23*—a level occupied by "...those who have recently left physical existence but who either have not been able to recognize and accept this or are unable to free themselves from the ties of the Earth Life System."[6]

If you find yourself inside this area of consciousness, it often feels like moving through a dark mist—a gray area where vision is blurred and devoid of any concrete perceptions. You can walk there for a long time without ever encountering anyone. Luckily, it is possible to get a good overview of the area from the "outside," such as in the following experience:

Journal Entry — Sunday, October 15, 2006, 3:15 am

I woke up in the middle of the night and quickly set the intent to phase out into the void, beyond anything personal. I soon moved upward with sufficient speed to give me the feeling that I might get somewhere.

After a period of moving upward in the void, my angle of ascent suddenly changed. I had not intended for this to occur. It was as if an invisible force was making me fly horizontally. Below me were hundreds of people, all of them isolated in separate locations, unaware of each other.

It was a peculiar view. Each person walked aimlessly through the darkness, as if there were some sort of ground under their feet. It made the scenery rather surreal, especially since many of the people seemed to be dressed in clothes from different eras.

I continued to fly across the area until I finally noticed some cohesion. A group of five people were having a fight.

I had no intention of getting involved. I glided over the conflict, trying not to attract any attention to myself. I was not too concerned. No one ever looked upward.

Not too far away, I could see an edge of sorts. As I approached it, I could see more clearly what it consisted of. It was made of different lights, or what looked like old-fashioned street lanterns, encircling the entire area. Except for a few in the far distance, most were not turned on.

I descended next to one of the lanterns to examine it more closely. To my surprise, I found a switch that I assumed would turn it on. For a moment, I wondered what this was all about but then got a sudden percept. Turning on the lanterns was meant to attract the attention of those wandering in the area.

Not having forgotten about the group of people fighting, I decided against experimentation and awoke soon after.

Homecoming Events

Another relatively frequent occurrence relating to the exploration of life after death is *homecoming events* when lending a helping hand to those who identify themselves as lost or deceased. If these events are successful, they are not infrequently followed by the perception of a white light in the distance, which gives the impression of moving through a tunnel very much like those reported in near-death experiences. These events may also include a joyful reunion with others.

Interestingly, the eventual destination of the assisted person often remains unknown to the projector. Despite several attempts on my part, it has never appeared to be possible to enter the white light myself. This appears to suggest a certain barrier that cannot be crossed or, at least, it seems difficult to do so. Nonetheless, the symbolic representation of an individual consciousness finding its way "home" can still be quite profound.

Journal Entry — Sunday, April 20, 2008, 4:00 am

I had a second OBE after the verification experiment. This time, I decided to visit the void and seek out a random afterlife environment. I felt slightly nervous since, when doing it blindly, you never really know what you're going to get.

I exited and flew up into the void and almost immediately found myself in a vaguely defined environment. I seemed to be standing on a road, but it was quite dark and misty. I was unable to see more than ten feet ahead of me.

Luckily, it did not take long before I got a percept of the overall environment. I grew up on the outskirts of a small town, with a lot of open land behind the house that had never been developed. The only thing out there was a road that ended abruptly behind our house. There were no streetlights, either, and it used to be pretty desolate there at night. This environment seemed similar.

Yet, this place was different as well. I began to notice people wandering past me. They did not appear to see me. Many of them were children; others were teenagers, no older than sixteen years of age. Strangely, they were all in some sort of nightwear, either a hospital type of outfit or pajamas, walking barefoot. It looked cold.

I looked down at my own body. I seemed to be well dressed, wearing a black leather trenchcoat. It was well suited to the environment as protection from the cold. The blackness of the coat made me virtually invisible.

Curious, I checked the pockets of the coat and found a cigar and a lighter. Preferring cigarettes, I normally don't smoke cigars, let alone in the out-of-body state, but I lit it anyway. It tasted exactly like a cigar.

Then, I saw a group of kids moving straight in my direction—two girls of around fifteen years old and three younger-looking boys. They almost bumped into me.

Without saying anything, one of the girls extended her hand quite politely for a handshake.

"What are you guys doing out here?" I asked.

I expected a regular answer, but instead I suddenly found myself bombarded with images. A cargo ship ... maybe a ferry ... shipwreck ... photographs flashing by in front of my eyes ... a child with her mother ... somewhere in the late '60s ... beginning of the '70s ... that long ago?!

"Are you telling you me you have been dead for more than thirty years?" I asked.

The girl shrugged, as if disappointed with my response, and without any goodbyes, the group went off into the darkness.

Not knowing what else to do, I let them go.

I threw away my cigar, which I no longer enjoyed. I felt uneasy about that last encounter, as if I could have handled it better. I knew they were going in the wrong direction. The road ended where they were going, just like in the town where I grew up. There was nothing beyond it except for more darkness.

I focused on a small figure whisking by not far from where I stood. It was a boy of around fourteen years old moving in the wrong direction as well.

"Hey kid! Where are you going?" I yelled out. "We have to move this way. Come, follow me!"

The kid looked at me, puzzled and unsure of what to do. I started to run, not looking back. I did not want to show any hesitancy or give him time to think.

It worked. I soon heard him running behind me.

I was not exactly sure I was going in the right direction myself or what I was doing to begin with, but if the environment in any way resembled my childhood environment, we were headed toward town.

My instinct proved correct. The mist began to disappear, and the environment became a lot lighter. It did not take long for the outskirts of the town to appear, and before I knew it, we were running toward the center of the town.

"I know this place!" the kid said excitedly, still running next to me. "I used to run through these streets with my dad."

"Good!" I said. "But we have to get to the center of town."

We continued to run through streets and alleys until finally I saw the center of town. The entire area was ablaze in white light with music originating from its center.

The music was comforting and uplifting. It reminded me of that teenage song Bad Day by Daniel Powter. I felt little emotional response to it, but the boy reacted. He took off in a sprint. Soon, he was running ahead of me toward the light and music. I could barely keep up with him.

Around the edges of the white light, I saw a parade of some kind going on, with large blue trucks and people cheering at each end of the road. This only seemed to excite the boy even more.

I now had almost reached the light. The boy had already disappeared inside of it. Then, just as I was about to jump into it, I woke up, abruptly ending the experience. Yet again, I was not privy to the ending, as if not allowed to go there.

H-Band

Aside from homecoming events, another common phenomenon you can expect to encounter is what Robert Monroe referred to as the *H-Band*— the uncontrolled thoughts and emotional patterns emanating from all human beings.[7] According to Monroe, the H-Band itself is part of the emanations originating from the wider spectrum of consciousness, or what he referred to as *(M) field radiation*. You are quite likely to come across it even in your early experiences.

It is generally perceived in the form of a wide array of sounds and voices intermingled with one another. It can also be perceived in its entirety, but that is not advisable. You will experience an extremely loud, high-pitched metallic screeching that is literally painful to listen to. The sound is not dissimilar to the Nazgul scream from the movie *Lord of the Rings*. It is disturbing.

If you do want to perceive the H-Band, your best option is to approach it slowly from the void. From there, with some practice, it is not too difficult to isolate certain sounds and voices as you fine-tune the connection and follow them all the way back to their origin. Even so, you might not always be interested in following up on every sound and voice you hear. Regrettably, not that many are uplifting, even if you are in a calm state of mind.

Journal Entry — Wednesday, January 11, 2008, 5:10 am

I had a brief OBE last night. I fairly quickly ended up in the void, with the impression of hovering somewhere over the city. I decided to tune in to the H-Band and directed my attention across the area below me. It did not take long for a cacophony of voices to rise up. There was a lot of wailing and screaming, as usual. There seemed to be no end to it.

I reached out further and deeper with my awareness, no longer trying to pick out sounds from the city but rather somewhere further away. I did so in a horizontal fashion, expecting some sort of emanation from a physically alive person. A dark, singular voice emerged.

"I'll cut you up, bitch! I know how to do it!"

I moved my awareness closer to its origin and then perceived the vague outline of a figure. It was a pretty big guy with an animal-like posture. I tried to shield my thoughts and emotions as much as possible by keeping my hearing tilted sideways instead of moving my entire attention toward him.

It seemed to work. I was now only a few feet away from him, yet he remained unaware of my presence. In the meantime, the ranting went on for a while. He seemed to be mostly talking to himself. I could not detect anyone else there, which was just as well. The guy was in a foul, bestial mood.

I then turned away, not wanting to push my luck. I found myself back in my body soon after.

According to the popular out-of-body literature, the voices and sounds you may hear in the void are not limited to the living but may come from the deceased as well. Yet, at the same time, the amount of noise caused by human thought and emotion is considered to decrease in intensity the further removed you are from physical time-space, until far outward into the outward rings or the at edge of the void, the level of uncontrolled human thought and emotion is at a minimum. In that scenario, the void is extremely suitable as a point of communication from where it is possible to converse with just about anyone you can think of. Initially, it may take some time to get a clear connection, but there will usually be a response from the person you intended to contact.

Journal Entry — Saturday, May 20, 2006, 4:00 am

I woke up in the middle of night and felt myself able to OBE. Yet, there were no energy sensations, which was quite unusual. For a while, for the purpose of practicing, I moved back and forth out of my body, and as I did, I decided to try to contact Monroe by extending my mind into the void.

Then in a crackling voice: "Can you hear me?"

"Yes, I can hear you!" I responded excitedly.

There was a lot of crackling and white noise. It was like trying to find the right frequency on a radio. But then I got the inner sense percept that I needed to lie still. I had been moving back and forth out of body throughout the experience.

I lay back and then felt pressure near my throat, as if it was being manipulated somehow. Energy surges began to flow through my throat area.

No other communication occurred after this, except for a newsletter that appeared in front of my eyes. There were different words written on it. My eyes only fell on one of them. It was a single word.

Interpret.

Note: The throat chakra is symbolic of communication and expression, I found out after this experience. Perhaps I subconsciously knew this already, but it still came as a surprise.

REPOSITORY FIELDS OF CONSCIOUSNESS

Repository fields of consciousness are yet another form of collective field, closely tied to the wider field of human consciousness. Unlike the other collective fields, these fields are mostly based on information and knowledge. There is no impression of interacting with other sentient consciousness. Rather, you are accessing information and knowledge seemingly stored inside a wider field of energy. It includes great inventions, beautiful musical compositions, dreadful mass events, the most amazing forms of art, horrific accidents, brilliant thoughts, and great vistas of hope for humankind.

Repository fields are accessed in the same manner as any other environment, either through entering an environment from the void or in the form of *partial* engagement from the void. For example, you can maintain a more detached stance toward the imagery, as if viewing it from a distance, which is preferable in the case of the more negative vistas. You may also use auditory information alone, without any visuals, which is my preferred method because there is the least risk of losing lucidity.

The information gleaned from repository fields of consciousness is difficult to attribute to your own personal psyche. You can, for example, tune in to the words of a long-dead famous philosopher. This will generally consist of listening to a one-sided monologue of his work rather than an actual conversation. There does not appear to be any sentience behind the words; rather, it is as if you are accessing an audio voice on a looped tape. Meanwhile, you will recognize that you would never be able to produce the same thing in ordinary waking consciousness.

Regrettably, some information gleaned from repository fields of consciousness is difficult to bring back into ordinary reality. It is rather like attending a scientific conference on a topic you know nothing about. For example, I have read many technical pages on quantum mechanics in the out-of-body state. In both situations, I would have difficulty reporting on what I heard or read.

Accessing information in the repository fields does not appear to be an illusory phenomenon. There are many reported instances throughout history in which artists, inventors, intellectuals, and scientists access these repository fields of consciousness, usually while drifting in between waking and sleeping. For example, the melody of the song *Yesterday* by Paul McCartney came about in this manner. After he made sure that the song was not already in existence and belonging to someone else, it became one of the most famous Beatles songs.

Similar stories of creation come from the fields of science and literature. For example, the structure of the DNA molecule was not discovered by expensive laboratory equipment; rather, it came when Dr. Francis Crick used hallucinogenic drugs, during which he saw two intertwined snakes in the form of a helix. Charles Dickens wrote most of his poetry while near the borderline of sleep. Mozart seemed to be able to access such fields of consciousness even while fully awake.

Once you begin to access repository fields of consciousness in your own out-of-body activity, you can expect to initially find yourself accessing information that is already in existence. The information is out there, distributed in a non-local manner as part of the wider field of human consciousness that can be accessed from any position inside of the void—your own intent being the most important factor.

You may, for example, open up auditory perception in the void with the intent to listen to one of your favorite songs. The melody and lyrics will be there, even if you were not able to reproduce them in ordinary states of consciousness. The sound quality will be better than any technology presently in existence. Then, as you become more familiar with connecting to repository fields, you may begin to hear songs that are not (yet) in existence. Unless you want to bring back the songs to physical reality, no talent for composition is required.

It is difficult to overestimate the potential significance of repository fields of consciousness. I have only scratched the surface, and yet I feel more comfortable with the "reality" of this field than any other. In fact, there is little doubt in my mind that controlled access to these repository fields of consciousness by a significant number of talented individuals has the potential to lead to a renaissance in culture, politics, literature, science, technology, and art unlike any ever before seen in human history. It would be wonderful if this indeed came to pass.

Journal Entry — Saturday, September 16, 2006, 3:15 am

I spent a long time in the void last night. Initially, I was listening to the H-Band—the usual disturbing cacophony of voices. One screaming voice of a woman dying in a fire stood out. I didn't have the stomach to follow up on it. Instead, I decided to reach out a little further with my mind, deeper into the void.

I soon found myself listening to monologues of several different writers on the out-of-body experience. At times, long stretches of text floated in front of my eyes, but it was auditory, for the most part. All the while, there was no interaction. It felt like tuning into a recorded audiotape, as if there was no sentience behind it, just thoughts floating "out there."

After a while, I began to provoke some music in the void. Initially, I listened to several pop songs, both known and unknown. One of the unknown songs was in my native Dutch language. I did not really like the song, but I could see it easily going to the top of the charts. It was a popular genre.

After a while, I decided to focus on something I did like. I tuned in to the finale of Once Upon a Time in the West *by Ennio Morricone. The angelic soprano voice was breathtaking, the melody and sound out of this world.*

After this song, I woke up. For a while, I tried to memorize the melody and lyrics of the unknown songs, still trying to catch my breath from the last song. By the time I got up in the morning, it was all gone.

PART FOUR

Theory and Practice

Chapter 8
A Preliminary Hypothesis

THE GHOST IN THE MACHINE

Most approaches to the out-of-body state make a clear distinction between the objective and the subjective. The out-of-body state is either entirely real, or it is imaginary and unreal. It is expected that you evaluate the validity of your experiences against physical reality as a litmus test for anything real. As long as what you perceive is the same as what exists in physical reality, perhaps it might be a real experience. Otherwise, it is not. But what are we really comparing it to? What is this distinction between subjective and objective really based on? What is physical reality?

Throughout human history, philosophers and scientists have attempted to come to grips with the notion of reality. The distinction between objective and subjective represents one of these attempts. The term *objective* refers to the external world—the real world of objects and events. *Subjective* refers to everything coming from *within* the subject—your own inner experience. On the surface, it seems like a straightforward distinction. However, the distinction is not without its problems.

The notion of objectivity—the idea that there is a fixed reality consisting of objects and facts independent of the mind—is closely related to *direct realist* accounts of perception. This realist model holds that reality is exactly as it appears to us—entirely physical, solid and touchable, existing independent and apart from the observer.

Realist models tend to have a materialistic view of consciousness as well, with matter considered the only real thing, and consciousness being a mere by-product of matter. Consciousness is reduced to brain function, with electrochemical processes considered to be responsible for any sort of subjective experience.

One of the problems with the realist model is that it very poorly accounts for perception under conditions of ambiguity in which people perceive the same thing in different ways. According to the direct realist model, these differences in perception cannot occur. Yet, perceptual illusions often lead to different perceptions among different people, such as in the case of Wittgenstein's duck-rabbit or the Necker Cube (See Figure 8.1).

Duck-Rabbit [1]   Necker Cube [2]

Figure 8.1. Perception Under Ambiguity

The realist model also fails to account for those organisms that perceive the physical world differently than humans do. For example, a bat perceives the physical world as something entirely different than we do. So what we refer to as physical reality, as we perceive it, does not exist entirely apart from the observer, human or otherwise.

Given the inability of direct realism to account for these perceptual differences, the realist model no longer holds much sway in modern-day scientific accounts of perception. Rather, most scientists these days propose a *mediational* model of reality. Reality is said to be mediated by the observer, who plays a role in the manner in which external reality is perceived. Some who subscribe to this mediational model adhere to an entirely materialistic explanation, in which the world is mediated by the brain, whereas others hold perception to be the result of an internal representation or mental model of the world. Others combine both approaches, suggesting that these internal representations are somehow "stored" inside of the brain.

Despite recognizing the role of the observer in perception, a mediational model of reality insists that there are physical things "out there" existing apart from me. It holds that I, with my senses, notice them or don't notice them because my senses are tuned in or not tuned in to pick up physical characteristics relayed through my brain as ambient light, sound, or touch. My brain, through its mediational faculties, makes sense of it accordingly.

At the same time, reality must be represented in my mind in order to be perceived. If there is an elephant and I see a hat, my representation is inaccurate, and I am not perceiving physical reality correctly. In other words, my representations must correspond to an external, objective reality to be valid. In that sense, a mediational model is not any different from a realist model, which also believes that an objective world exists apart from the observer.

Yet, we do not really know what exists out there on any objective level. We might try to reduce objective reality to sensory experience, but perception itself is not easily reducible to electromechanical impulses and nerve cells. Nor is external reality easily reduced to matter, which, if one goes into it deeply enough, reveals vast amounts of empty space in between atoms. Matter does not even appear to be very stable, ultimately consisting of quantum particles that continuously blink in and out of existence. In that sense, ultimate reality, if there is such a thing, continues to elude us all the time, which would make *all* perception an ever-ongoing distortion.

In a manner of speaking, mediational models of reality attempt to have it both ways, holding on to divisions between subjective and objective, inner and outer, while throwing the observer a bone. In particular, what mediational models fail to recognize is that almost everything about what they call objective reality occurs *inside* of consciousness, and that very little is known about what exists outside of it. We can try to delve "deeper" into reality and prematurely allude to quantum fields and particles, hoping to find some sort of ultimately reality, but doing so certainly does not lead to an objective reality. So for now, let's talk about what we do know something about, and which we are inside of all the time, which is our *experience*.

INNER AND OUTER

As noted by Edwards and colleagues, reality is essentially defined by consensus, not by physical criteria.[3] Even if we were to consider physicality a valid criterion for reality, it does not really distinguish between ordinary physical life and the out-of-body state.

For example, it is perfectly possible to bump your head in the out-of-body state. You can also experience very realistic pain in the out-of-body state. Yet, few realists would be willing to conclude that the out-of-body environment is therefore real and external.

The realist argument is incoherent because inner and outer experience is very closely linked, not easily divisible into one as subjective and the other as objective. Both imagination and perception often operate simultaneously, such as when you drive to work and imagine yourself lying on a beach at the same time.

You may not even remember how you got to work and be unaware of the actual drive, while your earlier perception of the beach still exists firmly in your mind. This lack of a clear boundary between imagination and perception is even more evident in the out-of-body state, such as when your own inner psyche leads to the manifestation of a corresponding environment.

This is not to say that there are no distinctions between imagination and perception. In particular, externalized perception does not respond as well to intent and expectation as does the imagination. For example, it is easy to rearrange furniture in your mind. It is another matter to actually move furniture from one room to another and then back again, if it does not work out to your liking. This would involve actual perception.

This distinction between imagination and perception also applies to the out-of-body state. It is only after setting intent, as well as some sort of expectation, that an external environment will appear, and this environment is never as amenable to change as your inner life. You may be able to defy the laws of physics in these environments and change the environment on a relative whim, but they are still nowhere near as malleable and transient as your own inner life—your imagination.

Otherwise, however, the distinction between perception and imagination is purely relational rather than defined by objective criteria. What is previously imagined can be subsequently perceived, and vice versa. It primarily depends on how you relate with either your inner life or the world around you. Neither that which is inner, nor what is outer, is ever fixed.

For example, if I were to imagine a dancing elephant and build up the image as if I owned it, it would continue to appear to be coming from inside of me. Yet, if I treated that dancing elephant as something that happens to me, losing some sense of ego in the process and becoming fully absorbed in the image, I might actually perceive it as if coming from the outside. In that case, it would be *perceived* rather than imagined.

We can turn this around as well, where what is initially perceived as external can subsequently be experienced as if coming from the inside. For example, when you are inside a car and are focused on the interior, you appear to be separate from the car itself. However, over time, as you focus on the street while you drive, the interior of the car will no longer appear as external to you as it did earlier. In fact, your body boundaries will have expanded significantly, enveloping the entire car as if it were made of your own skin. In those moments, you *are* the car.

These shifts between inner and outer experience occur all the time in daily life. You are simply not aware of them until you catch yourself in the middle of them. For example, a shift will frequently occur when looking out the window of your house or apartment. If you catch yourself doing it, you will notice the house itself shift toward the margins of your awareness, often even occupying an internalized position as if coming from within. In that regard, it is not surprising that any break-in into your home environment often feels like a mental and physical violation. Road rage can be explained in a similar manner, where being cut off by another driver is experienced as if someone literally pushed your physical body out of the way.

THE CONTEXTUAL NATURE OF PERCEPTION

Consciousness is relational.[4] It is always *about* something, which grounds your being in the world. The boundary of consciousness is therefore always between you and the world. This is not a fixed boundary, defined by the outlines of your physical body. Rather, the boundary between you and the world continually changes, depending on how you interact with the world.

For example, you may focus on a single leaf on a tree, with a very near horizon, and you will remain entirely unaware of the remainder of the tree. Or alternatively, you may expand your horizon far beyond the tree itself, even into that which is unseen.

Consciousness continuously contracts and expands as it travels through time and space. And while doing so, there is no clear boundary between perception and imagination. There are always unseen and unmanifested aspects of the environment in the periphery of your awareness. Consciousness is always surrounded by a wider context.

This wider context surrounding your cognitive focus is essential to perceive and think about because it provides the background against which any perception or thought occurs. You may liken it to a piece of white paper with black printed text. It is readable because of the contrast created by the black text on white paper. If there were no contrast—for example, if the paper were black—you would be unable to read anything. Without contrast, the primary focus of your perception and thought cannot exist.

To use a more complex scenario, if I were to perceive attending a barbecue without knowing how I ended up there, I would get very confused. The background context I need here includes the preceding events that led to an invitation and having traveled and arrived there as well as some expectation of how events typically unfold at barbecues. I need a wider set of possibilities surrounding my primary focus at the barbecue in order to make sense of the situation. Without such a background context, which is entirely implicit and not perceived, we cannot really function.

Context is therefore always present in all of our perceptions and thoughts. If I perceive a dancing elephant in my front yard, I never just perceive a dancing elephant. It is part of a larger context, such as where I might have ever seen a dancing elephant before. I might expect a circus to be nearby, or if that possibility seems unlikely, perhaps expect animal control to arrive soon. I might feel sorry for the elephant, and I would expect someone to take action.

If this situation occurs in the out-of-body state, you can expect these possibilities to very easily appear inside the environment. You may, for example, take a look around a street corner and indeed perceive a circus tent. From there, the story may unfold further, and you may see parents with children gathering, or you may notice different stands on the street where hot dogs and hamburgers are sold, and so forth. Alternatively, you might see police cars or animal control arriving.

While this situation seems quite absurd, perception in ordinary states of consciousness does not really function any differently. In physical life as well, when faced with a dancing elephant in your front yard, there will be a wider context surrounding that perception. Perhaps a circus will indeed come into view as you begin to explore the environment. Perhaps you are able to imagine another possibility that might explain the situation. Again, however, just as in the out-of-body state, what previously existed in the margins of your awareness as a possibility will eventually become part of your perception and thoughts. In both cases, it is possibility that defines reality.

A MODEL OF POSSIBILITIES

The notion of *possibility* as a key defining psychological characteristic of consciousness has recently been introduced in a possibilistic model of reality by O'Connor and Aardema.[5,6] In this model, possibility does not only cover what might be; it also covers what is here now—that which is seen or focused upon in the moment. In other words, some possibilities exist at the margins, not yet in view, while others are seen and directly experienced.

The context surrounding each of your perceptions and thoughts can be represented graphically in the form of a possibility distribution that peaks at your immediate focus, while the wider context surrounding your perception tapers off into the margins of consciousness (see Figure 8.2A). What exists at the margins are themselves possibilities, but of lesser likelihood than the peak of the distribution—your immediate perception and thought. Surrounding this maximum likelihood at the margins is the context in which these perceptions and thoughts occur.

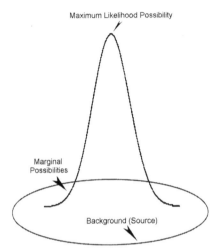

Figure 8.2A. A possibility distribution with a maximum likelihood possibility and the wider context surrounding it tapering off into the margins against an unmanifested background

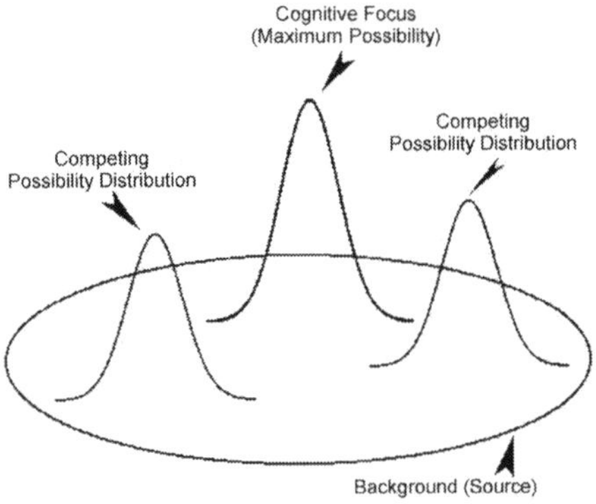

Figure 8.2B. Horizontal view of competing possibility distributions allowing for meta-cognitive positioning toward different maximum likelihood possibilities

In a wider perspective, there are also other possibility distributions surrounding your present one, either with a different context or an overlapping context (see Figure 8.2B). This particular landscape comes into view when you entertain multiple possibilities. It allows for a metacognitive positioning toward different possibilities and the quick interchange of one maximum likelihood possibility for another, even though their individual contexts might be entirely different. You may, for example, juggle around different possible destinations for your next vacation, each surrounded by a somewhat different context.

It is important to realize that possibility distributions are dynamic and in a constant state of flux. The peaks and valleys across a larger field of possibility continuously wax and wane. What initially existed at the margins will begin to peak as a maximum likelihood possibility as soon as you direct your attention toward it, according to your intent. For example, the simple act of moving your eyes sideways toward the periphery of your attention has a huge effect on the possibility distribution. What I see about a particular object depends on what I intend to do with it. It is my project that determines what I see, while other, irrelevant possibilities remain "out of view."

There is, then, a *dialectical logic* to consciousness, which is that being aware of something implies not being aware of something else. Every event or possibility in consciousness implicitly incorporates every other possible event. Some of these possibilities may be closely associated with your primary focus, whereas others exist far into the margins, but what is seen is still qualified by that which is not seen.

The dialectical nature of consciousness is a precognitive fact of human existence; it does not need any psychological explanation. At the same time, however, it creates a space between what is there and what is not there, where we as human beings psychologically position ourselves as determined by our intent and project. It is *intent* and my relationship toward the world that defines what I will perceive.

The realist model might argue that even though I do not notice everything about a particular project, it still exists independent of me. But even when going back to an object to discover attributes I had not noticed before, anything I perceive will still be wound up in a project or intent, as in a "going-back-to-see-missed-attributes project."[5] I will notice things in accordance with that project or intent. I would not be able to perceive anything without this intentional context.

For example, if I intend to drive to work, I never merely drive to work. The project includes all the possible destinations I could drive to, but quite purposefully do not. I can also widen or change the context when, for example, I still choose to drive to work but decide to follow a different route than usual. As such, there are always future possibilities opening up in the midst of any project, according to your intent. Initially, these possibilities go unseen, but eventually they will become seen and manifest inside of physical reality.

FIELDS OF CONSCIOUSNESS

The notion that reality is constructed on the basis of shifting possibility distributions is a quantum view of consciousness. It is compatible with the view that ultimate reality is a wave-particle spatiotemporal paradox.[7] The possibilistic model also explicitly adds that a possibility space encompasses a rich array of qualitatively distinct human projects and intents.[5] In that sense, quantum fields of consciousness are as much psychological realities as they are perceptual realities. Indeed, several quantum physicists have already advocated a more subjective form of physics in order to understand reality.[8,9]

A possibilistic model of reality does not propose that worlds or minds other than your own do not exist. Senses still function as senses. They provide what we refer to as physical reality with a certain level of predictability and permanence. They also allow for consensus between different observers. Simply put, my intent to perceive a dancing elephant on my front lawn is unlikely to make it so, and even if I were to perceive it, it is unlikely that anyone else will.

However, the point to keep in mind here is that what you perceive in physical reality still remains a maximum likelihood possibility. Sensory information does not transmit a *fixed* world out there. It is continuously being *created* as an active process occurring in consciousness.

We might even speculate that sensory information is really nothing more than a powerful and encompassing possibility distribution that affects the distribution of many other possibility distributions involved in the perception of physical reality. Sensory input would only be a sideshow of a more fundamental process that is occurring inside of consciousness.

In a similar vein, we might also view the influence of sensory input as "spikes," just like any other maximum likelihood possibility, but peaking even higher than usual. Practically speaking, this ensures that you will not be confronted with dancing elephants when you leave the house. Meanwhile, the world itself is more like a field of consciousness than anything else. It does not exist apart from you.

The Physical Field

The out-of-body state is most easily established by the pragmatic use of natural sleep cycles, when sensory input naturally retreats into the background. Taken-for-granted, self-defining body boundaries are more easily transcended than under ordinary circumstances.

When you leave the body, perception will no longer be as stable as before because the spikes mentioned earlier have disappeared from the possibility distribution. A much wider range of possibilities now compete for your attention.

There is still a maximum likelihood possibility, however, at least as long as you perceive something. If not, you would likely be inside of the void, where very little is perceived. The possibility distribution would be quite flat, with very little contrast at the margins.

The appearance of the void following the transition into the out-of-body state is no coincidence. The physical context ordinarily surrounding your perceptions will have disappeared, which leaves you with empty black space. However, the void is not *entirely* without context. It still has spatial depth, which is the primary dimension that allows for perceptual existence, preceding perceptual form and shape.[10]

While inside of the void, intent is the driving force behind any new perceptions. You can engage with any environment you wish, or more accurately stated, you can actively construct any environment you want, just as you do in ordinary states of consciousness. If your intent is directed toward where you just came from, the physical environment will be reconstructed, quite reminiscent of the original, but this time without the spikes mentioned earlier.

The environment you will perceive is no longer *informed* by the senses. However, at the same time, it is as real as anything else. In fact, the chair you perceive in physical reality is the same chair you perceive in the out-of-body state because they are generated by the same mental faculties. *Both* are actively constructed in consciousness.

This does not mean that everything you perceive in the out-of-body state will correspond exactly to perception in the presence of sensory input. In terms of a possibilistic model, without the spikes provided by sensory input, you are forced to operate in a relatively flat distribution in which many different perceptions become possible. It is only your intent that can keep the possibility distribution stable. Not surprisingly, veridical perception in the out-of-body state remains quite elusive.

Again, however, the fact that you do not perceive reality in the same manner in the out-of-body state that you do under ordinary circumstances does not make it unreal. The entire notion of veridical perception is based on a realist model, which mistakenly insists that there is an immutable and fixed world out there against which "reality" should be measured.

It might be possible to obtain convincing proof of veridical perception in the out-of-body state, but it would require a more complete recognition that reality is actively constructed. This would include a consideration of the natural lived-in context in which perception occurs.[11] In particular, it would likely benefit such research to focus on the *subjective level of correspondence,* rather than objective similarities, between the perception of the projector and a particular target object.

For example, if I try to perceive an apple in the out-of-body state, and if I ordinarily only think of apples in the context of apple pies, I am more likely to perceive an apple pie than an apple. The apple pie takes precedence over an apple in my personal possibility distribution. This is not a perceptual distortion. Nothing can ever be distorted if the world is constructed by you to begin with.

Veridical perception might also become more likely if perception as a whole more closely resembled physical reality, such as may be the case under conditions of high environmental and mental stability. Even so, it would be unrealistic to expect every aspect of the out-of-body environment to correspond with physical reality. There may be situations in which this can occur, but they are quite rare.

While inside the physical field, it is possible to operate with a high level of lucidity. At the same time, the relatively flat distribution easily leads to more remote perceptions. Your intent may succeed in keeping the possibility distribution stable for a while, but over time, little of what you perceive will correspond to what we ordinarily refer to as physical reality. This phenomenon has elsewhere been described as remote perception and the externalization of the inner psyche in the out-of-body state.

During remote perception, the level of lucidity is often threatened as well. This can be understood as dissociation between intent and perception, which appears crucial in order to maintain lucidity. Specifically, non-lucidity occurs when the *form* in which perception occurs is no longer tied to your expectations or intent. For example, you may be flying over a city and then suddenly flying an airplane afterward. Your intent in the project of flying over the city has not changed, even though the environment has changed considerably. Worse, because of the dissociation between intent and perception, you fail to notice that the shift even happened.

It is easy to see how these phenomena lead some researchers to consider the OBE closely related to dreaming. Indeed, given the phenomenological similarities, I suspect dreaming occurs quite often in a particular mode of consciousness that can be adopted in the out-of-body state. However, none of this diminishes the potential significance of an experience in which consciousness experiences itself beyond the confines of the physical body.

The Personal Field

Possibility distributions contain an important psychological dimension that does not ordinarily manifest inside of the physical world. However, in the out-of-body state, there are no such limitations. Even if you start out in the physical field, it generally does not take long for the inner psyche to take over entirely.

During externalization of the inner psyche, the psychological context surrounding perception takes on a prominent role. What initially existed at the margins of the possibility distribution, and is ordinarily kept at bay during perception, easily comes to the foreground as a maximum likelihood possibility. You will therefore be able to interact with your inner psyche as if it were an externalized reality. There are many positive applications here, limited only by your own imagination.

As stable as these environments may appear, they do not exist apart from you. They reflect the content of your inner psyche. For the sake of convenience, the personal field has previously been referred to as subjective. To an important extent, however, subjectivity is intrinsic to all perception and not unique to the personal field. Rather, what characterizes the personal field more than anything else is the conscious or nonconscious intent behind your perceptions.

It is always intent and attention that define which particular field of consciousness you will occupy. For example, a physically oriented mode of consciousness leads you to perceive the physical world, whereas a focus on your inner psyche leads you into the personal field of consciousness. As such, the divisions between different fields of consciousness are rather arbitrary. You are only "located" anywhere to the extent that you construct yourself to be there.

Interestingly, this is unrecognized in esoteric approaches to the out-of-body state. Here, the realist model is not only applied to physical reality but also to astral planes, which are made out of finer matter. The notion of astral planes is taken quite literally, existing independent of and external to the observer, just as in a realist model of physical reality. You are therefore also quite literally thought to occupy certain environments. This is not really the case.

Of course, environments in the personal field can be quite stable. They can be even more stable than a construction site in the physical world that changes on a daily basis. This is because the psychological dimensions defining these environments are quite stable, representing relatively permanent fixtures in your own inner psyche or the collective psyche. None of this is ever fixed, however, just as physical reality is never finished, either.

Collective Fields

Collective fields of consciousness represent yet another mode of consciousness. They are usually characterized by an intent to interact with other-than-self consciousness. This may include an interaction with people who identify themselves as deceased as well as other forms of consciousness.

From a realist point of view, it can be difficult to differentiate between personal and collective fields of consciousness. In those terms, it is conceivable that there is no such thing as a collective field of consciousness and that experiences occurring there are solely influenced by the mindset and belief system of the projector.

Yet, a large number of thought-provoking events may occur there, especially with respect to so-called repository fields of consciousness. Often, from a firsthand perspective, psychological explanations alone are not sufficiently convincing to account for perception in these fields, similar to the notion of archetypes and other primordial imagery.[12]

Still, collective fields certainly do not appear to be fixed environments. Often, perception is metaphorical and symbolic, which may make these experiences significant, but they are not always meant to be literal. This especially appears to be the case with regard to so-called afterlife environments.

Despite all of this, the idea of life after death is not an outlandish possibility to consider. After all, if consciousness is not bound to the physical body or the brain, interacting with other consciousness, including the deceased, is a perfectly logical possibility.

There are many oddities in mind-brain interaction to begin with, some of which suggest that the brain might not be essential to consciousness. For example, consciousness is not always threatened even when the cerebral cortex is missing.[13]

The lack of any clear relationship between brain and consciousness is also evident in near-death experiences. Conscious experience continues even in the absence of any apparent brain activity, such as during trauma. Near-death experiences have also occurred during general anesthesia during which the brain is being put into a controlled deep coma.

By definition alone, the near-death experience is an OBE in which the person is at a location other than the physical body. In both cases, the person frequently finds him- or herself initially hovering near the physical body, which is then often followed by moving through the void, including visions that arise from within it. The person may also perceive a white light in the distance while traveling toward it. It is a barrier that often represents a point of no return in the near-death experience, and it is not easily crossed in the out-of-body state, either.

BEYOND HUMAN CONSCIOUSNESS

In the hundredth issue of *The Psychologist*, scientists were invited to submit their ideas on the most important experiments never done, while casting practicalities and ethical concerns aside.[14] One experiment, suggested by Susan Blackmore, was to investigate the brain activity of people as they die. It might help to determine whether consciousness really needs the brain to survive.

Of course, some would claim that evidence is already there, in the form of anecdotal reports on near-death experiences during which brain activity appears to have ceased and conscious experience continues. However, these are rarely controlled studies, and as a result, there often tends to be some confusion about the exact timeline of loss of brain function and the continuation of conscious experience.[15]

Perhaps the experiment suggested by Blackmore will indeed be carried out one day. It might be difficult to accomplish, given ethical and practical considerations. It may also prove to be unnecessary. The out-of-body state might turn out to be just as informative. Projectors of consciousness are becoming increasingly adept at reaching beyond the confines of regular human consciousness.

To move beyond ordinary human consciousness requires giving up one of the most fundamental characteristics of physical existence—the idea of space. This means going beyond the void itself, which, even though it is non-local space, still has *illusory* spatial characteristics. To move beyond human consciousness, these illusory characteristics need to be transcended as well. When doing so in the out-of-body state, it does not seem unlikely that the level of unresponsiveness from the physical body is similar to that of general anesthesia—a state of consciousness similar to coma.[16]

Journal Entry — Monday, June 5, 2006, 3:30 am

I awoke with the familiar energy sensations last night. They came on strong but smooth. I relaxed and fell into them while staying fully alert and lucid. Soon after, I detached from everything physical and entered the void.

I immediately began to move through the void. I felt less physical and defined this time. Initially, there was not much sense of going in a particular direction. I would be able to go far—much further than usual.

I moved fast, upward, downward, and sideways, all the while with the feeling of going deeper and further into the void.

As I continued to move, pushing my mind forward, I wondered where I was going. It would be easy to enter a physical-like environment from the void, but that was not what I had intended. I wanted to go beyond it all, beyond my mind, beyond any sort of physical-like environment. I wanted to reach the essence of consciousness.

I pushed on through the void, continuing to go deeper and further. There seemed to be no end to the blackness. I had never gone this far. I wondered if this was a good idea. But I told myself to keep going, not to stop, so I kept going.

Suddenly, I quite literally "stepped outside" of myself.

I saw myself from a third-person perspective traveling through the void in the form of a small figure moving through darkness toward an edge with blue light on one side. It was peculiar, as if I were looking at a two-dimensional cartoon. It was like looking at me living in Flatland. Yet, it was I traveling to that edge.

I began to get a feeling about what lay beyond the void—a sudden inner percept. It felt like an abyss. I yelled at the little figure moving ahead. Turn back!

I then saw myself turning frantically, away from the edge. I was able to avoid the edge just in time, going in the opposite direction, still in this third-person perspective.

Suddenly, I remembered. I had dreamt about "the blue zone" a few days ago. In that dream, I was inside of the void, and someone told me to go beyond the void. It was supposed to be different—unlike many of the environments I had encountered so far. It had something to do with moving beyond <u>everything</u>.

I still saw myself flying, so I told the little figure to turn around again and move past the edge. No need to be afraid. Nothing can harm you. Just go!

"I" responded.

I saw myself turning back toward the edge. I approached it with some trepidation and then crossed over into the blue wall of light. As I did so, my perspective changed back to first person. I was now there, inside of it.

I couldn't breathe! What was this!? I had never felt anything like this. I had never been anywhere like this! This was too far out! I had never been so far out. Nothing was familiar. It was all gone.

It felt as though I was suffocating, falling apart. I didn't remember anything here. Who was I?! Where was I? Where did I come from? I did not want to lose myself. I was struggling to reach the surface of me.

I was <u>suspended</u>.

I tried to pull myself together. I could not get a sense of me. I did not remember who I was. I did not remember where I came from!

I looked around frantically, trying to get a hold of something—a concept, a perception, anything that was in any way concrete. But I only found blue static all around.

I never felt anything so alien. It was not just because I was lost. The fear was that I did not even know what <u>where</u> meant. The concept had disappeared. There was nothing there to help me find the way back to me.

I "yelled out" for help, and by an invisible force, I sensed myself going down. What did it mean? I did not even know what "going down" meant!

Then I felt something "underneath" me. I touched "ground." I remembered ground! How could I have forgotten what that means!? I told myself to move forward...walk...

The blue light began to disappear. I soon found myself moving in darkness, back in the void. I intended to get back to my body quickly. With that last thought, I awoke soon after.

I never imagined it was possible to be so "far out."

There is a certain coherency to the idea that the further your consciousness moves away from physical existence, the less involved your brain will be, ultimately resembling death. At the same time, most strikingly, your sense of *being* never appears to come to an end. You may lose many mental and perceptual faculties we so often associate with consciousness, yet you continue to exist.

Stripping consciousness bare of its presumed attributes seems like a logical approach to capturing its essence. In fact, transcendent states of consciousness may be nothing more than the loss of a selected array of perceptual and cognitive functions while it simultaneously becomes apparent that consciousness is not defined by these functions. After all, if consciousness precedes matter, then surely it must be capable of an existence that involves more than darting through meadows, parks, and cities. It should be able to exist in a non-three-dimensional environment, without any physical or evolutionary purpose for it to do so.

In my experience, it is able to do just that, even though venturing beyond human consciousness might feel like a second death. Severe drops in body temperature and heartbeat deregulation have been reported during these kinds of explorations.[17] This is in accordance with the hypothesis that the further one moves outward into the spectrum of consciousness, the less brain activity is involved, including depressed brain stem activity. Empirical studies might be useful in this area, not only to register brain activity during a typical OBE, but also in situations in which consciousness ventures outward much further. These studies could establish whether brain activity does indeed cease in some of these areas of consciousness. I suspect it indeed does. We just need a few bold and capable near-death explorers.

A FINAL WORD

The view that consciousness lies at the basis of everything has gained popularity in the last few decades. It has led many out-of-body explorers to explore the boundaries of consciousness in the hopes of touching on some sort of transcendental state of consciousness that would explain and encompass all else. The attempt is not dissimilar to the search for the "God Particle" in quantum physics.

It may be wise to tread carefully. It is far too easy to transpose theories and imagery on what such a reality might entail. Often, that is all that remains—mere theory and metaphor, while the core of the experience is lost in the interpretation, all too often heavily laden by personal desire, history, and cultural influence.

Obviously, it's not easy coming to terms with an ultimate reality that we still know so little about, and no amount of theorizing or quantum physics can disguise this. This is yet another reason why it is worthwhile to sometimes move away from theory and go back to the experience.

Experience is in fact the only true vehicle of understanding, whereas intellectual understanding is often just that—a bunch of beliefs and thoughts that do not automatically make a successful explorer of consciousness.

There is a way of learning from experience that can provide you with valuable insights about the larger reality in which it is embedded. Experience should always be part of the story, strengthening any sort of theoretical argument.

Ultimately, it has to be your *own* story. You can never ever truly understand the out-of-body state if you do not practice it yourself.

Personal practice will also shield you from those who make all sorts of claims about the out-of-body state, or exaggerate their achievements, yet offer little in terms of experience. Inauthentic experiences become easy to identify.

Regrettably, guruism or narcissism is still prevalent in this area. I suspect it has a lot to do with the fact that the out-of-body state is often confused with spirituality and power. It is one of the reasons I have attempted to avoid these concepts in the current book.

Establishing the out-of-body state is like learning any other kind of skill. It does not automatically make you more advanced than anyone else except for your ability to perform the skill. What you do with that skill can make a difference. It's up to you.

Chapter 9
Inducing the OBE

THE IMPORTANCE OF WAKEFULNESS

So you want to join the ranks of those who, in the words of the poet John Magee, have "...slipped the surly bonds of earth and danced the skies on laughter-silvered wings." You won't be flying an airplane, which inspired those words, but the rewards of learning how to project are even greater. So how do you make the OBE happen?

Clearly, the voluntary induction of the out-of-body state is associated with sleep. There are other situations in which the OBE occurs, such as during trauma or other extreme events, but the voluntary induction of the state is associated with the natural sleep rhythms of the physical body. In particular, Robert Monroe was the first to fully recognize the importance of being able to reach the MABA state (Mind Awake/Body Asleep) in order to effectuate the OBE.

The good news is that you already know how to accomplish at least half of the MABA state. You do it every night, over and over again, as your body falls asleep. This may seem rather obvious, but it is important to realize that letting your body fall asleep is not where the challenge lies.

Of course, you cannot really control the physical body falling asleep. It will do so when it is ready. Ultimately, however, letting the body fall asleep is not where the difficulty lies. The real difficulty in reaching the MABA state is to control your level of wakefulness *while* your physical body is falling asleep.

To realize the importance of wakefulness is your first key to success. It will ensure that your energy won't be scattered across all manner of other methods and techniques. And once awake and focused, there is really not that much stopping you from having an OBE.

Do keep in mind that staying awake is not as easy as it may sound. It requires a great deal of motivation and vigilance. Yet, it is the only thing you have any control over in order to induce the OBE. The entire method described in this chapter is geared toward enhancing that control.

PRELIMINARY CONSIDERATIONS

Time of Practice

Overall, the best time for practice is in the middle of the night after having slept some. Your mind will be flexible and alert, better able to hover near the borderline of sleep with less risk of immediately losing lucidity. At the same time, your physical body will have a natural tendency to fall asleep.

Ideally, you will practice multiple times at night in between sleep cycles. Each sleep cycle is known to last around ninety minutes. You will therefore be quite busy throughout the night, shifting frequently between waking and sleeping, with the goal of having an OBE never far from your mind.

Avoid practice immediately after retreating to bed. The physical body may be quite willing to fall asleep at that time, but so is your mind. There is barely any transition in between waking and sleeping. You are far better off going to sleep for a while, after which time your mind will have rested some, and then practicing.

If you like to experiment, you can also go to bed much *later* than usual or get up for a while in the middle of the night. This will often lead to a higher state of wakefulness as well. The phenomenon is not unlike the situation with children who go to bed too long past their bedtime and consequently are unable to sleep because their natural sleep rhythm has been disturbed. For the same reason, jet lag, insomnia, fever, and sleep deprivation can all be beneficial catalysts for practice.

Finally, some people report success with practice in the morning, as opposed to practice in the middle of the night. However, it is often more difficult to establish an entirely lucid transition into the out-of-body state. Especially at around 3 or 4 am, you are far more likely to experience a full-fledged OBE straight from the waking state, without any interruption in consciousness. So if you want a bit of magic, practicing in the middle of the night is your best bet.

Position

There is no ideal body position from which to practice the out-of-body state. Some occult approaches have proposed not crossing your legs during practice because it would put a strain on energy pathways. Others have proposed that your head should point toward magnetic north. However, none of these positions will have any effect on your ability to project.

There might be some benefit to the supine position (i.e., lying on your back). The outward focus can help to increase your level of wakefulness as your body falls asleep. But there are also a few drawbacks to this position. Many people feel too exposed in this position and are unable to fall asleep because of that. This position also increases the risk that you will end up in sleep paralysis, which is a complication to avoid.

In general, therefore, the best position for practice is simply the position you feel comfortable with. This may include lying on your side, on your back, or on your belly. Once you are in a preferred position, act as you normally would before falling asleep. Tossing and turning are often part of that process. So if you experience an urge to move, react as you normally would before your body falls asleep.

Purpose and Intent

The intent to have an OBE should never be far from your mind. You will have to keep it active throughout the night. It should also be active during the day. You will want to frequently think about projecting. It has to be a major priority in your daily and long-term goals.

Without purpose and intent, the mind easily wanders off into semi-sleep, and before you know it, thoughts take on a life of their own and you begin to dream. With intent and purpose, on the other hand, your level of wakefulness will be maintained. It is one of the driving forces behind a consciousness that is aware.

Intent and purpose also serve to ensure that you will wake up after each sleep cycle. It is merely a matter of being sufficiently motivated. For example, most people are probably familiar with waking up a few minutes before the alarm clock goes off because they have a plane to catch or an important meeting during the day. If you do experience difficulty waking up naturally, there are ways to get around it, such as by using an alarm clock.

Wakefulness throughout the night is also greatly enhanced by being in a good mood. Over time, you will learn to recognize those moments and take advantage of them. In the meantime, you will likely have some work ahead of you. So from here on out, let's continue with the practical aspects of out-of-body induction as a skill, and perhaps a little bit of art as well.

THE VIGIL METHOD: A SIX-STEP GUIDE

Step 1: Presleep Preparation

Immediately after retreating to bed, begin by reducing your inner dialogue—the usual chatter of your mind. The reason is to slow down your thoughts a little so that affirmations will have a greater effect. Thoughts will never cease completely, but they can be slowed down enough so that reactions are not so quick and your mind is quieter than usual.

A simple technique to slow down the chatter in your mind is to focus on a few single thoughts or a repetitive action for a while. Focusing on your breathing is a good way to accomplish this, especially in combination with another action. For example, each time you breathe in, focus on the darkness in front of your eyes, and each time you breathe out, defocus on the blackness in front of you. Doing so will slow down your mind fairly quickly.

This method of quieting your mind will also serve you well later in the night. For example, take note of how, during each inhale, you will feel slight muscle tension around the eyes, whereas these muscles relax with each exhale. This relaxation represents a point at which your mind moves into itself rather than outwardly into the physical world, which is exactly what you will need to do later on a more continual basis.

Once your mind feels relatively clear and alert, it is time to combine the exercise with some affirmations that reinforce your intent to project. Tell yourself you will wake up later on and that you are going to have an OBE. Envision yourself waking up in the near future rather than in the present, just as you would if you have an important appointment very early in the morning. It is a subtle but important difference.

Do not be afraid to back up your affirmations with some force and determination. You have to feel them in your gut as opposed to them merely being a robotic mantra. Any muscle tension is not a problem at this point—or later on, for that matter. You are not meditating. You are intending to wake up and have an OBE.

How often you will need to do this varies from individual to individual. If you do not wake up, double the time you spend on it the next time. Repeat the instruction to yourself as often as needed until the imprint in your subconscious is strong. Then, let it all go and allow yourself to fall asleep naturally with the knowledge and conviction that you will wake up later on.

Step 2: Establishing an Anchor

Immediately after waking up, or even while waking up, your first thoughts should be about having an OBE. If you're in luck and are relatively experienced, you might be able to trigger energy sensations almost immediately. Do not count on it, however. Usually, you will need to go through a good deal of preparation first. This begins with establishing an *anchor* in wakefulness.

An anchor is a repetitive mental activity focused on a fixed pattern of thought. Its primary purpose is to keep your mind active enough to prevent it from falling asleep. Its secondary purpose is to prime your subconscious for the activity of projection; as you drift toward the borderline of sleep, the anchor will help you remember your original intent.

Because the anchor acts as a reminder in the event that you lose some lucidity, it can be helpful to choose an activity that you in some way associate with the OBE. For example, a common anchor used by many successful projectors revolves around "energy work," such as imagining breathing in lights or colors while simultaneously visualizing the second body being charged and filled up with energy.

There are many variations on "energy work." You might prefer imagining energy sensations or high-energy vibrations surrounding your physical body. Alternatively, you can visualize your favorite color, or a variety of different colors, moving in front of your eyes as you establish a rhythmic, repetitive pattern. Just choose something you are comfortable with. In the end, it does not really matter what you do.

It is not unlikely that "energy work" only has a beneficial effect on achieving the out-of-body state because it functions as an anchor that provides the projector with some insulation from falling asleep. So do not hesitate to try different anchoring techniques, especially if you have no firm beliefs about these matters. The only real requirement is that the activity consist of a relatively simple mental action, which, albeit requiring some effort, should otherwise be fairly automatic and rhythmic.

It is important to be aware that anchoring may initially make you feel very sleepy. This is not because the anchoring activity fails to keep you awake but rather because your mind will resist the repetitive pattern and will have a strong tendency to wander off into uncontrolled thought, leading into oblivious sleep. The step of establishing an anchor is therefore not an easy task. You will need to exercise a great deal of vigilance to keep yourself from drifting toward the borderline of sleep. Repeat your affirmations to project. Keep your mind active. If you have to, use different anchoring techniques to break any boredom.

After around twenty minutes of anchoring activity, you will find yourself less inclined to move toward the borderline of sleep, at least in any non-lucid manner. Any sluggishness or drowsiness should have disappeared. Likewise, sleepy thoughts that initially tended to jump to the foreground and try to catch your attention will no longer arrive with the same intensity. Effectively, you will have created a barrier that prevents your mind from falling asleep while your physical body, due to natural sleep cycles, will eventually begin to insist on falling asleep.

The more time you spend building this barrier, the more impervious it will become. In fact, it is possible to build up this barrier enough to create an insomniac state of mind. You may find yourself frantically tossing and turning in bed. When this happens, do not worry too much about it. Your mind may feel quite hyperactive, but the natural tendency of the physical body to fall asleep will eventually catch up with you. It almost always does, even for those with real insomnia. And once it does, provided you have remained focused on your intent to project during all this time, it may even guarantee an entirely lucid transition into the out-of-body state.

Step 3: Drifting with an Anchor

Once the anchor is firmly established in your subconscious, either before or after reaching an insomniac state of mind, depending on your preference and ability, you can proceed to the next stage, in which you allow yourself to drift a little bit toward the borderline of sleep. You will continue to anchor, but you will intermittently allow your mind to drift, as if extending the connection between your anchor and awareness. You do this by taking on an unfocused perspective toward the edges of your awareness. The activity is quite similar to the unfocused perspective you took on earlier during presleep preparation while exhaling.

You will find that taking on this unfocused perspective will happen quite naturally. It is not something that requires effort or control. The mind will have a natural tendency to wander away from the boredom induced by anchoring. Ordinarily, such wandering leads straight to sleep. However, the anchoring activity of the previous step should ensure that you never drift away too far. Still, never give up on your anchoring activity for too long or else your mind will fall asleep.

As your mind drifts, you can expect some hypnagogic phenomena to occur, which, in the initial stages, typically consist of very momentary, vague, and undefined forms, such as different shades of gray or a sense of movement somewhere in the darkness in front of you. Alternatively, you may experience brief images or incoherent patterns of thought, which are yet another sign that your mind is moving toward sleep. Each time this occurs, you should go back to your anchoring activity for a while and then allow your mind to wander yet again.

Over time, as you continue to intermittently anchor and drift, you should be able to perceive increasingly complex imagery. You will be able to drift further away, extending the link between your attention and your anchor, but without much risk of completely losing lucidity. You may experience seeing faces, landscapes, objects, houses, animals, people, or anything else you could possibly imagine. When this occurs, you may no longer need to anchor each and every time after an image occurs.

Do not concern yourself too much with the content of these images. Your purpose at this point is not to analyze all these different phenomena and wonder what they all mean. You can always do that later on. Do not try to hold onto these images, either. Early on, you will not be able to, nor is it necessary.

After a while, you will find yourself increasingly lucid during the experience of these images—perhaps not as lucid as you might like, but you will know you're getting somewhere when you start to experience some level of synchronicity between your mind and the visual scenes. That is, the scenes will start to naturally follow your thought patterns, emotions, and concerns. For example, while having a thought about some work you might need to do tomorrow, you might see an office desk in front of you, or alternatively, while thinking about having forgotten to turn off the stove, you might see a house on fire.

You might even be able to invite certain selected images into awareness through your intent. Some personal favorites are looking at trees, large-scale nature scenes, lakes, seascapes, and beautiful mansions and other houses. Start playing around with seeing your favorite images in your mind's eye, but don't create the image in terms of creative visualization. Rather, you try to "see" a favorite image for only a very brief period of time as if it comes out of nowhere. If it's vague, do not try to make it more vivid. Get on with the next one.

As you continue to pick up imagery, expect energy sensations to occur every now and then. These energy sensations will often relate to the type of anchoring activity you engage in. For example, imagining light may lead to some stroboscopic effects, whereas imagining an aura around your body may lead to feeling a short burst of vibrations.

These are all good signs, but do not expect too much to come of them. For these sensations to really take off, your physical body has to fall asleep or be very close to doing so. If your body is indeed ready to fall asleep, that's great, but otherwise, just ignore these sensations. Do not try to hold onto them.

Finally, be aware that in your practice of drifting with an anchor, a *yo-yo effect* will take place.[1] You will shift into semi-lucidity, an image will begin to appear, and as soon as you start to notice, you'll shift back to complete wakefulness. You want this to happen! There is no need to go "deep" as if you were meditating and trying to reach some elusive state of consciousness. It is simply about waiting for that moment when your physical body is ready to fall asleep while your mind is not.

Step 4: Free-Flow

So far, the anchor has served to provide you with some protective insulation from falling asleep, as well as to prime your subconscious toward the goal of projecting. In the next step, the anchor will continue to perform these functions but without the need to actively engage in any anchoring activity. Rather, you will engage in a free-flow exercise in which you allow your awareness to drift without paying any attention to your anchor.

The reason for dropping the anchor is that it has served its purpose, and it is far too rigid an activity for your body to easily fall asleep. Having gone through the activity is important, however, as the anchor will continue to exert an effect, even while not actively maintained. Only if you are highly practiced can you skip the previous steps and go straight to free-flow in your practice. Even then, vigilance will have to be maintained to prevent you from falling asleep.

Begin the free-flow exercise by once again allowing your mind to drift toward the margins of your attention. At the same time, do realize that the absence of an anchor considerably increases the risk of losing lucidity. Consequently, remind yourself often of your intent to OBE, and exercise an appropriate level of mental vigilance throughout your practice. In a sense, these reminders act as an anchor, but one that you use only to the extent that the situation demands.

As you let your mind drift, do not solely try to catch any imagery, but give yourself some leverage to engage in all manner of incoherent thoughts and feelings, as you usually do before falling asleep. This may also include tossing and turning now and then or moving your pillows to get into a more comfortable position. These things will help your body fall asleep. You might even allow yourself to lose lucidity for a while, though never so much that you find yourself unable to return to wakefulness. This is an area of practice in which projecting is more of an art than a skill. You need to be able to intuitively assess how likely it is that you will lose lucidity as you approach the borderline of sleep. It is never exactly the same.

Allowing yourself to drift further may also mean that you may occasionally experience non-lucid dream vignettes. These short dreams develop from the sort of isolated imagery you experienced during your anchoring practice. Be very careful about getting too involved in mini-dreams. They are only one step removed from oblivious sleep, and you should be more awake than is the case during mini-dreams.

For example, if you have spent the entire day working in the garden, do not be surprised to find yourself engaged in exactly the same activity during a mini-dream. These short dreams are okay to have for perhaps a few seconds, but if you lose yourself in one for any longer, it is a clear warning sign that you are about to lose lucidity entirely. Pull back into full wakefulness as soon as you find yourself engaging in a mini-dream. Repeat the anchoring exercise for a couple of minutes if you need to.

Throughout the free-flow exercise, continue to balance on the borderline of sleep, picking up imagery as you go along and watching any incoherent thought patterns develop while intermittently reminding yourself not to fall asleep. Eventually, you will reach a delightful pattern of free-flow, easily moving in and out of sleep, but without any real risk of completely losing lucidity. Your body will become increasingly relaxed, while your mind will simply be enjoying the flow. From here on out, once your body is ready to fall asleep, energy sensations are likely to ensue. You do not need to do anything specific to generate them.

Step 5: Transitioning

Once a sufficient buildup in sleep pressure has been established, energy sensations will begin to occur that are strong and persistent enough to carry you into the out-of-body state. For most novice projectors, this is more likely to happen in a semi-lucid stage of consciousness, in a partial state of sensory reduction in which an image, thought, or feeling suddenly catches your attention. Fearful imagery, an especially strong trigger in this regard, can be put to use quite successfully, although it may not be advisable to purposely seek out such imagery.

Keep in mind that energy sensations may *not* occur if you gain lucidity while deep inside the hypnagogic stage of sleep. You are no longer connected to the physical body in any way, and as such, there will be an insufficient level of sensory input to allow for the perception of energy sensations. This is an unproblematic phenomenon, however, since you will have largely completed the transition process without knowing it. You may still engage in some sort of separation, such as, for example, "swinging" or "rolling" out of the body, but usually there will not be much of a transition left to complete.

While semi-lucid transitions are common as you start out, do not underestimate the degree of desynchronization between mind and body that you might be able to establish during the free-flow exercise. Transitions into the out-of-body state do not need to be semi-lucid or mentally clouded affairs. Energy sensations can be triggered with complete physical body awareness.

Under ideal conditions, you can even move around physically in bed, with ongoing energy sensations, completely wide awake and yet able to project at any point in time without any lapse in consciousness. This situation is often accompanied by a sense of "quickening," a heightening of arousal that, paradoxically, does not remove you further from sleep. Instead, it brings you closer.

For example, have you ever been tossing and turning in bed, unable to get any sleep, until a point when all the chatter in your mind comes to a sudden halt and your physical body feels as if it were made out of a pleasant, warm liquid or jelly that trembles and rocks ever so lightly? Under these conditions, if you relax your mind just a little more, touching ever so slightly on the borderline of sleep, a sense of quickening will follow—a sudden increase in arousal. Once it does, energy sensations will ensue almost immediately.

The further progression of the transition process is primarily guided by your mind by nudging itself toward sleep. It is the same mental movement as when you dipped into the hypnagogic stage of sleep, except that you will be entirely lucid. It will feel like moving more deeply into the energy sensations. They will intensify as you do so.

Ignore any feelings of dread or terror that may coincide with this movement. There may be a sense of approaching the object of your fear, which is disconcerting, but once you have completed the transition process, everything will be quite calm and peaceful. Eventually, this layer of fear will disappear from your experiences, and you will be left with the accompanying heightened sense of arousal alone, now fully claimed as your own.

Until then, especially if the sense of terror is strong, you will have to be braver than you ever imagined. A great deal of courage will be required. You should feel very proud of yourself if you continue to push through. It is a significant accomplishment when a person is willing to risk life and limb for a greater goal. You are not really doing that, of course, but it will certainly feel that way, which makes it quite a heroic feat.

Finally, be careful not to move too quickly through the transition process. Your physical body is in the process of falling asleep, and if you are not careful, you will lose lucidity in the process. It is a very fine thread of consciousness on which you have to maintain your balance. Then, as you move further in the transition process, you will notice the energy sensations intensify until they reach a peak. It is here, or shortly thereafter, where you are free of physical limitations and have established the out-of-body state.

Step 6: Separation and Engagement

If you experience difficulty in separating from the physical body, you have simply not yet completed the transition process. You will need to nudge your mind closer toward the borderline of sleep until your physical body falls asleep more completely. Also, remember that you do not necessarily need to go through any "exit" technique. In theory, although it won't be so easy the first time, you should be able to simply get up out of bed in your phantom body, which will have replaced your physical body at the end of the transition process.

If you experience difficulty, it can be useful to go through an exit technique. The act of moving "out" of the body will give your mind something to occupy itself with, which is likely to further deepen the process of sensory reduction. However, always try to use a technique that is natural and effortless. For example, rolling over, as you would normally do when lying in bed, is an excellent technique that will provide you with the feeling of leaving the body. If you get stuck, try not to force it—this will only make things worse. Instead, relax your mind a little bit more, which will result in the further intensification of energy sensations, and you will find that moving out of body is much easier to accomplish.

Usually, upon exiting, if you have maintained body awareness during the transition, you will see the environment that you physically occupied moments before. If you have maintained no body awareness during the transition, the environments you encounter will tend to be of a more nonphysical nature. If you slow down the process, you may also find yourself inside of the void preceding the appearance of an out-of-body environment. When you are inside of the void, you have completed the transition process, and you will only need to get up, fly away, or engage visually in order to enter an out-of-body environment.

Welcome to the club!

SUPPLEMENTARY METHODS AND TECHNIQUES

The vigil method has been fine-tuned for more than two decades as I have become more proficient at inducing the OBE over time. It is in fact how I induced my first experience, rather accidentally, by merely preventing myself from falling asleep for a prolonged period of time. In essence, it is that simple. The stepwise approach in combination with anchoring makes it even more effective than would otherwise be the case. If properly applied, it should allow a substantial number of people to induce an OBE within a reasonable amount of time.

Of course, it is unlikely that the vigil method will work for everyone.

There is still a lot that remains to be done in the area of voluntary OBE inducement. However, do not get frustrated if you're not successful right away. No energy is wasted since the efforts of the previous night carry over to the next. If you are not successful after two or three weeks despite putting in the time and effort, it's likely that another problem stands in the way, which you will need to identify in order to get any further.

If you are successful and you stick with it, you'll find that it becomes progressively easier to induce the out-of-body state. You may find yourself easily waking up with a single intent instead of having to repeat it to yourself endlessly before sleeping. You might be able to jump straight to the free-flow stage without using any specific anchor other than your intent and without the risk of falling sleep. You might wake up with ongoing energy sensations and be able to project immediately. You might also get lazy, skipping steps because you are in a rush and failing as a result.

Of course, becoming a frequent flyer does not mean you will have an OBE every night for the rest of your life. A more reasonable goal would be to have one or two each week when you're working on it, while at other times, when things get too busy in real life, you may have none at all for a prolonged period. Do not ignore your daily responsibilities.

Keep in mind that your activities in the out-of-body state and how you are in the world are not separate. As you become stronger and more effective in daily life, this will also be the case for your activities in the out-of-body state. So nothing is lost, even during periods of time when you are not focused on OBEs.

In the meantime, when you do have time to practice, a number of supplementary methods and techniques can increase your overall level of proficiency. These include 1) manipulating the transition, 2) keeping a dream journal, and 3) Hemi-Sync.

Manipulating the Transition

The type of transition you will experience primarily depends on your focus of attention during the transition process. For example, if you primarily maintain a visual focus during the transition process, you will experience energy sensations of a more visual nature, such as lightning or flashes. As a result, an asomatic transition is more likely to occur.

Conversely, if you remain focused on the physical body, you are more likely to experience tactile sensations, such as vibrations or trembling. Under these circumstances, a parasomatic transition is more likely to occur.

None of this should really concern you too much in the initial stages of your practice. It is generally best to flow with whatever that comes. However, as you become more practiced, you may wish to effectuate a specific type of transition. You might prefer an asomatic transition, which is effectuated by maintaining a solely visual focus and paying very little or no attention to your physical body. Or you might want to engage in a parasomatic transition by remaining mainly focused on energetic sensations of a tactile nature.

This may prove to be difficult to accomplish since usually, once energy sensations have been triggered, you will find yourself on a roller coaster with a clear path carved out in front of you. For example, if your experience starts out with vibrations, it is quite difficult to change them to something of an entirely visual nature. It is here where the anchoring activity you have engaged in previously is important.

For example, if the anchoring included imagining vibrations across your body, you can expect energy sensations of a tactile nature to occur. This is then naturally followed by a parasomatic transition, during which body awareness is maintained. Conversely, if your anchoring activity was more visual in nature, such as when imagining only lights or colors, you can expect energy sensations of a visual nature to occur, giving rise to an asomatic transition. You will therefore be able to make one type of transition more likely than the other, even before energy sensations have started, depending on the anchoring technique you use.

This is certainly not a foolproof method. Ultimately, the type of energy sensations you will experience depends on where your attention goes at the onset or during the transition process itself. If your attention is all over the place, as is initially the case for most, you can expect a plethora of energy sensations across different sensory modalities. However, matching up your anchoring technique with the type of transition you prefer to experience will at least give you a good head start. The following are some examples of anchoring techniques to use until you find your own:

Color Breathing: Imagine breathing in your favorite color and filling up your entire body from top to bottom. This method leads to parasomatic transitions, including many visual phenomena in the course of the transition. You may also imagine breathing in sparkling energy, in which case tactile sensations are more likely to occur during the transition.

Swinging: Imagine yourself swinging back and forth in bed or moving back and forth on a swing. This is likely to lead to a parasomatic transition with pronounced sensations of movement as well as various tactile sensations.

Flying: Imagine yourself flying over a relatively monotonous landscape such as a desert, forest, or mountain area. Increase the complexity of the environment, or the imagined flight path itself, when too much boredom begins to set in. This anchoring technique tends to lead to an asomatic transition, provided that a visual focus is maintained at the onset of energy sensations. This does not mean you will automatically be flying over the imagined landscape at the end of the transition process. Flow with whatever imagery occurs when energy sensations of a visual nature commence.

Light Show: Visualize your favorite color, or a variety of different colors, moving in front of your eyes. Establish a rhythmic, repetitive pattern by allowing the colors to move in patterns. Try to remain visually focused without attention to any sort of (imagined) body. This will make an asomatic transition more likely to occur.

Walking, driving, or paddling: Imagine a favorite scene that includes a rhythmic, repetitive movement where you walk down a path, drive down a road, or paddle down a river without much focus on an imagined body while doing so. Do not focus too much on the imagined bodily activity itself (e.g., driving, walking or paddling). Instead, focus on the imagined environment. This will ensure an asomatic transition. The method generally gives rise to a gentler visual transition than an anchor involving flying.

Third-Eye Method: Imagine an infinite reservoir of purple energy at the center of your forehead, and whirl it in a band of energy around your head. Keep whirling it around your head, each time picking up more energy from the infinite reservoir, until the energy becomes increasingly vital and expansive around your head. This anchoring technique tends to lead to a powerful semi-asomatic transition. It will be accompanied by strong background awareness of the head space but without any other sort of body boundary. Expect a roller-coaster experience. It's not for the faint of heart.

Keeping a Dream Journal

In the course of your practice, especially as you are starting out, maintaining a dream journal is highly beneficial, likely even mandatory. It will thin the veil between waking and sleeping, and as a result, your intent to have an OBE will have a greater chance of getting through. It will also increase the frequency of wake-ups, which usually occur immediately after you have a dream and which provide opportunities for practice.

To maintain a dream journal, begin by writing down every sliver of a dream you remember right after waking up, even if it is only one word or sentence. If you don't remember any dreams at all, write down that you do not remember anything. Sooner or later, you will begin to remember something, even if it is just a hunch or a feeling. Write down every snippet diligently, and after a while you will begin to remember your dreams in more detail.

Maintaining a dream journal will also increase the likelihood that you will wake up with energy sensations, which will give you the opportunity to project immediately, without any lengthy preparation. It will also make you a much lighter sleeper, and as such, it is especially helpful for deep sleepers, who are generally at a disadvantage in this area.

Another benefit of maintaining a dream journal is that it will help you to develop the skills needed to have an OBE. For example, if your goal for the night has been to have an OBE, expect that intent to bleed into your dream life. If these dreams do not already happen naturally, you can also provoke them by telling yourself to work in the dream state toward having an OBE.

Common themes in your dreams may include flying, high-speed running, and even running in slow motion. Alternatively, you might find yourself attempting to perform almost impossible tasks and actions in your dreams that would require some sort of supernatural talent to complete successfully. All of these represent situations in which your mind is coming to terms with the mobility of consciousness, which will have a positive effect on your overall ability to project.

A dream journal may also produce lucid experiences initiated from the dream state. It is not as exotic as initiating an OBE from the waking state, but it is an entirely legitimate launch pad. If you use this approach, however, developing some navigational skills will probably need to be your first order of business. As far as the purposeful induction of these experiences, I am happy to refer to other writings in this area, such as Stephen LaBerge's classic book *Lucid Dreaming.*[2]

Hemi-Sync

Hemi-Sync is a process developed by the Monroe Institute to induce a state of synchronicity between the two hemispheres of the brain through the use of audio technology. Specifically, it utilizes binaural beats delivered to each ear to create a frequency-following response in the brain in order to induce certain states of awareness conducive to the induction of an OBE.

Hemi-Sync quite effectively induces certain altered states of consciousness and, as such, can be useful in your practice to effectuate an OBE as well. It is no magic bullet, however. Its use won't guarantee an OBE, nor is it specifically intended to do that. However, it does facilitate the exploration of consciousness in a similar way as remote viewing or meditation, during which some background awareness of the physical context usually remains.

One of the more effective uses of Hemi-Sync technology might be as a preliminary step toward establishing the out-of-body state. For example, utilizing the tapes prior to sleep, while practicing your affirmations, is quite beneficial. They also greatly assist with inducing imagery or the provocation of all manner of other sensations. You can use them as a prelude to the OBE in the middle of the night as well.

The technology is also quite useful for learning how to induce a state of sensory reduction without heavy reliance on natural sleep cycles. It is indeed quite possible to directly induce such a state of sensory reduction, although for most people it remains quite difficult to reach the required depth for an OBE to occur. I suggest you try it out for yourself to establish whether this technology is useful to you.

There are also new technologies on the horizon to assist people in reaching the out-of-body state. For example, a promising new audio technology recently released by the Monroe Institute is Spatial Angle Modulation, which is based on quantum mind hypotheses.[3]

Ultimately, however, technology will only carry you so far, and it is probably a good idea to not become too dependent on it. But, given the difficulty of establishing the out-of-body state, a little helping hand is always welcome. Perhaps one day, a magical device will indeed be invented.

Chapter 10
Navigating Consciousness

THREE-DIMENSIONAL MODES OF TRAVEL

Perhaps one of the most ignored aspects of the OBE in the literature is the issue of travel. Travel is usually not a problem if you choose to stay "local." You separate from the physical senses, get out of bed with your phantom body, and simply walk or fly where you want to go. More problematic is reaching "long-distance" destinations, especially those that are often referred to as *nonphysical* locations. There are neither road signs nor highways to heaven anywhere to be found. So how does one reach these types of environments?

Traditional conceptualizations typically objectify nonphysical locations as "astral planes" that are located around Earth's atmosphere, as if these locations are somehow part of physical reality. Consequently, most methods of reaching nonphysical locations are relatively straightforward extensions of physical travel that involve "flying there." Robert Bruce, for example, advises flying upward into the sky at a 45-degree angle in order to reach so-called "astral plane structures."[1] Other variations of travel include moving through tunnels or magical doorways or entering mirrors in order to transport oneself from one environment to another.

Even more modern approaches that explicitly adhere to the notion that the OBE involves travel in consciousness still use similar geographic metaphors. Robert Monroe, for example, in his earlier work, envisioned nonphysical locations to be organized in layered rings surrounding Earth.[2]

However, three-dimensional modes of travel, in which distance needs to be traversed, essentially constitute a metaphorical confusion, not only conceptually but experientially as well. No matter what it may feel like, you do not actually move through three-dimensional space when trying to reach a nonphysical location. Likewise, there are no tunnels, magical doorways, or astral-plane structures leading to nonphysical locations—at least not in any objective manner.

If you do experience such a physical-like or objectified mode of transportation, it is only because a *change in attention* is represented in a perceptual format that makes sense to you. Some of these symbolic modes of transportation may be highly individualized, whereas others may be more widely shared, such as, for example, the experience of traveling through a tunnel of light before reaching one's destination. They do, however, always represent indirect translations of what is really happening.

While the issue of travel may appear trivial for the pragmatic projector, it is important to realize that navigating consciousness in a physical-like manner brings along problems associated with physicality. For example, traveling in consciousness *with* a second body automatically invites the sense that distance will have to be traversed to get from one place to another. If you are not careful, you might be flying forever without ending up anywhere. Or alternatively, you might not be able to pick up enough speed, or even fall down, due to yet another physical belief (i.e., gravity). As such, traveling in a physical-like manner creates several *psychological load factors* that keep you relatively immobile in the wider spectrum of consciousness.

The problem with three-dimensional flight is further compounded by beliefs that you have to put in a great deal of effort in order to reach certain locations. For example, if you believe more spiritual environments are more difficult to reach, or that you have to move through lower-level environments in order to reach them, this belief easily becomes a self-fulfilling prophecy.

The difficulties associated with three-dimensional modes of travel are the result of numerous habits, assumptions, and beliefs imposed by our physical experience. It is virtually impossible to get rid of them overnight—the idea of having a body being one of them. However, it is essential, at least on a conceptual level, to understand that consciousness is a nonlocal phenomenon. It does not need to travel to get anywhere. Nowhere is this more evident than inside of the void, which is *nonlocal* space.

TRAVEL IN THE FOURTH DIMENSION: BEYOND TIME AND SPACE

To fully understand the void, it is important to realize that it does not only occur at the end of the transition process. Rather, the void constitutes a space of nothingness that exists in between *all* OBE environments. It is the invisible glue that permeates all conceivable environments you could possibly encounter.

Donald DeGracia offers the following helpful metaphor for understanding the void:

> "We all know that on the radio there are radio stations you can tune into up and down the dial. And what is in between these radio stations? Nothing is, and when you tune into a place on the dial where there is no radio station you get STATIC. The way I figure it, when I'm in an OBE episode, this is just like tuning into a radio station, and when I'm in the void, this is just like tuning into the static between radio stations where nothing exists."[3]

The void is always a *preamble* to a three-dimensional location. It is not a location itself. Spatial dimensions do not really apply in the void, and while you will perceive three-dimensional depth inside of the void, this is an illusionary phenomenon. You are looking into nonlocal space—the vast depth of consciousness.

You are, in fact, at the quintessential center of all the perceptual environments you could possibly encounter. No environment is located any further away than another. You merely have to "tune in to" an OBE environment from inside of the void. This makes the void extremely well suited as a launch pad from which to delve into OBE environments.

REACHING THE VOID FOLLOWING TRANSITION

Transitions into the out-of-body state can occur in the space of only a few seconds, making it easy to bypass the void and become part of an OBE environment before you know it. Indeed, most projectors pass through the void without even noticing it is there.

However, to experience nonlocal consciousness and benefit from the navigational opportunities it offers, it is crucial to learn how to hold still at the void before you immerse yourself in an OBE environment. You may have to learn how to slow down the process of transitioning to ensure that you actually end up in the void.

Also, to avoid premature immersion in an out-of-body environment, you will need to block out visual perceptions of your immediate environment in the course of the transition process. This will ensure that the external environment remains completely dark so that you arrive at the void at the end of the transition process.

The Void Following a Parasomatic Transition

Following a parasomatic transition, you will generally have body awareness. You will likely also still feel yourself lying in bed. Nonetheless, as long as you only perceive darkness in front of you, you may consider yourself to be in the void.

If you find yourself lying in bed following a parasomatic transition, it is advisable to fly up a little bit in order to lose any remaining tactile sensations. This may also allow you to perceive white "stars" inside of the void, which will make it easier to connect with nonphysical environments.

Again, however, do not assume that you are actually located somewhere. After flying up, it might feel *as if* you are floating in a dark bedroom or above your house. but you are not actually located anywhere. Of course, if you do engage visually, it is likely that your house or bedroom will appear, but this is simply due to your intent and expectation.

Once you have established yourself in the void, try to relax as much as possible and enjoy floating around without doing anything else. In general, as long as you do not associate the blackness with anything negative, the void is a very pleasant place to be. You can feel very much like "yourself" there, especially when body awareness has been maintained.

You can also look into the void without any increased risk of waking up as long as you do not fixate your gaze too much. The void is not an easily lost, momentary state of consciousness where you only briefly lose contact with the physical body, as is commonly the case with meditative practice. Once you're there, you are *really* there.

The Void Following an Asomatic Transition

An asomatic transition leads to a "purer" manifestation of the void since without body awareness, your perception is at a minimum. You will be approaching "zero-point energy" as pure mind floating inside a blackness that is absolute. If you were to reach deeply into the void with your mind in order to reach a destination, it would almost be as if you were already there. Psychological distance can be traversed in the blink of an eye. If any sense of movement occurs, it is felt as a mental movement where you "phase into" the environment.

Journal Entry — Wednesday, November 19, 2008, 2:10 am

It was my second OBE of the night. Energy sensations came on quickly as a high-pitched wave of energy, more auditory than vibrational. I soon lost contact with my body, including any sense of spatial position. There was no second body. I had no outline. No form. There was only mind.

The void surrounded me, and even though I was separate from it, my mind seemed to be part of it. I was able to "see" in multiple directions. It was as if "vectors of attention" were extending outwardly from my mind—a most peculiar sensation.

I began to follow one of the vectors with my mind—like following a thread of mind extending deep into the void. In a way, it felt like physical movement except that I moved along the thread mentally. The speed at which I moved was directly related to how quickly I shifted my attention.

I moved up and down a couple of threads without intending to arrive anywhere. There was a "destination" at the end of these threads, but I was far too fascinated with the mental movement itself. I pulled back each time just before I was about to reach the end of a particular thread.

I then focused on a thread that extended very deep into the void. It went off in a sideways direction. Even though I could not sense what was at the end of it, the destination felt interesting—something different.

It did not take long to "travel" down the thread. There was a sense of mental movement, and then, at the end of it, an environment appeared around me. There, I quickly lost my ordinary sense of self.

I watched "myself" on the phone with a salesperson, ordering a microphone. Apparently, I was in the process of getting some new hardware for two computers located next to me. The microphone went with a router. My wife was with me, listening to the conversation.

As I experienced myself talking to the person, I wondered what a microphone had to do with a router. It was an unfamiliar piece of technology, yet it was familiar to this other self. I objected to the price at first, but the salesperson said it was an excellent brand.

After I informed the salesperson that I would take it, he transferred me to a female operator to get my name and address. I gave her my information, which was exactly the same address where I live now. Even the postal code was the same. Shortly after finishing the conversation, I found myself back in bed.

THE QUICK-SWITCH METHOD

The *quick-switch method* of transportation through the void was initially defined by Robert Monroe.[4] While his early experiences were strongly characterized by geographic metaphors, they took a different turn when he discovered a new mode of transportation.

Initially, he described this method as stretching his awareness like an elastic band to his intended destination, letting go, and then being catapulted toward it. Over time, however, this process began to increasingly resemble a change in attention, and he came to use the *phasing* metaphor to describe his experiences.

Using the quick-switch or phasing mode of transportation is as close as any projector can come to experiencing travel in consciousness in a nonsymbolic, direct manner. During the switch itself, there is no body awareness involved, at least not until you arrive at your destination. Rather than moving your phantom body to get there, you move your *attention* from one place to another. This is relatively easy to accomplish under less-than-lucid circumstances, but quite difficult when highly lucid and aware. The method can be learned, however, and once fully controlled, it extends your reach in consciousness considerably.

Phasing In

Phasing in is the process by which you connect to an out-of-body environment. This process is best initiated from the void, which therefore begins with very little perception and in complete darkness.

If you have body awareness inside of the void, which is typically the case following a parasomatic transition, phasing in will be a little more difficult to accomplish. The presence of a second body will tempt you to *fly* to a destination rather than merely changing your attention.

Even so, phasing into an out-of-body environment from the void can also be accomplished with body awareness. You will just have to forget about your phantom body as you phase into the environment. This will usually happen automatically.

Keep in mind that imagination in combination with outward engagement toward the void is a very powerful tool in the navigation of consciousness. You may become part of an OBE environment in the blink of an eye.

However, it is still worthwhile to practice slowing down the process of phasing in to increase your overall level of proficiency in the navigation of consciousness. This is rather like learning how to fly a fighter jet at near-stalling speed. The activity may seem at odds with the purpose of a jet, but being able to do so makes you a much better pilot.

The process of phasing in starts with moving some of your attention *away* from the blackness surrounding you. Focus on your own thoughts and inner life. Meanwhile, maintain a relaxed outlook toward the void as if watching it out of the corner of your eye.

Next, actively imagine your destination, or state your intent as to where you wish to go, while simultaneously reaching out with part of your attention *as if* there is something behind the veil of darkness. It may take some practice before you are able to do both at the same time, but if properly applied, vague forms and shapes will begin to appear in the void.

You may, for example, perceive small patches of gray or perhaps several streaks of light and color intermixed with the blackness of the void. There might be a sense of movement or emanation, as if there is some sort of activity behind the veil of darkness. Whatever your perceptions might be, initially maintain a relaxed outlook toward them. Then, as these perceptions begin to increase in complexity, focus more of your attention toward them until the *movie-screen effect* occurs.

The movie-screen effect is rather like sitting in a movie theater in which you watch the screen in living color with darkness surrounding you. You are watching the screen from a distance, with most of you remaining inside of the void. If you were to completely focus on the scenery, however, you would forget about the void surrounding you, and you would become part of the environment, similar to the process of becoming engrossed in a movie.

The benefit of the movie-screen effect is that it allows you to *preview* out-of-body environments. If an environment is not to your liking, you only have to remove your attention from the movie screen and return it back to the void surrounding you. Conversely, if the environment seems interesting and you wish to become part of it, all that is required is to allow yourself to become captivated by it.

In some cases, there might be a sense of mental movement before you become part of the environment, but in most instances, it will happen quite naturally. If you did not already have a body, you will generally have one as soon as you are part of the environment. Environments tend to impose body awareness.

PHASING IN FROM THE VOID

1. Move your attention away from the void and actively imagine your destination. You may also simply set a strong verbal intent.

2. While imagining your destination, move part of your awareness back toward the void, as if looking out of the corner of your eye. Find the correct balance—the point of manifestation.

3. Preliminary abstract perceptions will begin to form in the void. Maintain the proper balance between inward focus, where you actively imagine your destination, and outward focus toward the void until perceptions begin to increase in complexity.

4. The movie-screen effect will begin to appear. You may now divert all your attention toward the scenery.

5. Watch the scenery and allow yourself to be captivated by it until you become part of the environment as an active participant.

Journal Entry — Sunday, February 8, 2004, 3:00 am

[Continued from p. 52] ...I decided to trigger some imagery in the void above me. I relaxed my awareness while reaching out with my mind at the same time. A scene popped up almost immediately. Two dogs were fighting, one of them quite viciously.

I berated myself for not having reached out further. It seemed like some lower-level phenomenon playing itself out in front of me. One of the dogs was my own. She was only a little pug. Luckily, she seemed to handle herself quite well against the much bigger, vicious dog.

So far, I had been observing all of this from a distance. I had no intention of putting myself in the middle of the fight and broke the connection before I got immersed in it. The scenery promptly disappeared as I turned my attention away from it.

I was still lying in bed, staring up into the void, and decided to try to reach out a second time. This time, however, I reached as far as I could. Almost immediately, my entire perceptual field was filled with an imposing scene.

A huge golden chariot surrounded by white light raced toward me. Inside the chariot was a tall, larger-than-life individual. He had long white hair and a wild white beard.

The chariot came at me fast, and while I was only observing, the white surroundings had already almost enveloped my position inside of the void. It would not take long for the chariot to reach my position and for me to become part of the environment.

I decided to break the connection yet again. I did not want to end up under the chariot's wheels. This time, I found myself back in my real body.

Phasing Out

Phasing out is the process by which you *disconnect* from an out-of-body environment back into the void—that is, by leaving any environment without returning back to the body and without having to start the transition process all over again. As such, phasing out is a practice that has the potential to significantly extend the duration of your projections.

Phasing out essentially consists of phasing in, in reverse. So the first step involves not being an active participant in the out-of-body environment. You cease all interaction with events occurring in the environment, which is best accomplished by finding a quiet corner somewhere.

Next, observe the scenery as if you were watching an unimpressive B movie. This detached stance will result in a destabilization of the environment, often accompanied by "special effects."

For example, it is not uncommon for the environment to start to shake and tremble. Then, once a crescendo is reached, the environment disappears from view. Alternatively, your entire perceptual field may shatter into separate pieces as if it were made of glass. Yet another effect is a misalignment of the environment with your visual field, wherein only part of the environment remains visible while the other has fallen out of view. This is similar to the effect that used to occur in movie theaters now and again when the film got misaligned with the projector track.

PHASING OUT FROM THE VOID

1. Find a quiet spot in the out-of-body environment that gives you a general overview. Act as if you are not really part of the environment.

2. The environment will destabilize. Focus on any darkness that becomes apparent.

3. Allow the dissolution of the environment to unfold naturally.

4. Complete the process by turning all of your attention toward the void.

There are as many variations of phasing out as there are special effects in movies, and the manner in which it occurs is not very important. The primary thing to remember about phasing out is to focus your attention on any blackness that occurs as a result of the environment beginning to break up. Meanwhile, it is vital that you allow the environment to dissolve naturally, without too much focus on any of the remnants of the perceptual environment. Then, as you divert an increasing amount of attention toward the void, empty blackness will slowly fill up your field of vision until you are once again "in between" worlds.

Journal Entry — Monday, November 6, 2006, 4:30 am

[Continued from p. 209] ...I found myself sitting on a chair in a theater. There were many other attendees, most of them facing the podium up

ahead. Apparently, however, the "show" had not yet started. There were still a lot of people walking around, not yet having taken their seats.

I then noticed someone trying to get my attention. It was my father running up to me. He told me that the gathering was a special event organized for our family—a celebration of some kind. This all seemed rather odd to me, which was good because I regained some of the lucidity I had lost earlier.

I walked to the back of the theater, leaving my father and everyone else behind. From the back, I had a better view of the entire place. On the stage, someone was telling a story or perhaps reciting a poem. I was too far away from the podium to be able to hear anything.

I quickly lost interest as I remembered my original intent. I had to leave the dream and return to the void. No sooner had I realized this when the entire dream environment began to dissolve, quite literally breaking up into shattered pieces of mirrored glass as the darkness of the void became evident in between the pieces. It was a spectacular effect.

For a moment, I was captivated by the implications of a coherent dream unfolding in separate pieces. I could actually see dream fragments continuing to play out on the separate pieces! I had no time to waste, however.

I quickly focused my attention toward the blackness that appeared in between the pieces of glass, which then soon disappeared entirely from view. I once again found myself back in the void... [Continued on p. 209].

INTERMEDIARY METHODS OF NONLOCAL TRAVEL

The quick-switch method is not something you will learn overnight. It took Robert Monroe, who first described the process, nearly twenty years before he became adept at it. The reason lies in the fact that the method challenges beliefs that are intimately tied to our physical existence, most notably the idea that in order to get somewhere, you have to *move* there. This is an extremely ingrained belief, and because of that, you will often be tempted to fly to your destination, especially when you have body awareness inside of the void.

Likewise, even though spatial distance does not apply literally in the void, there is still a *psychological distance* between you and any potential environment you may encounter.[5]

For example, if you are in a fearful mood, the "distance" between you and fearful environments decreases. Unconscious mood factors and belief systems may affect your destination as well, sometimes for the worse, sometimes for the better. This includes any beliefs and assumptions you carry regarding the organization of out-of-body environments in the void.

Given these habits and beliefs, which you will not overcome overnight, there is nothing wrong with relying on intermediary methods of nonlocal travel to some extent, which may include flying to your destination as well as flying in directions you feel most comfortable with. Time spent out of body is limited, and a pragmatic approach is often necessary in order to deal with travel effectively. So if you feel you have to fly in the void in order to get somewhere, do not let a purist approach stop you from doing so.

Of course, when flying in the void, sooner or later you will have to perceptually engage to enter an out-of-body environment. If you fly for too long, expect the OBE to be cut short and to find yourself back in your body. You cannot fly without intent and still hope to end up somewhere. You will have to *do* something to get somewhere.

By far the most effective technique is to make a *tactile entry* into an environment. Try to feel for ground below you as if there were actually an environment there. Almost invariably, you will feel ground under your feet, and in many cases the environment will immediately become visible as well.

You can also combine a tactile entry with visualizing the environment you wish to enter. This is a practice that comes very close to the quick-switch except for the fact that it includes body awareness during the switch.

If you experience "blindness" after having made a tactile entry, do not peer *into* the darkness as if you were really unable to see. Instead, try to open up perception by using the phasing-in technique discussed earlier. If that fails, engage in whatever activity feels like a convincing method to make an environment appear.

Journal Entry — Friday, April 27, 2007, 2:45 am

I woke up in the middle of the night, induced the vibrations, and floated upward a few feet until I had firmly established myself inside of the void. I then began to descend, falling deeper into it.

I moved down for what felt like around fifty feet, at which point I began to feel for ground under my feet. It did not take long before I was standing on a surface. It remained completely dark, however. I had not yet engaged visually, nor did I previously have any specific destination in mind.

I peered into the darkness, hoping to trigger my vision, but nothing happened. I then imagined an environment around me for a while, but again, nothing happened. Finally, I got down on my hands and feet, feeling my way around. Still, no environment appeared.

Then an idea occurred to me. Looking back, I have no idea how I came up with it. But I stood up from a crouching position and intertwined my fingers while leaving an empty space the size of a golf ball between my palms. I then squeezed my palms together as if compressing the empty air between my hands. Sure enough, I could actually feel some sort of mass beginning to form between my palms.

I continued to squeeze, and after a while, slivers of light began to shoot out of the mass enclosed between my hands. Seeing the light made me squeeze even harder, and now a whole beam of light was shooting out from between my fingers. I opened up my palms, curious about what I had created.

It was an odd, small, rectangular object, like a small flashlight with light coming out of one end. Even though I did not exactly understand my actions, nor the nature of the object, I had known the purpose of my actions all along—to create light and see the environment.

Without hesitating, I pointed the light device at the environment around me. It did not have a wide spread, but wherever I pointed it, the environment lit up in bright white light. It was a bit like a regular flashlight, but the light itself seemed different.

After pointing the device in several places, I got an overall impression of the environment. It was quite exotic. I was standing in a bright green field with some sort of ground cover that reminded me of the tropics. There were trees and bushes surrounding me as well. I had never seen these particular types of vegetation before. The environment seemed really unspoiled. There only seemed to be plant life here. I woke up soon afterward.

LIGHTENING THE LOAD

Body awareness inside of the void limits your overall mobility in consciousness. You will be almost forced to fly to your destination, and especially when body awareness is strong, it may interfere with reaching your destination. In contrast, if your body awareness is not very firm or solid, such flight will more closely resemble a change in attention, and your reach will be considerably increased.

Luckily, body awareness is quite flexible in the out-of-body state. The less attention you direct toward it, the more abstract it will become. The more attention you direct toward your own form, the more concrete it will become. Hence, the most straightforward way to get rid of body awareness inside of the void is to divert attention away from your second body. Doing so will make it a bit less solid than before, and you may even find yourself entirely formless after a while.

If this seems difficult, a more physical-like method is to leave your second body in a third body. Generally, after doing so, you will feel a little bit lighter than you did before. Of course, you are not really in an objective third body. We are dealing with habits and constructions of reality rather than any sort of objective, energetic phenomenon.

Journal Entry — Tuesday, June 27, 2006, 4:00 am

I woke up at around 4 am with the usual vibrations. I immediately relaxed my mind, which was quickly followed by the appearance of the void. I stepped out of bed without any feeling of separation and then flew out through the window, deeper into the void.

Despite a strong sense of body awareness, I seemed to have good lift and thought I might actually end up somewhere. For a while, I was distracted by hearing a barking dog in the void. I ignored it since I wanted to move further out instead.

While moving, I felt a pleasant breeze blowing through my hair. This was unusual. I never experienced physical sensations in such detail in the void. Even more curious was the fact that my hair was long, which is not the case in real life, nor do I have any plans to grow it.

I was losing speed. I felt far too heavy to get anywhere. I quickly tried to get some impressions from the void before waking up and briefly saw the face of a woman, but nothing else. I then had a sensation of pain on the right side of my body just under my ribs. I awoke soon after.

AVOID STAR CHASING

While inside of the void, it is not uncommon to perceive various pinpricks of lights in the distance, which may be symbolic of a more expansive state of consciousness or simply the result of residual neuronal activity. The colors vary; they may sometimes be entirely white or may consist of different hues of yellow, green, or orange. They strongly add to the impression of spatial depth in the void and may even lead you to believe you are floating in outer space. However, they are not real stars, and trying to reach any of them should be avoided. If you do, you will not actually get closer. It will be exactly like following a carrot with a stick and rope tied to your back. Likewise, avoid fixing your gaze on any of these lights, as they will activate your physical eyes, and the OBE will abort prematurely. Anything other than these stars can be focused on in the void without an increased risk of waking up.

Journal Entry — Monday, July 14, 2004, 7:00 am

After waking up from a dream, I immediately found myself in the proper state for separation. There was no need to go through any routine, as I was able to fly upward immediately.

I quickly found myself in the void, surrounded by hundreds of light specks piercing the darkness. Most of them were white in color, interspersed with a few that were yellow or green.

I had tried to reach these lights in the past, thinking perhaps they represented something significant—a potential destination inside of the void. However, I had never seemed to arrive, and unlike any other lights in the void, they never got any bigger as I approached them.

I decided to give it one more try and focused on one of the green ones. This was a mistake since, almost immediately, I became partially aware of my physical eyes. To avoid waking up entirely, I quickly diverted my attention away from the light, turned around in the air, and flew downward.

My nonphysical vision opened up almost immediately, and I found myself hovering above the street in front of our house. Strangely, the entire environment was enveloped in a greenish hue—the same color as the light I had just stared at. Unable to prolong the experience any more, I awoke soon after.

EMISSION CONTROL

While the void is generally a pleasant place to be, do realize it is *thought responsive* in that thoughts and emotions can easily lead to the appearance of a corresponding OBE environment. This means that if you are fearful inside of the void, it might lead to the manifestation of that fear. Rest assured, however, that a considerable level of control is possible in the void. You will not be swept willy-nilly from one environment to another if you have a basic idea of what you are doing.

Firstly, the void is not as thought responsive as the hypnagogic stage of sleep, in which the slightest thought leads to the manifestation of corresponding imagery. Usually, there is a time delay between your thoughts and emotions and their subsequent manifestation inside of the void.

Secondly, a certain level of *engagement* is required for anything to be perceived inside of the void. Without engagement, you'll be able to float in the void for a long time with nothing else happening, no matter what you think or fear. It is therefore possible to be extremely frightened in the void without anything bad happening, as long as you do not engage.

Thirdly, related to the second point, over time you will learn how to remain entirely "closed" inside of the void, directing most of your attention inward, without any leakage of your own thoughts and emotions into the void, and yet still keep an eye on the environment. Robert Monroe referred to it as "...a nice trick to have, even in the physical waking state."[6]

Journal Entry — Tuesday, May 2, 2006, 2:10 am

I was back in the void last night. At first, I tried to connect with an environment, but nothing seemed to be happening, so I decided to float around a bit. I was calmer than usual, feeling little fear, alone with my own thoughts.

Thoughts came and went. Some were about my goals, others about worries, and yet others were calming. In short, there was nothing unusual. It was like any other pattern of thought.

After enjoying floating around for a while, I began to notice a pattern. As soon as I directed my attention outward, the void began to respond to the thoughts I was having in the moment. There was a sound of sorts—a particular frequency or radiation that emanated from me.

The sound changed in intensity with each specific thought I had. Whenever I had a calming and relaxing thought, I appeared to make very little sound. However, when I had a thought associated with fear or even a slight worry, the volume increased quickly, which at its peak resembled a very unpleasant metallic screeching.

I continued to play around with this phenomenon for a while, even purposely scaring myself with fearful thoughts about the unknown. The effect was unmistakable. The worrisome thoughts quickly led to an increase in the unpleasant noise, while thinking calming thoughts had the opposite effect...

PRAGMATIC MODES OF TRAVEL

Travel in consciousness may also be accomplished in a far more opportunistic manner than discussed up to this point. Such modes of travel rely on the fluidity of out-of-body environments and the opportunity it offers to quickly exchange one environment for another.

For example, if you were to go through the front door of your house with the intent to end up at a different location, you might find yourself somewhere complete different from your front yard. Any sort of physical boundary, such as windows, closets, corners, walls, or stairs, is well suited to this kind of navigation.

These pragmatic modes of travel are also very well suited to reaching the void. For example, flying through a dark window while ignoring everything that is left behind may assist in quickly substituting the out-of-body environment for the void. Moving through mirrors often has a similar effect.

The drawback of pragmatic modes of travel, unless used to reach the void, is that it is easy to get caught up in a negative spiral of increasingly fluid environments. The environment you enter will often be more unstable than the one you have left behind. So if you decide to use pragmatic modes of travel, try to set a clear intent each time and firmly reestablish yourself inside the new environment before going any further.

PANORAMIC VIEWS OF CONSCIOUSNESS

Panoramic views of consciousness reveal the larger underlying structure and organization of consciousness—a glimpse into the totality of consciousness. For example, Robert Bruce reports on the perception of "astral plane entrance structures" covered in a multitude of different mandala-like shapes that provide the entry point into a particular out-of-body environment.[1]

Likewise, Monroe describes different circular structures, or fields of consciousness, surrounding Earth's atmosphere, perhaps indicative of a more technocratic or scientific orientation.[2] I quite regularly perceive multicolored "planets" inside of the void, perhaps because the void is so reminiscent of outer space. At other times, I experience rather abstract geometric patterns or different regions of consciousness separated by color.

In any case, there is a lot of variation between different projectors, which makes it seem likely that enculturation plays a strong role in the way these overviews are perceived. Hence, as impressive as encounters with panoramic views of consciousness may be, they do exist in the eye of the beholder to some extent, at least in terms of the particular *manner* in which they are perceived. So trust your own experience and do not try to replicate the experience of others.

Journal Entry — Early 1990s, date and time unknown

I had an exciting OBE last night. The experience again started with trying to remain balanced at the borderline of sleep, during which I momentarily lost consciousness. However, shortly after I regained consciousness, I floated upward into the void, and without making any effort to perceive anything, a grandiose scene unfolded in front of me.

I saw an awe-inspiring helix-shaped structure extending far up into the sky. I could not quite see how far up it went. There seemed to be no end to it. It was made of the most beautiful colors, brighter and more vivid than I had ever seen before. Every conceivable color was there, extremely saturated and bright, including flashing reds, deep purple, and golden yellow.

As I got closer, I noticed that it was in fact a double helix, consisting of two separate strands with amazing hues of color connecting them. It was like a massive DNA strand. In fact, the helix consisted of more than shapes and colors alone. The strands were held together by millions of human bodies, each a different bright color, lined up next to each other.

None of these people were alive, nor were they dead in the ordinary sense of the word. Rather, it was as if the strands were made out of an "imprint" of the many who had gone before me, leaving behind their memories and all they had learned in life.

This helix was the ultimate result of their efforts.

I moved on top of the imprint of bodies that held the strands of the helix together. It felt like a soft cushion, and they held me with ease. Next, I began to move almost immediately, with the speed and feeling of gliding down a slide, except that I was going upward, with the human forms and shapes flashing before my eyes.

Then, I came to a halt. There was something in front me, a mirage of sorts, as if the air was moving. Visually, it looked like vibrating air— a layer of turbulence where hot and cold air came together. I was not sure what would happen, but I moved forward nonetheless, passing through the vibrating air.

I did not feel anything out of the ordinary, but to my amazement, there was another "I" coming out the other end. It was the exact mirror image of my present position. As one went up, the other went down.

The idea of a "null point" came to mind. I had no time to waste, however, and continued to glide upward until finally, at what seemed to be the end of the helix, I was thrown out.

I found myself standing in darkness with the silhouette of a tall, slender man in front of me. He was dressed in a black tuxedo with white gloves, holding what appeared to be a long black magic wand with a white tip. He reminded me of the actor Christopher Walken—the same deadpan expression.

For a while, he just stood there staring at me with the slightest flicker of amusement in his eyes. He seemed familiar. There was something eerie about him as well, but I did not feel uncomfortable. Then, he moved toward me, lifted his magic wand, and touched my left shoulder.

Before I knew it, I found myself going downward, moving along the helix again. Again, I passed the midpoint, and sure enough, as I moved through it, another "I" was going upward.

I awoke soon after, baffled...

Happy traveling!

Appendix

The Mental and Environmental Stability Scale (MESS)

Score	Description
0	Level of mental clarity is extremely high, approaching hyper-lucidity, with a sense of being more awake than in physical life. Virtual correspondence of the OBE environment with the known physical environment. Objects, people, and events appear with great vibrancy and perceptual richness.
1–3	Level of mental clarity is normal. No bizarre or impossible events during the OBE. Layout of walls corresponds completely to the physical environment. Furniture and objects are, for the most part, in place. Few objects are missing, and any displacement of objects is no more than a few feet from their actual position. Objects and people generally appear as they are, although they occasionally appear as remote representations of the original. For the most part, lighting schemes in a house correspond with physical reality. Seasons and weather broadly correspond to physical reality as well.
4–6	The mind feels somewhat drowsy and heavy. There is some lack of alertness and lucidity, including a certain level of poverty of perception. Walls and rooms are located where they are supposed to be. There may be some bizarre or impossible events occurring during the OBE, but they remain relatively controlled. Furniture and objects might be missing, or there may be objects lying around that should not be there. Alternatively, objects and people may be somewhat different than how they look in real life. Day and night may be mixed up as well. The weather might be different from reality.

Score	Description
7–9	A low level of lucidity. The environment corresponds to physical reality only in a very broad sense. Walls in a house may have rearranged themselves, and rooms are not where they should be. The surrounding landscape and neighborhood are different from reality. There is a relatively high frequency of bizarre and impossible events with a tendency to take on a life of their own. Objects and furniture are out of place or missing, or alternatively, the out-of-body environment contains objects, furniture, creatures, and people that should not be there. Weather, seasons, and lighting are frequently out of order as well.
10	Non-lucidity. Virtually no correspondence between the OBE environment and the actual physical environment. Any sort of resemblance is extremely remote.

Glossary

Asomatic Transition — A transition into the out-of-body state without any body awareness, usually accomplished by maintaining a visual focus during the transition process. Energy sensations accompanying this transition tend to be of a visual nature. Once the transition is completed, you may find yourself in the void without any body awareness, thereby significantly expanding your reach in consciousness.

Aspects — Fairly well-rounded characters in the out-of-body state that symbolically represent facets of your own inner psyche. Often, their appearance and behavior symbolically correspond to the particular parts of your inner psyche that they represent.

Atmospheric Influences — The manifestation of objects and events in the out-of-body environment that originate from sources other than the projector's own mind. These may include the consciousness of others as well as past or future events that leave an imprint on the out-of-body environment.

Barrier Zones — Barrier zones typically occur with initial attempts to move beyond the personal field of consciousness when the projector is confronted with psychological limitations that manifest inside of the environments as objects and events. They often represent occurrences in which projectors are faced with the wider context of their own intent, including any fears associated with that intent, without actually ending up in the environment where they wanted to be.

Bilocation — Bilocation (or trilocation, etc.) in its advanced form is a fairly rare and thought-provoking phenomenon in the out-of-body state. It involves finding yourself in more than one environment at the same time, potentially even including separate streams of consciousness and identities.

Bleedthrough Effects — A situation in which one environment exerts an effect on another environment. Most commonly, these effects involve marginal levels of sensory input with tactile stimulation of the physical body felt as if originating from the second body. However, bleedthrough effects may also involve interaction between two different nonphysical environments.

Collective Fields of Consciousness — A mode of consciousness in which the intent of the projector is to perceive beyond his or her own personal psyche, leading to the perception of "other-consciousness." From a realist perspective, in which experience is either subjective or objective, the actual existence of such fields of consciousness remains an issue of debate.

Displacement — A relatively common occurrence in which the projector finds him- or herself in a different environment than initially expected. This may, for example, include finding oneself in a strange hotel room or the bedroom of one's childhood. The phenomenon is often due to a loss of lucidity in the course of the transition process, but it may occur in other situations as well.

Energy Sensations — Any type of sensation associated with the onset of the OBE, including vibrations, noises, and light effects. They occur at the highly energized "fault line" between the physical world and entry into the out-of-body environment.

Externalization — The process by which internal and what is ordinarily considered subjective experience is viewed as if coming from the outside in the form of objects, people, and events in an out-of-body environment.

H-Band — An energy pattern or "radiation" produced by uncontrolled human thought and emotion. Often experienced as a cacophony of loud voices or as metallic screeching, it is relatively easy to pick up on from the void. It often occurs independent of the projector's own feelings and emotions at the time. The H-Band is less disturbing when further removed from regular time-space, deeper into the void, and is more likely to instead be experienced as whispering.

Inner Sense Percepts (ISPs) — ISPs represent an "inner knowing" in the out-of-body state without any apparent explanation for that knowledge. They often take the form of percepts that bubble into awareness without any active effort on the part of the projector. ISPs play an important role in advanced forms of nonverbal communication as an exchange of imagery and concepts without anything being spoken aloud.

(Lucid) Dream — A mode of consciousness in which the projector adopts a dreaming state of consciousness in the out-of-body state. This situation often leads to a convergence between different fields of consciousness wherein meaning and symbols take on a multilayered quality, which makes the experience difficult to interpret or dissect.

(M) Field — A wider energy field representing the entire spectrum of consciousness permeating both the nonphysical and physical worlds. The (M) Field appears related to what is currently understood to be the zero-point field in quantum physics.

Mind Awake/Body Asleep (MABA) — A situation in which the mind is awake and the body is asleep. It is all that is required to induce the out-of-body state, provided the physical body is indeed asleep.

Mindscaping — An activity in which you actively manipulate an out-of-body environment inside the personal field of consciousness in order to effectuate a change in your own psyche.

Movie Screen Effect — An effect that may occur shortly after the projector begins to engage with an out-of-body environment from the void. It is experienced as watching scenery from a distance as if sitting in a movie theater while darkness surrounds you. Further engagement and absorption lead to becoming part of that environment as an active participant.

Panoramic Views of Consciousness — Wider, symbolic views of consciousness that incorporate multiple out-of-body environments or even the entire spectrum of consciousness. The manner in which these views are experienced appears partially dependent on the mindset and background of the projector.

Parallel Fields of Consciousness — A physically oriented field of consciousness with its own separate history and timeline that exists parallel to current space-time reality.

Parasomatic Transition — A transition into the out-of-body state that coincides with body awareness. It occurs when the projector remains partially focused on tactile sensations in the course of the transition process. Then, as sensory input diminishes, nonphysical body awareness seamlessly replaces physical body awareness. If carried out from the waking state under entirely lucid conditions, there is no gap in body awareness or consciousness.

Phasing In — The process by which a projector becomes part of an out-of-body environment. It is a mainly visually oriented process in which the projector phases into an environment by interacting with perceptions inside of the void. This can be accomplished with or without body awareness immediately preceding phasing in. An intermediate form of phasing in is carried out with body awareness where you make a tactile "phasing" entry into an environment, which often also involves flying inside the void.

Phasing Out — The process by which a projector leaves an out-of-body environment, preferably back to the void. This is best accomplished by minimizing your interaction with a particular environment while maintaining a very detached stance. Once controlled, it can significantly prolong the duration of OBEs.

Physical Field of Consciousness — A mode of consciousness in which the intent of the projector is to perceive the physical world, leading to perceptions in accordance with physical reality. Excursions into the physical field tend to be brief and do not appear entirely natural to the out-of-body state.

Perceptual Blending — A situation in which two distinct perceptual categories combine, or "fuse" together, to form a new "blended" perceptual category.

Personal Field of Consciousness — A mode of consciousness in which the intent of the projector is directed toward the constructs of his or her own inner psyche, leading to perceptions in which the inner psyche manifests as external objects, events and people in the environment. The personal field is easy to access, requiring only a minimal amount of intent.

Psychological Load Factors — Habits and beliefs that keep you relatively immobile in the wider spectrum of consciousness. They may include fears but can also consist of taken-for-granted physically based concepts such as gravity and body awareness. The most fundamental habits and concepts tied to physical existence are also the most difficult to overcome, such as, for example, the notion of three-dimensional space. Once you do overcome them, you are likely to move beyond human consciousness altogether during your experiences.

Rebooting — The direct manipulation of perception by treating your visual field as a canvas or window that can be wiped clean. Rebooting can be accomplished by a simple movement of the hand or any other method in which you temporarily blind yourself to your surroundings.

Repository Fields of Consciousness — Fields of consciousness that contain limitless amounts of information related to human existence. They are relatively easy to access from the void, especially by focusing on them in an auditory format.

Sleep Paralysis — A situation that occurs at the borderline of sleep in which you are not only immobilized in a physical sense but in a nonphysical sense as well. You are likely to come across it now and then as you try to transition into the out-of-body state, especially when sleeping in the supine position. The hallucinations often accompanying sleep paralysis are best ignored. They will abruptly disappear into thin air as soon as you manage to break out of it, as no sensory input remains to sustain them.

Veridical Perception — Veridical perception refers to perceptions in the out-of-body state that correspond to physical reality, without any prior knowledge of the actual physical environment. It is also sometimes referred to as extrasensory perception (ESP). The term *veridical perception* is preferable, however, because perception in the out-of-body state is always *extra*sensory.

Void — A minimum-perceptual environment, characterized by spatial blackness, that becomes apparent at the end of the transition process once all contact with the physical senses has been severed. The void represents a very deep state of consciousness, highly sought after in Eastern disciplines and not easily accessed through meditative techniques or hypnosis. It will generally only reveal itself once the physical body has fallen asleep. It is only there that you are completely free of physical limitations.

References

Chapter 1

1. Monroe, R. A. (1971). *Journeys out of the body.* New York: Doubleday.
2. Tart, C. (1990). Multiple personality, altered States and virtual reality: The world simulation process approach. *Dissociation, 3,* 222–233.
3. Ibid, p. 227.

Chapter 2

1. Blackmore, S. J. (1982, 1992). *Beyond the body: An investigation of out of body experiences.* Chicago: Academy Chicago Publishers, p. 1.
2. Green, C. (1968). *Out-of-the-body experiences.* New York: Ballantine Books, p. 17.
3. Monroe. R. A. (1985). *Far journeys.* New York: Doubleday, p. 3.
4. Irwin, H. J. *Flight of mind: A psychological study of the out-of-body experience.* Metuchen, N.J.: Scarecrow Press, p. 5.
5. Tart, C. T. (1974). Some methodological problems in out-of-the-Body experiences research. In W. Roll, R. Morris, & J. Morris (Eds.), *Research in parapsychology, 1973.* Metuchen, NJ: Scarecrow Press, p. 117.
6. Blavatsky, H. P. (1888, 1988). *The secret doctrine.* Pasadena, CA: Theosophical University Press.
7. Arundale, G. S. (1926, 2003). *Nirvana.* Whitefish, MT: Kessinger Publishing.
8. Bailey, A. C. (1925, 1989). *A treatise on cosmic fire.* New York: Lucis Publishing Company.

9. Leadbeater, C. W. (1909, 2007). *Man visible and invisible.* Whitefish, MT: Kessinger Publishing.

10. Jinarajadasa, C. (1997, 1921). *First principles of theosophy.* Whitefish, MT: Kessinger Publishing.

11. Powell, A. E. (1926, 1998). *Astral body and other astral phenomena.* Whitefish, MT: Kessinger Publishing.

12. Ibid, p.8.

13. Leadbetter, C. W. (1896, 1997). *The astral plane: Its scenery, inhabitants and phenomena.* Whitefish, MT: Kessinger Publishing.

14. Powell, A. E. (1926, 1998). *Astral body and other astral phenomena.* Whitefish, MT: Kessinger Publishing, p. 134.

15. Ibid, p. 130.

16. Powell, A. E. (1927, 2006). *The mental body.* Whitefish, MT: Kessinger Publishing.

17. Ibid, p. 232.

18. Besant, A. W. (1895, 2003). *The path of discipleship.* San Diego, CA: The Book Tree, pp. 146–147.

19. Arundale, G. S. (1926, 2003). *Nirvana.* Whitefish, MT: Kessinger Publishing, pp. 67–68.

20. Green, C. (1968). *Out-of-the-body experiences.* New York: Ballantine Books.

21. Muldoon S. & Carrington, H. (1929, 1992). *The projection of the astral body.* London: Rider & Company.

22. Buhlman, W. (1996). *Adventures beyond the body.* New York: HarperCollins Publishers.

23. Bruce, R. (1999). *Astral dynamics: A new approach to out-of-body experience.* Charlottesville, VA: Hampton Roads Publishing Company, Inc.

24. Monroe, R.A. (1971). *Journeys out of the body.* New York: Doubleday.

25. Monroe. R. A. (1985). *Far journeys.* New York: Doubleday.

26. Ibid, p. 242.

27. Monroe, R. A. (1994). *Ultimate journey.* New York: Doubleday.

28. Atwater, F. H. (2001). *Captain of my ship, master of my soul.* Charlottesville, VA: Hampton Roads Publishing Company.

29. Monroe, R. A. (1994). *Ultimate journey.* New York: Doubleday, p. 201.

30. Ibid, p. 242.

31. Ibid, p. 249.

32. Russell, R. (2007). *The journey of Robert Monroe.* Charlottesville, VA: Hampton Roads Publishing Company, p. 246.

33. Monroe, R. A. (1994). *Ultimate journey.* New York: Doubleday, p. 274.

34. Ibid, p. 100.

35. Russell, R. (2007). *The journey of Robert Monroe.* Charlottesville, VA: Hampton Roads Publishing Company.

36. LaBerge, S. (1985). *Lucid dreaming.* New York: Ballantine.

37. LaBerge, S. & DeGracia, D. J. (2000). Varieties of lucid dreaming experience. In R.G. Kunzendorf & B. Wallace (Eds.), *Individual differences in conscious experience.* Amsterdam: John Benjamins.

38. Levitan, L. & LaBerge, S. (1991). Other worlds: out-of-body experiences and lucid dreams. *Nightlight, 3,* 1–5, 1991.

39. Van Eeden, F. (1913). A study of dreams. *Proceedings of the Society for Psychical Research, 26,* 431–461.

40. Blackmore, S. (1984). A postal survey of OBEs and other experiences. *Journal of the Society for Psychical Research, 52,* 227–244.

41. LaBerge, S. & DeGracia, D. J. (2000). Varieties of lucid dreaming experience. In R.G. Kunzendorf & B. Wallace (Eds.), *Individual differences in conscious experience.* Amsterdam: John Benjamins.

42. Metzinger, T. (2005). Out of body experiences as the origin of the concept of a soul. *Mind and Matter, 3,* 57–84.

43. Blackmore, S. J. (1982, 1992). *Beyond the body: An investigation of out of body experiences.* Chicago: Academy Chicago Publishers, pp. 121–132.

44. Hartwell, J., Janis, J., & Harary, B. (1975). A study of the physiological variables associated with out-of-body experiences. In Morris, J. D., Roll, W. G. and Morris, R. L. (Eds.), *Research in parapsychology 1974.* Metuchen, N.J.: Scarecrow Press.

45. Rogo, D. S. (1985). Out-of-body experiences as lucid dreams: A critique. *Lucidity Letter, 4,* 43–47.

46. Monroe. R. A. (1985). *Far journeys.* New York: Doubleday, p. 239.

47. Persinger, M. M. (2001). The neuropsychiatry of paranormal experiences. *Neuropsychiatric Practice and Opinion, 13*, 521–522.

48. Blanke, O., Ortigue, S., Landis, T., & Seeck, M. (2002). Stimulating illusory own body perceptions. *Nature, 419*, 269–270.

49. Palmer, J. (1978). The out-of-body experience: A psychological theory. *Journal of the American Society for Psychical Research, 9*, 19–22.

50. Blackmore, S. J. (1982, 1992). *Beyond the body: An investigation of out of body experiences.* Chicago: Academy Chicago Publishers.

51. Ehrsson, H. H. (2007). The experimental induction of out-of-body experiences. *Science, 317*, 1048.

52. Metzinger, T. (2005). Out of body experiences as the origin of the concept of a soul. *Mind and Matter, 3*, p. 61.

53. Rogo, D. S. (1986, 1993). *Leaving the body.* New York: Simon & Schuster.

54. Clarke, C. J. S. (1995). The nonlocality of mind. *Journal of Consciousness Studies, 2*, 231–240.

55. Hameroff, S. R. & Penrose, R. (1996). Conscious events as orchestrated space-time selections. *Journal of Consciousness Studies, 3*, 36–53.

56. Wigner, E. P. (1970) *Symmetries and reflections: Scientific essays.* Cambridge: MIT Press.

57. Monroe, R. A. (1994). *Ultimate journey.* New York: Doubleday, p. 101.

58. Van Lommel W., Van Wees R., Meyers V., & Elfferich I. (2001). Near-death experience in survivors of cardiac arrest: a prospective study in the Netherlands. *Lancet, 358*, 2039–2045.

59. Van Lommel, P. (2004). About the continuity of our consciousness. In C. Machado, C. and Shewmo, D. A. (Eds.). *Brain death and disorders of consciousness.* New York, Boston, Dordrecht, London, Moscow: Kluwer Academic. Plenum Publishers, pp. 130–131.

60. Blackmore, S. (2006). *Conversations on consciousness.* New York: Oxford University Press, p. 121.

61. Merleau-Ponty, M. (1945). *Phénoménologie de la perception.* Paris: Gallimard.

Chapter 3

1. Monroe, R. A. (1971). *Journeys out of the body*. New York: Doubleday, p. 209.
2. Blackmore, S. J. (1982, 1992). *Beyond the body: An investigation of out of body experiences*. Chicago: Academy Chicago Publishers.
3. Levitan, L. & LaBerge, S. (1991). Other worlds: Out-of-body experiences and lucid dreams. *Nightlight, 3*, 1–5, 1991.
4. Monroe, R. A. (1994). *Ultimate journey*. New York: Doubleday, p. 279.
5. Hartwell, J., Janis, J. & Harary, B. (1975). A study of the physiological variables associated with out-of-body experiences. In Morris, J. D., Roll, W. G. and Morris, R. L. (Eds.), *Research in Parapsychology, 1974*. Metuchen, N.J.: Scarecrow Press.
6. Osis, K. & Mitchell, J. (1977). Physiological correlates of reported out-of-the-body experiences. *Journal of the Society for Psychical Research, 49*, 509–524.
7. Harary, K. & Weintraub, P. (1989). *How to have an out-of-body experience in 30 days*. New York: St. Martin's Griffin.
8. Muldoon S. & Carrington, H. (1929, 1992). *The projection of the astral body*. London: Rider & Company.
9. Bruce, R. (1999). *Astral dynamics: A new approach to out-of-body experience*. Charlottesville, VA: Hampton Roads Publishing Company.
10. Bruce, R. (2007). *Energy work: The secret of healing and spiritual development*. Charlottesville, VA: Hampton Roads Publishing Company.
11. Peterson, R. (1997) *Out-of-body experiences: How to have them and what to expect*. Charlottesville, VA: Hampton Roads Publishing Company, p. 211.
12. Blackmore, S. J. (1982, 1992). *Beyond the body: An investigation of out of body experiences*. Chicago: Academy Chicago Publishers.
13. The Monroe Institute (1989). *The gateway manual*. Faber, VA: The Monroe Institute.
14. Albuquerque, W. & Bronstein A. M. (2004). "Doctor, I can hear my eyes": report of two cases with different mechanisms. *Journal of Neurology, Neurosurgery and Psychiatry, 75*, 1363–1964.

15. Bentov, I. (1979, 1990). Micromotion of the body as a factor in the development of the nervous system. In John White (Ed.), *Kundalini, Evolution and Enlightenment*. St. Paul, MN: Paragon House.

16. Haisch, B., Rueda, A., & Puthoff, H. E. (1994). Inertia as a zero-point-field Lorentz force. *Physical Review, 49,* 678–694.

17. Monroe, R. A. (1971). *Journeys out of the body.* New York: Doubleday.

18. Green, C. (1968). *Out-of-the-body experiences.* New York: Ballantine Books.

19. Waelti, E. (1983). *Der dritte Kreis des Wissens.* Interlaken, Switzerland: Ansata.

20. DeGracia, D. J. (1999). In the theater of dreams: Global workspace theory, dreaming and consciousness. http://www.med.wayne.edu/degracialab/metaphysics/Dreams_GWS.pdf.

Chapter 4

1. Bruce, R. (1999). *Astral dynamics: A new approach to out-of-body experience.* Charlottesville, VA: Hampton Roads Publishing Company.

2. LaBerge, S. & DeGracia, D. J. (2000). Varieties of lucid dreaming experience. In R. G. Kunzendorf & B. Wallace (Eds.), *Individual differences in conscious experience.* Amsterdam: John Benjamins.

3. Roberts, J. (1972). *Seth speaks: The eternal validity of the soul.* New York: Bantam Books, pp. 96–97.

4. Van Eeden, F. (1913). A study of dreams. *Proceedings of the Society for Psychical Research, 26.*

5. Monroe, R. A. (1971). *Journeys out of the body.* New York: Doubleday.

6. Wolf, F. A. (1990). Parallel universes: The search for other worlds. New York: Simon & Schuster.

7. Bohm. D. & Hiley, B. J. (1993). *The undivided universe: An ontological interpretation of quantum theory.* London: Routledge.

8. Stockton, B. (1989). *Catapult: The biography of Robert A. Monroe.* Norfolk, VA: The Donning Company.

Chapter 5

1. Monroe, R. A. (1971). *Journeys out of the body.* New York: Doubleday.
2. Blackmore, S. J. (1982, 1992). *Beyond the body: An investigation of out of body experiences.* Chicago: Academy Chicago Publishers.
3. Tart, C. (1968). A psychophysiological study of out of body experiences in a selected subject. *Journal of the American Society for Psychical Research, 62,* 327.
4. Tart, C. (1998). Six studies of out-of-the-body experiences. *Journal of Near-Death Studies, 17,* 73–99.
5. Ibid, p. 89.
6. Swann, I. (1975). *To kiss earth good-bye.* New York: Dell Publishing Company.
7. Mitchell, J. L. (1973). Out of the body vision. *Psychic, 4,* 44–47.
8. Rogo, D. S. (1978). *Mind beyond the body.* New York: Penguin, pp. 17–34.
9. Blackmore, S. J. (1982, 1992). *Beyond the body: An investigation of out of body experiences.* Chicago: Academy Chicago Publishers, p. 199.
10. Bruce, R. (1999). *Astral dynamics: A new approach to out-of-body experience.* Charlottesville, VA: Hampton Roads Publishing Company.
11. Monroe, R. A. (1971). *Journeys out of the body.* New York: Doubleday, p. 57.
12. Fox, Oliver (1962). *Astral projection: A record of out-of-the-body experiences.* New Hyde Park, NY: University Books.
13. Targ, R., & Puthoff, H. E. (1977). *Mind reach: Scientists look at psychic ability.* New York: Delacorte.
14. Targ, R. (2007). *Limitless mind: A guide to remote viewing and transformation of consciousness.* Novato, CA: New World Library, p. 53.
15. Smith, P. and Irwin, H. (1981) Out-of-body experiences, needs and the experimental approach: A laboratory study. *Parapsychology Review, 12,* pp. 65–75.

Chapter 6

1. Monroe, R. A. (1971). *Journeys out of the body.* New York: Doubleday, p. 74.
2. Buhlman, W. (1996). *Adventures beyond the body.* New York: Harper Collins Publishers.
3. LaBerge, S. (1985). *Lucid dreaming.* New York: Ballantine.
4. Bruce, R. (1999). *Astral dynamics: A new approach to out-of-body experience.* Charlottesville, VA: Hampton Roads Publishing Company, p. 376.
5. Russell, R. (2007). *The journey of Robert Monroe.* Charlottesville, VA: Hampton Roads Publishing Company, p. 61.
6. Roberts, J. (1972). *Seth speaks: The eternal validity of the soul.* New York: Bantam Books.
7. Monroe, R. A. (1994). *Ultimate journey.* New York: Doubleday.
8. William, J. H. & William, G.D. (1993). *Mythical trickster figures: contours, contexts, and criticisms.* Tuscaloosa, AL: University of Alabama Press.
9. Muldoon S. & Carrington, H. (1929, 1992). *The projection of the astral body.* London: Rider & Company, p. 35.

Chapter 7

1. Monroe, R. A. (1994). *Ultimate journey.* New York: Doubleday.
2. Metzinger, T. (2005). Out of body experiences as the origin of the concept of a soul. *Mind and Matter, 3,* 57–84.
3. Verman, M. (2005). Reincarnation in Jewish mysticism and gnosticism. *Shofar: An Interdisciplinary Journal of Jewish Studies,* 24, 173–175.
4. Greyson, B. & Evans-Bush, N. (1992). Distressing near-death experiences. *Psychiatry, 55,* 95-110.
5. Leland, K. (2001). *A field guide to non-physical reality for the out-of-body traveler.* Charlottesville, VA.: Hampton Roads Publishing Company, 2001.
6. Monroe, R. A. (1994). *Ultimate journey.* New York: Doubleday, p. 249.
7. Ibid, p. 272.

Chapter 8

1. Jastrow, J. (1899). The mind's eye. *Popular Science Monthly, 54,* 299–312.
2. Necker, L. A. (1832). Observations on some remarkable optical phaenomena seen in Switzerland; and on an optical phaenomenon which occurs on viewing a figure of a crystal or geometrical solid. *London and Edinburgh Philosophical Magazine and Journal of Science, 1,* 5, 329–337.
3. Edwards, D., Ashmore, M., & Potter, J., (1995). Death and furniture: The rhetoric, politics and theology of bottom line arguments against relativism, *History of the Human Sciences, 8,* 25–49.
4. Merleau-Ponty, M. (1945). *Phénoménologie de la perception.* Paris: Gallimard.
5. O'Connor, K. & Aardema, F. (2005). The imagination: Cognitive, pre-cognitive, and meta-cognitive aspects. *Consciousness and Cognition, 14,* 233–256.
6. O'Connor, K. & Aardema, F. (in press). Living in a bubble: Dissociation, relational consciousness and obsessive compulsive disorder. *Journal of Consciousness Studies.*
7. Bohm. D. & Hiley, B. J. (1993). *The undivided universe: An ontological interpretation of quantum theory.* London: Routledge.
8. Goswami, A. (1995). *The self-aware universe.* New York: Putnam's Sons.
9. Wolf, F. A. (1999). *The spiritual universe: One physicist's vision of spirit, soul, matter, and self.* New Hampshire: Moment Point Press.
10. Morris, D. (2004). *The sense of space.* Albany, NY: State University of New York Press.
11. Parker, A. (2003). We ask, does psi exist? But is this the right question and do we really want an answer anyway? *Journal of Consciousness Studies, 10,* 111–134.
12. Jung, C. G. (1964). *Man and his symbols.* United States: Del Publishing.
13. Merker, B. (2007). Consciousness without a cerebral cortex: A challenge for neuroscience and medicine. *Behavioral and Brain Sciences, 30,* 63–134.

14. Jaret, C. (Ed.). The most important psychology experiment never done? Celebrating the 100th issue of the Research Digest—A selection of responses from top psychologists. *The Psychologist, 20,* 658–659.

15. Augustine, K. (2007). Does paranormal perception occur in near-death experiences? *Journal of Near Death Studies, 25,* 203–236.

16. Brown, E. N. Lydic, R., & Schiff, N. D. (2010). General anesthesia, sleep, and coma. *The New England Journal of Medicine, 363,* 2638–50.

17. Monroe, R. A. (1994). *Ultimate journey.* New York: Doubleday, p. 220.

Chapter 9

1. Aardema, F. (2006). Focus 10: Mind Awake/Body Asleep. From: http://www.explorations-in-consciousness.com/focus10.html.

2. LaBerge, S. (1985). *Lucid dreaming.* New York: Ballantine.

3. The Monroe Institute (2011). A new initiative: Spatial angle modulation™. Retrieved, September 12, 2011, http://www.monroeinstitute.org/resources/spatial-angle-modulation.

Chapter 10

1. Bruce, R. (1999). *Astral dynamics: A new approach to out-of-body experience.* Charlottesville, VA: Hampton Roads Publishing Company.

2. Monroe. R. A. (1985). *Far journeys.* New York: Doubleday.

3. DeGracia, D. (1994, 2004, 2006). Do_OBE. Astral Projection/OOBE class notes, conducted on the Compuserve New Age, p. 39. From http://www.med.wayne.edu/degracialab/metaphysics/do_obe.pdf

4. Monroe, R. A. (1994). *Ultimate journey.* New York: Doubleday, p. 105.

5. Leland, K. (2001). *Otherwhere.* Charlottesville, VA: Hampton Roads Publishing Company.

6. Monroe. R. A. (1985). *Far journeys.* New York: Doubleday, p. 241.

Index

sleep, 2, 20, 22–23, 26–27, 35,
38–39, 42–46, 54, 63, 80, 120,
231, 245, 255–273, 301
borderline of, 1, 34, 36, 231, 256,
260–261, 264, 266-267, 304
see also hypnagogic stage of
sleep
sleep paralysis, 36, 40, 52, 54,
100, 257, 304
soul, 15, 17, 157, 159, 185, 188,
202
subjectivity, 73, 104, 122, 158, 161,
166, 171, 179, 192–193, 202,
235–236, 238, 244, 246, 248
superior canal dehiscence, 39
symbolism, 51, 54, 71, 73, 77, 86,
99, 103–105, 122, 158–161,
164, 166, 171–177, 188,
213–214, 225, 249, 276, 281,
290
synesthesia, 39
Swann, Ingo, 121
theosophy, *see* mystical and
occult traditions
thought-responsiveness, 6, 126,
157, 159, 175, 196, 215
see also externalization
time travel, 110
transition process, 22, 33–35, 42,
46, 52, 58–60, 63–64, 73, 77,
102, 192–194, 245, 256–257,
261, 265–271, 277–281
with body awareness, *see*
parasomatic transition
without body awareness, *see*
asomatic transition
transcendence, 19, 196–197,
253–254

traveling, *see* navigation
tricksters, 177
Van Eeden, Frederik, 25, 80
Van Lommel, Pim, 31
veridical perception, 29, 117, 122,
135, 149–153, 182, 203, 246,
304
evidence of, 119–121, 149
vibrations, *see* energy sensations
vigil method, 258–268
virtual reality, 30, 164
void, 5, 57–59, 64, 78, 94, 97,
101–102, 161, 172, 202–203,
209, 221, 228–231, 245,
249–250, 267, 277–294
wakefulness, 82, 85–87, 131–132,
255–258, 260–264
Wolf, Fred, 110, 244
x-ray vision, 90, 92–93, 117
yo-yo effect, 263
zooming-in, 91–92, 117

About the Author

Frederick Aardema is a researcher and practitioner in the field of clinical psychology at the Fernand Seguin Research Center, which is affiliated with the University of Montreal. He has published widely in international scientific journals, including two books on obsessive-compulsive and related disorders. Other aspects of his research include dissociation, virtual reality, introspection, reasoning, and psychological assessment. He is a frequent presenter at international conferences. A more private aspect of his life has always been the exploration of consciousness through out-of-body experiences, lucid dreams, and altered states of consciousness. Originally born in the Netherlands, he now lives in Montreal, Canada.

To contact Frederick Aardema, visit his website and forum at www.explorations-in-consciousness.com.